W. P. B. BOTHA was born in Johannesburg in 1952. His background is Afrikaner working class. Having been granted a bursary by his stepfather's employers – the national chain-store, O.K. Bazaars – he became the first member of his family to go to university. He left South Africa in 1975, after graduating as a teacher, and has since taught in Papua New Guinea, the Transkei and Northern Ireland. He is currently teaching in London. *The Reluctant Playwright* is his first novel.

W. P. B. BOTHA

THE RELUCTANT PLAYWRIGHT

HEINEMANN

Heinemann International Literature and Textbooks
A division of Heinemann Educational Books Ltd
Halley Court, Jordan Hill, Oxford OX2 8EJ

Heinemann: A Division of Reed Publishing (USA) Inc
361 Hanover Street, Portsmouth, New Hampshire, 03801-3912, USA

Heinemann Educational Books (Nigeria) Ltd
PMB 5205, Ibadan
Heinemann Educational Boleswa
PO Box 10103, Village Post Office, Gaborone, Botswana

LONDON   EDINBURGH   PARIS   MADRID
ATHENS   BOLOGNA   MELBOURNE   SYDNEY
AUCKLAND   SINGAPORE   TOKYO

© W. P. B. Botha 1993

First published by Heinemann International Literature
and Textbooks in 1993

Series Editor: Adewale Maja-Pearce

British Library Cataloguing in Publication Data
A catalogue record for this book is available from the British Library.

ISBN 0-435-90589-9

Phototypeset by
Wilmaset Ltd, Birkenhead, Wirral
Printed and bound in Great Britain by
Cox & Wyman Ltd, Reading, Berkshire

93 94 95 96 10 9 8 7 6 5 4 3 2 1

For Tryphina

PART ONE

Prologue

A bright, cloudless day. A car slides sinuously along a narrow country lane where the dry stone walls contain the swish of its tyres. Its windows are down and the warm summer breeze brushes its fingers pleasantly through the occupants' hair. The sun bounces off the bonnet, flashes over the windscreen, over the front seats. A picnic basket nestling in the back, conceals plastic explosives.

Suddenly an army helicopter clatters overhead. The man and woman in the front of the car exchange frightened glances. In the back a boy tosses aside the book he has been reading. Unaware of the helicopter, he lunges forward and demands to be allowed to drive.

'Sweet Jesus. Now see what ye've done!' exclaims the woman, pointing to the brown liquid trickling from the broken seal of the flask which the boy has knocked over. 'Seamus stop the car!'

The boy's father glances over his shoulder. 'Ye're driving yer mother and me mad,' he growls.

'Seamus will ye leave the boy alone and pull over!'

'Whad, an' set the Brits an' tap a us like a pack a wild dogs? Nad an yer life!'

The boy's father accelerates. Silently the woman searches for a paper napkin and wraps it around the flask which she sets on the ashtray between the seats. The napkin soon turns soggy and begins to disintegrate into brown clots that slide towards the boy's feet. Again he lunges forward and demands to be allowed to drive. But the man and the woman have begun to argue between themselves and pay no attention to him.

With the underbelly of the helicopter hovering only inches above their heads, they swerve out on to the coastal road which climbs steeply upward over black cliffs. On the left, green fields sparkle crisply in the bright sunshine. There is a profusion of stone walls criss-crossing the higher slopes where yellow gorse bushes hide the barren soil. On the right is the sea – a vast sweep of scintillating turquoise. The woman sits quietly wiping the flask. The wind-slicing blades of the helicopter render the man speechless as he points to the horizon where a knuckle of land, red and swollen, smashes its way up out of the sea.

Immediately the helicopter sets down in the road and soldiers spill out of its sides like newly hatched eggs. The man swings the steering wheel round and the car leaves the road. As the soldiers shrink and vanish in the distance a mysterious silence washes over the occupants of the airborne vehicle. Terrified, the boy begins to shout. But his voice can't be heard. The silence is like a plate-glass window between him and his parents – his father raising a triumphant fist in the air while his mother sits blindly stroking the flask.

A flock of migratory geese sails toward them, their sleek white wings tinged with the ruby glow of the knuckle of land on the horizon. But as their paths cross the boy notices the birds' feathers are torn and clotted with blood. He shoves his fist into his mouth and quickly looks away, noticing that the liquid staining the floor of the car is turning bright red. His parents begin passing the leaking flask back and forth between them. When they finally attempt to hand it on to him he tries to jump out of the car but is prevented from doing so by his father. However, no sooner has his father locked the back door than the front bursts open, causing the vehicle to plunge downward. As his parents are sucked out they are followed by the flask and the picnic hamper. The angry rush of wind tearing the clothes from their bodies reveals hard metallic shells that fall in neat sequence: father, mother, flask then hamper.

Alone in the back of the car the boy screams. The sea mysteriously vanishes, its place taken by a void – a silent infinity, like black silk into which the shells quietly drop, creating just enough draught to slam the doors of the car shut. The boy leaps to his feet, banging his fists on the window . . .

1

A white tree explodes as a thousand egrets take to the sky.

'*Molweni! Molweni!*' the women cry.[1]

The sun spurts over the horizon.

'*Molweni, titsha!*'

He carries on sweeping.

'*Unjani?*'

The home-made broom tattooes the wall with bits of glass from a broken whisky bottle. The dung floor dries and begins to disintegrate, emitting a sour smell. Soon the interior of the hut is bathed in a luminous cloud of amber. Doyle opens another bottle and washes down the dust.

'*Unjani titsha?*'

He looks up as they swing past the mission. Awash in a surfeit of petticoats and pinafores they remind him of extras in an Edwardian musical. Their movements are a flurry, the hands jubilant, the colours garish and loud. The flash of pearly teeth – cracking open the masks of their mud-daubed faces – is accompanied by the clash of bracelets as they return boisterous greetings at every kraal. Their lavish headscarves bobbing in the long grass where liquid hemlines crackle, they chatter and chant as they sweep through the veld, scattering birds and livestock like old props from the stage. Their eyes gleam behind the sunflower masks; their bare feet polish the shiny earth. Brandishing their hoes they laugh: '*Sala khakuhle, titsha! Sala khakuhle!*'

He senses their laughter is self-mocking, hiding the hurt, the injustice they feel. For as extras – as women – *African women* – they have mastered all the roles handed out to them. Only to find that the show has moved on, leaving them behind.

'Sala khakuhle,' they call.

[1] Xhosa words are translated in the glossary on page 233.

5

But the stalls are empty – except for Doyle, a solitary figure who sees their quiet desperation but makes no move towards them.

◇

Full name: Seamus Paeder Doyle.

Date of birth: He recalls the photocopy of his application form lying, like a discarded programme on the floor of the police station, a bootprint obscuring the date and place of his birth.

Marital status: Single.

Identity number (Although he would deny it, he too is one of the cast): 6520842173.

Secondary education: A horizontal fold separated St Joseph's from St Peter's, uncannily mirroring the line running through his memory. The former lay beyond recall; the latter – redemption.

Higher education: University College, Dublin.

Degree obtained: The same bootprint, this time the heel, obscured a degree he had never used.

Previous experience: Waiteha, Solomon Islands – Catholic boarding school: roll 400 (co-ed). Colombo, Sri Lanka – State High School: roll 300 (boys). St Martin's, El Salvador – Independent College of Language Studies: roll 250 (mature students). Bitter Creek, Northern Territories, Australia – School-of-the-air: roll 200 (mixed).

With this miscegenous background he had won the hand of Transkei, a universally ostracised 'republic' born of in-breeding, though given both their past records the relationship was unlikely to last. Already, after barely a year, the strain was beginning to tell, largely thanks to the efforts of the Security Branch which, like a jilted lover, had returned to confront him with spurious tales of a past he had all but forgotten, even going so far as to shove a photocopy of his application form in front of him in case he tried to deny his infidelity: '. . . Your reasons, Mr Doyle, for coming to Transkei?'

The villagers didn't seem to care what his reasons were. '*Molweni, titsha! Molweni*!' they cried whenever they passed his hut. Whether this was because they were happy their school had a teacher, any teacher, or they were just better at hiding their uneasiness, he couldn't tell. Perhaps it was only a matter of time before they, like the police who regarded his presence in the village as a threat – a sign that he was involved in the struggle – began to expect something

6

more of him. Was marking books enough? How long before someone like Majogo demanded to know where he really stood? Demanded proof of his affiliation. Of his commitment to the people's fight for freedom.

He had made no such commitment, since struggles grow out of ideologies and ideologies out of meaning – a meaning to life which, in Doyle's view, did not exist.

Thankfully there were only eight weeks left to the end of term. All he had to do was comply with the villagers' sanguine fantasy: 'Au! Titsha in your hands all our children will be passing their final exam!'

Mentally surveying the derelict church – their only classroom – the broken windows, dung floor, the rain drumming on the iron roof, corroding the mud walls; the heat and the flies and the pained faces of pupils crushed together like beetles in the fetid gloom . . . he despaired of their optimism. How could his appointment – as temporary replacement for the incapacitated Pilot Mjozi – guarantee the success of pupils whose destiny was always likely to lie in exile, martyrdom, unemployment or mutilation on the mines . . .? Assuming, of course, the Security Branch did not jump the queue.

But then they already had.

'It's not detention, sir, as such. We have no order to that effect.'

'Then what are your orders?'

'We would just like to ask you a few questions.'

'About?'

'I think Lieutenant Mbanjwa will be able to inform you on that.'

'Where is the lieutenant?'

'At the police station.'

'So you are detaining me?'

'No sir.'

'You'd just like me to go along with you to the station?'

'Yes sir.'

'Voluntarily?'

'Of course we could detain you. It would only be a matter of . . .'

'Then why don't you?'

'I think you will agree that it is not necessary.'

'No, I suppose it isn't.'

◇

Yet 'they' had detained him – in Waiteh, San Salvador, Bitter Creek (twice) and Colombo (three times). Each time for no longer than twenty-four hours. Each time for his own protection. 'You drunk, they steal your clothes,' an armed Sinhalese police officer had told him after finding him laid out in the car park of a popular hotel. 'Come, it is safer you sleep in jail. Tomorrow we let you go.'

Doyle usually drank alone, colleagues arriving at the same bar tiptoeing out on to the verandah where the fires of their fierce political altercations – these were a modern breed of expatriate: professional, well-informed, well-intentioned, well-paid – raged safely out of range of the notoriously morose figure who was known to ruin many a lively and stimulating debate, not with his drunken oratory but by a propensity to see all sides, as he invariably did, with the same jaundiced eye. Love, politics, religion, the relationship between man and society, between men and women, man and himself, were all seen in the blackest light, brightened only by his withdrawal to another bar, to another hotel. There he would spin a cocoon of languid forgetfulness about himself so that by the end of the evening he would not only fail to recognise aquaintances when they left, but would have difficulty in remembering where he was. Stumbling off into the night with a bottle under his arm, he'd be found in the morning – police permitting – fast asleep on the bonnet of someones car, his own having been stolen since Doyle, arriving drunk, would inevitably forget to lock it.

Occasionally words like disgrace and shameful, or scandalous resurfaced among the old breed. But for the new, driven by a spirit of bureaucratic idealism – everyone Doyle knew seemed to be employed either directly or indirectly by the UN – it was his indifference to their work, above all his insinuations of self-interest and hypocrisy which angered them. For these honest, right-minded people, to get too close to Doyle was to encounter a disturbing negativism.

'The trickle down theory?' he'd groan, as though he were returning a bungled answer paper to one of his pupils. 'The only thing that trickles down is our rubbish – the cardboard boxes and plastic wrapping which become the walls and roof of a shack in the shanties. And even that's on loan, until the next urban renewal programme –

8

utopian-speak for multi-storey car park or office block – takes it all back again, reminding them that nothing's for free, least of all the crumbs from a rich man's table. You put down a non-returnable deposit: your land, your labour, your life so that the men in their shiny limos can decide what to build next, where, when and why . . . can decide which crumbs to release, which 'loans' to call in. Three hundred years ago we offered them baubles. We followed that up with Christianity. Today it's called trickle down . . .'

Tousled and streaked with amber his beard obscured a disappointing face. A face with as much life in it as an old washboard. It had no light, no resonance or passion. Its contours were worn and indistinct. They lacked depth. Indeed they were like a shallow imprint in the sand. A tenuous suggestion. The sort of face children produced when they were learning to draw. What it cried out for were a few skilful strokes, a couple of deft squiggles to bring out the character, to free the stifled spirit.

Instead the nose was slight, the eyes baggy. A dull brow casually obliterated the long, curved lashes. Skin peeled from his lips. His cheeks were colourless, his jaw faint. He wore sandals, loose-fitting trousers and frayed shirts whose pockets were usually ink-stained. His hair cascaded down over his collar like a barrow-load of seaweed, dark, labyrinth curls that teased out of his elusive gaze a hint of nostalgia, fleeting perhaps, like a shoreline fog, yet black and vivid as a rock over which gulls wheeled noisily. It was this hidden regret that those who had worked with Doyle would always remember.

'Reminds me of a character out of Conrad.'

'One of those anarchists.'

'Worn-out visionary.'

'At thirty?'

'Oh, difficult to say how old he is. Much younger than he looks.'

'Unhappy childhood?'

'Family emigrated to South Africa.'

'Odd destination considering their Republican loyalties.'

'A popular place with informers.'

'Ah! Sins of the father.'

'Might explain the vagabonding.'

◇

So would Majogo's boycott now that it had attracted the attention of the Security Branch. Doyle had felt certain the boycott wouldn't last. It was too small, Majogo only had four or five supporters, and it had been badly timed, so close to the exams. He'd expected it to peter out. But it hadn't. It was already two weeks old.

He did not begrudge them their brief hour of fame. They were young, the products of their History, though mercifully the people of Ngagabhaleko did not portray History as burning with quite the same intensity as in the townships. For life in the village was bare, stripped of passion as the land had been stripped of its vegetation. It was true migrant workers returning home over Easter and Christmas brought with them some of the ashes of the terrible fires that had scarred them, but these were quickly swept away by village routine, the timeless tilling of soil, fetching water, felling wood, herding . . .

Mornings, when he hadn't been to bed but had stayed up all night drinking, he watched them set out for the fields.

'*Molweni titsha! Molweni!*' they cried.

With the hollows of their cheeks nestling like the graves of infants in the brightly coloured mud, it wasn't hard to see why they only had bit parts. For in spite of their fluency, the real stars were the stage and its props: the veld, sun, sky, drought, dust, their indestructibility towering over and yet failing to daunt them.

Watching them swing their hoes over their shoulders as they disappeared into the distance he tried to picture them the way colonial commentators used to in the old days; tried to 'admire' the 'primitive' gait, the 'majestic' forehead, the wide, 'sensuous' eyes, 'exquisite' cheekbones . . . the 'noble' carriage with its 'shameless' nudity, its 'tawny' hips, and lips that 'pouted' and 'teased' with a flash of teeth, with the warm thrill of 'savage' laughter . . .

But all he saw was the uncertainty the villagers tried to hide, the fever of suspicion that drained all romanticism from the African stage. For the truth was, even though the fire of History burned low in Ngagabhaleko, it could never be extinguished.

'*Molo titsha!*'

'*Unjani titsha?*'

Just how difficult was it for them to accept his presence in the village? How much courage had it taken to grant him the necessary space in which to work? A space they skirted round with care, compassion, always with the utmost politeness, unlike the authorities who, decidedly less stoical, had come crashing through the febrile fence.

'If we may begin, Mr Doyle . . .' Swallowing the unfamiliar name like a hard-boiled sweet; clearly resenting his passivity, as if he wasn't taking them seriously; trying to unpick in a single afternoon the century's sores – not blatantly, for they weren't, he suspected, as sadistic as their Afrikaner godfathers, but with a carefully nursed innuendo, revealing in moments of frustration, the despairing assertiveness of a mutilated history; revealing above all, the threat of vengeance by those who had managed to survive it.

'If we may begin with your reason for coming to Transkei.'

2

Eight weeks to the end of term. Another year of his contract to run. Was it worth the risk? Was it worth going back to the village at all? Doyle's shoulders rose then fell in the dark. Fogbound, the road to Ngagabhaleko drifted in and out of view like a firefly on the diaphanous dress of the night.

Beside him Alexia wrestled with the wheel of the pick-up, showing that she too resented his indifference. After the smell of the police station – his clothes saturated with the miasma of communal latrines, stale sweat, floor wax and paraffin – her liberal use of perfume emphasised her disgust, helping to push him further away from her, though now and then he caught a whiff of the cow dung that clung to the soles of her high-heeled shoes lying under the seat. Two worlds grappling over one soul. Grappling to the death. For neither could win. Alexia would carry the battle inside her wherever she went. Everything she touched would become a weapon, a double-edged sword. For the moment the pick-up was her weapon and the speedometer needle was swinging wildly.

They were on a remote, dirt road, with corners looming out of the dark like ghosts. Rises remained unmarked; drifts a matter of memory. Villages lay concealed in the distance like corpses awaiting burial; the ill-fitting doors of the pick-up rattling in an hysterical wake while stones ricocheted off the chassis. A stray animal or phantom villager materialising out of the fog would have stood little chance. Yet as Alexia shoved her food down even harder on the accelerator Doyle leaned back and shut his eyes, cradling the by now almost empty whisky bottle which he had kept hidden under the seat.

Perhaps he was indifferent. Perhaps he was failing to take her seriously. Having secured his release, she at least deserved his . . . gratitude? sympathy? understanding? What exactly did she want from him? What had brought her storming into the quiet country station, demanding they free him before they'd even had time to button their tunics or scrutinise the paper she brandished under their noses?

'Go back? You want to go back to Ngagabhaleko? What about Mazeppa? Doyle we should celebrate!'

Celebrate? Jesus, this wasn't an act of heroism. It was Alexia at her most wanton, cavalier and dangerous, heedless of the questions that were bound to be asked, not least by her uncle, the Reverend Benedict Xolile, head of the local Lutheran church and chairman of the school committee with whom she lived at the mission in Ngagabhaleko.

Doyle had sensed the danger and yet even now the more he thought about it, the more reckless her 'heroism' seemed, posing a threat to him that was just as serious as Majogo's boycott, or even the attention of the Security Branch – any one of which made his leaving urgent, indeed more urgent than he had earlier realised. He now felt he couldn't risk staying even to the end of term. He felt he had to get away that night, though it meant a 700 kilometre drive to the airport in Johannesburg.

It would also mean abandoning his pupils on the eve of their exams. And yet what else could he do? What more could he achieve in the short time that was left? The *umlungu* as conjuror? 'Mister Mjozi principal,' they would fret and fuss, 'few children pass. Mister Doyle in charge, all our children pass!'

Strange how even in the storms they endured they clung to the coat-tails of their arch-old enemy, reflecting, to his surprise, just how conservative the inhabitants of Ngagabhaleko were. Perhaps this had sustained them in their years of suffering. Or had it been their undoing? *His* would be to remain.

◇

'If we may begin, Mr Doyle, with your reasons for coming to Transkei. What is it exactly that has brought you to our poor country?'

Note: not 'What has brought you *back*?'; simply: 'What has brought you?' – though of course he knows what they mean. The scuffed curriculum vitae lying at his feet gives it away. It's a self-indicting history. No doubt the Security Branch have obtained a copy

13

from the Department of Education. Having concealed or distorted nothing in it Doyle realises he is vulnerable. Yet he makes no effort to hide the sheet at which everyone entering the room studiously glances. Instead he ignores it, just as he has always ignored the past, or rather, the resentful symbol he identifies with it: his father's grave which, his interrogators also know, lies less than 200 kilometres from Ngagabhaleko, in the Lusikisiki district of Transkei.

'Work?' he feebly suggests and is bemused by his co-star's reaction, which is hurriedly to search the script.

'You are not certain?'

'I know *you're* not,' Doyle replies.

'That shouldn't surprise you.'

'It doesn't.'

'So you are also a sceptic. We should find it easy to get along.'

'Ah! Marital bliss.'

'That depends,' the lieutenant warns hastily.

'On?'

'Whether we are able to trust each other.'

'Trust? You're asking a lot. Do you know what the divorce rate in this country is? One in three.'

'You yourself have never married, Mr Doyle?'

'It's on my . . .' Doyle is about to point to the document on the floor. He stops, allows his hand to flop by his side like a discarded handkerchief and says: 'You know I live alone.'

'Nevertheless,' the lieutenant insists, 'you can understand a woman wishing to know whether her husband is faithful or not.'

Doyle slides down his chair. 'Not being a romantic . . .'

'But you are a man. And at one time or another all men have been questioned about their fidelity. They also have to put up with a woman's constant need for reassurance. Women always want to know whether they still have that certain something, whether their lover will be moved to pick them out from among the . . .'

'Look, I've picked out no one, Lieutenant. You chose me.'

'But clearly you have chosen Ngagabhaleko.'

'Which makes you an interloper.'

'If that were true,' sniffs the lieutenant, 'I would leave gracefully. Unfortunately, as history shows it is you, Mr Doyle, the white man, who . . .'

'Your government invited me here,' Doyle sniffs in return. 'They advertised the job in the paper.'

'You were attracted by a *bundu* school?'

'This is a *bundu* station.'

'Yes but we are well provided for. Unlike the people at Ngagabhaleko we have permanent houses with running water, electricity . . . You've seen the generator. It even runs a television.'

'Or would if the government could afford to pay its bills.'

'I admit we are a poor country. Nevertheless we enjoy most of the creature comforts.'

'Like grenade wire over the windows?'

'Oh but it's just a precaution. I'm sure you lock your door before you go to sleep at night.'

The thought of Alexia's discrete visits brings a wan smile to his lips.

'Life is cheap in the village, Mr Doyle.'

'I can't say I've experienced any personal danger.'

'Even so, your blood is just as likely to be spilled as the next man's. It all depends on whose belly is empty.'

'Most bellies are.'

'That is true. So perhaps the villagers have a vested interest in you.'

'In *me*?'

'White men who come to Africa always promise a lot – everything from glass beads to the kingdom of heaven.'

'Charlatans, I agree. Disguised by history as great adventurers.'

'Surely you are not a charlatan, Mr Doyle?'

'Nor a great adventurer.'

'Then what are you? A lover who has come back because he feels guilty? Because in the past you paid Africa so little attention? Do you, by offering your skills in this empty corner of our country, intend to win her back? After so many years of neglect?'

'Africa,' sighs Doyle, running his fingers through his greasy hair, 'doesn't care how much attention you pay her. She'll always be indifferent. Dreams, pious hopes, human vanity . . . they all crumble like dust in her blank stare. Africa consumes people, Lieutenant, she's like some mythical beast stretched out in timeless lethargy, her hunger's insatiable, her tastes catholic. Not many get to look her in the eye and survive.'

15

'For you the hunger of a creature out of mythology; for me, that of a *tsotsi* wanting to fill his belly. Both pose a threat to the journey you have undertaken, Mr Doyle.'

'All journeys carry a risk. My only fear is arriving somewhere and finding the way out blocked.'

'What if the Department were to offer you the post of permanent rather than acting principal? Would a sense of ambition not overcome this . . . eh?'

'Claustrophobia? On the contrary. My instinct would be to resign.'

'You are happy to lead the life of a migrant worker?'

'It's a life like any other.'

'But not one a man would ordinarily choose.'

'The men of Ngagabhaleko have.'

'Please. You have seen the conditions in the village, Mr Doyle.'

'We all have our "conditions".'

'Not everyone suffers from an empty stomach.'

'When was the last time you visited a village, Lieutenant?'

'I talk not of the amaXhosa, but the *abelungu*. His hunger is in the eyes, not in the belly.'

'The *abelungu*'s eyes? Or the Security Branch's?'

$$\diamondsuit$$

Lieutenant Mbanjwa shakes his head. It's supposed to be a gesture of contempt but it fails to soothe his nagging incomprehension. Fortunately he senses that Doyle is unaware of his discomfort. Or could it be the *umlungu* doesn't take him seriously? The lieutenant doubts it. Nevertheless, Doyle's attitude is puzzling. There is the usual liberal scepticism. The self-effacing humility, the lack of edge, or bite. But he also displays a peculiar indifference – indeed a marked lack of respect though, it would seem, for none other than himself. Is it the self-loathing of a drunkard? The state of his clothes and the way he slouches would suggest so. Yet the lieutenant is convinced Doyle is playing some sort of game with him. The *abelungu*, he has learned, like to play games even though they soon become bored by them. He can see Doyle is bored, pretending not to understand the line of questioning. Really he doesn't want to understand. There is no fire in his eyes. He is like a beggar going from village to village yet scarcely expecting to be handed a crust of bread. It doesn't seem possible.

What *umlungu* could endure such shame? He must be playing a game. But what sort of game? Can a man ignore his own past – even when it is lying, printed in his own hand, on the floor in front of him?

3

The stage: a cell in a remote, country police station. The reek of paraffin as a constable brews tea in a smoke-blackened corner of the passage outside; the smell of wax. A floor, polished that morning, stubbornly refuses to shine; every now and then its wooden boards crack, like a bone breaking. On the walls graffiti lurk beneath a recent skin of yellow paint. Scratches near the door resemble pieces of a broken comb – suggest a calendar. A dark stain, just off-centre, hints at dried blood; the ghosts of past occupants lingering . . .

High in the corner is a solitary barred window. Free of dust, it shimmers in the bright light, like the scales of a gutted fish. It is not a window for gazing out of: scorched countryside surrounds the protagonists. Overhead a torn canvas ceiling hangs like an open fly, pouring heat down upon them; heat as thick as boiled sugar, blackened by paraffin smoke; drugged insects writhe in a brief paroxysm, before they expire.

The props: Doyle's c.v. This, as already indicated, lies in a state of neglect on the floor. Doyle understands the statement the Security Branch are making. They know his parents once farmed near Lusikisiki and that he previously had attended boarding school nearby in the Eastern Cape.

There is nothing here that Doyle has tried to hide. What concerns him is the lieutenant's stomach. For the ghosts of History are on the loose. And their parts, Doyle's and the lieutenant's, are bit parts which seldom lead anywhere since Africa is a star that brooks no competition.

The props (continued): a single straight-backed chair – antique. It is unlikely the rest of the set survives in the brushless expanse between Butterworth and Ngagabhaleko and so its isolation is fitting. For it echoes the confinement not only of the cell, but of the station – to a remote corner of the countryside. Indeed it symbolises the very isolation of Transkei itself. In addition there is Doyle's own estrangement and the loneliness of the lieutenant – cut off from the people he purports to serve.

Lieutenant Mbanjwa leans against the wall. His arms are folded. A cigarette dangles from the pod-like lips. No, he is not another Marlow. His reading does not extend that far. He has obviously watched and is now imitating his superiors. He is no slouch at it either. He is fit and lean and waits with a keen sense of anticipation for Doyle to join him in transforming an uneventful career into something more glamorous. Well, not necessarily glamorous, something more solid. The lieutenant isn't after fame. All he dreams of – this in the face of History's continuous onslaught – is rapid promotion followed by early retirement, and a tiny farm in the foothills of the Drakensberg, where the soil is rich, the water plentiful and a man's worth has nothing to do with the number of acres he owns. A dream which, in Doyle's view, would make him a hopeless romantic.

Doyle himself sprawls carelessly across the chair, propping an elbow on the only other item of furniture in the room, ironically a school desk. Although it is old and the seats have been torn from the wrought-iron frame, its writing surface gouged, it embodies a haunting indestructibility. But not to Doyle or the lieutenant. In this unlikely setting the lieutenant regards the desk as a symbol of the end of colonialism, greeting the sight of the headmaster draped over it, with a quiet if puzzled satisfaction. Doyle, on the other hand, glances at the empty inkwells and is reminded of the vain hopes of the hundreds of pupils he has taught.

He rests his head on the wooden surface, drugged by the heat like the flies buzzing in the window. His back aches. Every now and then he stirs to rub it, but it's a feeble gesture and his hand repeatedly plops on to the desk. He has removed his tie and stuffed it into his shirt pocket. The shirt is faded and torn at the shoulder though one hardly notices as it hangs open to his waist. His chest is thin and sunken like an old mattress. Its northern translucency belies the years he has spent in the tropics. But then Doyle has never been one for the sun. Great half-moons stain his armpits while his hair sticks to his scalp. His beard remains untrimmed and his fingernails are black.

Yet there is soap, water and a basin in his cell. He has suffered no indignity. He hasn't been assaulted, denied sleep or food. He is even free to wander about the compound. In fact it's only the second day of his 'confinement' and questioning has hardly begun.

In spite of this, his mood can only be described as fatalistic which, unknown to the lieutenant, is an integral part of Doyle's character. Had the lieutenant known something about accents, the disappearance of Doyle's would have warned him. For having long ago abandoned his northern burr, Doyle, like a chameleon blending in with its surroundings, frequently imitates his host's. Thus while the lieutenant sees anonymity all around him and strives to rise above it, Doyle embraces it as a method of survival. It is his ultimate, no-hype definition of existence.

So the play continues. Doyle, having slipped in as a member of the audience, finds the authorities are determined he should play a more leading role; *the* leading role in their hackneyed production of 'A Liberal Hero'.

◇

'If I may ask, what attracts you to working among the poor, Mr Doyle?'

'My own poverty?'

'But you are not poor.'

'I'm not optimistic either.'

'A man of your education? Surely you are ambitious.'

'Maybe you should ask the people of Ngagabhaleko.'

'They themselves do not lack ambition.'

'The old? The unemployed? Sick and bereaved? Children without fathers? Grandparents without children? They can't afford the illusion.'

'But they have retained their faith. You yourself are a witness to the success of the Lutheran mission under Reverend Xolile.'

'I wouldn't call it an unqualified success. The witch-doctor still has a large following.'

'The form of belief is not relevant. I raise the matter of the villagers' faith only in order to contrast it with . . .' The lieutenant pauses to light a fresh cigarette from the old, which is pinched and wet. 'Forgive me if I am mistaken, Mr Doyle . . .' Smoke steams from the dilated nostrils. The discarded stub is allowed to burn itself out on the floor. ' . . . But you do not strike me as a man of any religious conviction.'

Doyle, wondering whether this is a subtle dig at his relationship with the Reverend's niece, examines the lieutenant's face for any sign of irony. However, he soon gives up for the lieutenant's eyes are quite blank. And besides, what if he did know about their secret affair? It would merely be a diversion, an unneccessary sub-plot that obscured the simple message of the 'Liberal Hero'. On the other hand, he feels a diversion at this moment would be welcome.

'You see,' the lieutenant intones, 'although you work among the poor I can detect no evidence of any spiritual motive. The people of Ngagabhaleko are poor but they are ambitious. The Reverend Xolili is ambitious. He has built many churches throughout the country, including the one at Ngagabhaleko. Yet in spite of the opportunity you have had to witness the triumph of his mission, you share none of your illustrious neighbour's enthusiasm. On the contrary, you suggest that you have come to Transkei not only without ambition, but without a choice in the matter. That is, you say you faced a similar choice to that of the men of the village who have to decide between hunger and the gold mines. You imply that man has no control over his destiny, that all of us are just onlookers. Yet how is one to reconcile such fatalism with your role as a teacher? We are a young country building for the future, Mr Doyle. We have no place for those who merely shrug their shoulders when they are offered something fresh and idealistic.'

But Doyle neither shrugs his shoulders nor, indeed, shows any sign of hearing the lieutenant. Managing to lose himself in the diversion, he wonders what the reaction in the village would be if they found out he was sleeping with the Reverend's niece. Who would pose the greater threat, Christians or non-Christians? Undoubtedly Alexia would say it was none of their business but that was hardly a sentiment the Reverend could be expected to agree with. It was even possible he had feared that very thing might happen – hence his attempt, as chairman of the school committee, to dissuade the department from offering Doyle Pilot Mjozi's job. Or had that merely been one of Alexia's stories, designed to win him over in the fight against her uncle?

'Come, Mr Doyle, if you have not chosen for yourself this life of a migrant, then who has chosen it for you?'

'*Who*?'

'Some doctrine, perhaps?'

'I'm sorry. I was . . . well, what do you want me to say? *Communist* doctrine?'

'They are never onlookers.'

'We are all onlookers.'

'You must please explain.'

'Well, we're both actors and onlookers if you like, but actors only because as an audience we can't make sense of the script. So we charge up out of our seats and on to the stage, chasing the cast away, or rather, the leading character. We wait for the spotlight and our own personal moment of glory. Then it arrives but unfortunately it doesn't last very long: our lines are hastily edited; sometimes they become incoherent. In a matter of seconds we are yesterday's show.'

'You talk of chasing the leading character?'

Doyle kneads the small of his back. The corrugated-iron roof pops in the heat.

The lieutenant says, anxiously: 'You are referring to the violent overthrow of . . .'

'1789? 1848? 1917? Take your pick, Lieutenant.'

'I am not an Historian, Mr Doyle.'

'Though History consumes you. African history: our mythical beast.'

'So History is the leading character!'

'No. It's just a chronicle of the audience's repeated invasion of the stage. Take a night, say, in 1823. Adam Smith's *Wealth of Nations* seduces the public to insurrection. Everyone is invited to strip off their onlooker rags. A part, a leading part, is promised to all. In the end we are bombarded with clichés. History as a continuous soap opera. Today we are still stripping off our rags, clamouring for a part. Hovering on the edge of the spotlight, we conveniently forget the unfortunate death of our hero whose role we have usurped and whose identity is forgotten. Inevitably each of us believes we are the leading character. Me! Me! Me! we cry, demanding the audience's attention, forgetting our place in the vast scheme of things, re-writing the rambling script as if it were an autobiography. Actors? Suddenly we're all bloody playwrights!'

'And you have no such ambition?'

'Haven't had since my lines were torn up as a child.'

22

'Children tear up their lines every day, Mr Doyle.'

'I didn't do the tearing.'

'If someone else did, why didn't you protest?'

'Everyone protests.'

'So why didn't you re-write the script; attempt to put yourself back in the centre of your own drama?'

'It wasn't my script to re-write any more. The plot and its characters were forced on me, lines shoved down my throat. Meanings became and remain distorted to this day.'

'You are a widely travelled man,' says the lieutenant, sombrely stroking his jaw. 'Surely your experience has given you some insight into the complexities of our time; enabled you to discover fresh meaning, a new sense of vision?'

Doyle drags a hand through the air. It is thin and pale and collapses into his lap like an exhausted egret. 'Vision? Yes – of a crumbling stage and the final curtain.'

'But surely that is still some way off.'

'Is it?'

'It's in our own hands.'

'Try telling that to the villagers – that they have the power, indeed the right to alter the script; the ability to become their own playwrights. It's an illusion even the Reverend Xolile's congregation would quickly see through.'

'So you have seen through it? Is that why you are no longer a Christian?'

'That was part of the old script.'

'But if you abandoned your faith doesn't that show a desire to take personal control of your life?'

'Look, where are my lines?' cries Doyle, scuffing the floor with his sandal. 'I'm playing off the cuff. My stage is empty. The only sign of life is . . . is this vague figure emerging out of the wings, caught up in his own desire to gain the spotlight. So far he's been polite and surprisingly unhurried. But sooner or later he'll want to be noticed. I know because it's in his script. The only problem is the playwright he's stalking – or is it guerrilla? – is eluding him; just as the dead elude us all.'

'The dead?'

'Fantasy and sedition, Lieutenant. Aren't these what you're

looking for? Hopes, dreams, ambitions? They're all dead. Without graves or headstones; like the dead in a time of famine.'

Twin jets of smoke vanish into a thick fog. Lieutenant Mbanjwa tosses an empty cigarette packet on to the floor. A red-billed quelea brushes the wire mesh as it alights in the window. The lieutenant pays no attention to it. As he speaks the bird bolts.

'You imply we are chasing after phantoms, Mr Doyle. In which case allow me to quote Circular No. 53 to you, on the distribution of subversive literature at schools. You see it makes it quite clear . . .' Like a butterfly's wings, the lieutenant's eyes quietly close. Smoke and phlegm are evacuated.

'. . . "that opponents of educational advancement scatter and disseminate subversive pamphlets at the entrance to school premises. This and other nefarious acts, such as the promotion of class boycotts, is usually undertaken first thing in the morning before staff arrive" . . .'

The red-billed quelea returns, is nonplussed by the lack of space on the ledge and flies off again. The lieutenant's eyes remain shut.

'"In order to protect the innocent youth of our nation, responsible citizens such as chiefs, headmen, members of churches, school committees and teachers are all requested to be on the lookout for and to collect any seditious material before it reaches the students. This material, along with those who are found to be distributing it, should be taken to the principal who is responsible for handing the matter over to the police" . . .'

The blood-shot eyes snap open. 'What do you have to say, Mr Doyle? Does this not indicate that, far from being without ambition, you have resolved to follow your own script? Surely you cannot deny that you have deliberately ignored the instructions of the government?'

Slumped over the desk, Doyle's body has the appearance of a corpse that has just been fished out of the river. His clothes are awry. His head flops over one shoulder; greasy curls entangled about his neck. His flesh, in spite of a hard, bluish pallor, has a looseness about it, a precariousness, as if it might come away in ones hands. His jaw, hanging slackly, exposes through the sediment of beard, a row of rotting teeth. His legs are strung out in front of him, his eyes focused blankly on the wall which the lieutenant is leaning against.

Lieutenant Mbanjwa is not in uniform. Nevertheless, he is impeccably turned out in a grey tweed jacket which he keeps fastened, a pastel pink shirt, blue string-tie and polyester trousers from which he now and then flicks away bits of ash. His neat, orderly build is marred by a crushed nose that lends his expression a certain inner tension. The tips of his fingers are almost white. Squinting through the smoke, his eyes betray a surprising defencelessness.

'You do not answer, Mr Doyle.'

'History has distorted your hearing, Lieutenant.'

'I have told you I am not an historian.'

'And I have told you that I am not a playwright.'

'A process of elimination would be rather tedious, don't you think?'

'Then what about a process of positive identification?'

'Of what – goals?'

'I told you I don't have any.'

'Roles?'

'Easy. Migrant worker.'

'Not *mercenary*, Mr Doyle?'

'Pimp. Whore. Mercenary. If only money *were* the driving factor.'

'Only idealists are not driven by it.'

'Idealists? Jesus! You haven't heard a word I've said, Lieutenant.'

'I admit I haven't understood everything you have said. Perhaps it is my background which is somewhat different from yours. But the idea that a man can go through life without . . .'

'Precisely. You have understood. You've just refused to *believe* any of it. Given the disabling History of the country, I suppose that's understandable. But it's *your* disability and you'll have to live with it, as the people of Ngagabhaleko have to. I haven't set out to win their trust. It isn't my fight. They've allowed me into their village to teach and that's what I've done. *All* I've done.'

Thumbs hooked in the waistband of his trousers. A dramatic steel squint. Smoke jets once more through the lieutenant's nose.

'Allow me to point out, Mr Doyle, that while the villagers may be pleased to have a man of your experience instructing their children, your first responsibility is to your employer, namely the Government of Transkei. Either the Department of Education or the Security Branch should have been informed of the widespread unrest at your school. This you failed to do. Why? Was it because you were hoping to avoid the attention of your superiors? Perhaps you yourself tried to persuade the students to return to class? Maybe you were afraid that if the authorities learned of this lack of discipline, they would cancel your contract? Or is there another reason? Some possibly more sinister motive?'

Doyle glances up at the portentous bank of smoke. Two flies become entangled on the inside of the window, skid and buzz against the wire mesh before breaking free.

'Can we be clear about one thing, Lieutenant? There has been no widespread unrest. The handful of pupils who called for a boycott failed to persuade anyone to join them, not surprisingly since they're outsiders. They came here with their parents who kicked out of Johannesburg by the authorities. The boys were born and grew up in the townships around there. They have no allegiance to Ngagabhaleko. Unlike these . . . five or six . . . I'm not exactly sure how many there are, the rest are extremely proud of their school, even if all it consists of is mud bricks and a few rusty sheets of iron which leak in the rain.'

'Nevertheless,' the lieutenant frowns, unrelenting, 'you have allowed the first seeds of dissent to be sowed.'

'Nothing grows in Ngagabhaleko, I can assure you.'

'I think you should allow the Security Branch to be the judge.'

'Then I suggest you talk to the boys themselves. Ask them how much progress they think they've made. I'm surprised you've ignored them for so long. But then I forget. You're looking for something a little more sinister, aren't you?'

'The lieutenant lifts himself from the wall; unfolds his arms; hitches his trousers. 'You've heard of the monkey and the organ-grinder, Mr Doyle?'

Doyle knows better than to laugh. 'You're suggesting *I'm* the orchestrator of this whole thing?'

Twin jets of smoke emerge. Once again the iron roof pops.

'Or do you think I'm one of the monkeys? It would have to be a pretty long lead, stretching all the way from . . . where do you have in mind? London? Or Lusaka? Maybe even Dublin? Jesus I haven't been to Ireland in ten, eleven years . . .'

More disgorged smoke. Like stale flour it thickens the heat in the room.

'One would be negligent if one did not consider all the possibilities, Mr Doyle.'

'And paranoid to take them all seriously.'

'It is our job.'

'Well, they say a former head of MI5 may have been a Russian mole, so I guess anything is possible.'

An expression of contempt sweeps over the lieutenant's face. But then, like a wave crashing against a breakwater it retreats amid turmoil and confusion. He drags on the butt glued to his lips; hugs the wall.

◇

And so the play continues. The parts are cast and Doyle must play the role assigned to him. Many years ago he would have relished the challenge, but his heart is no longer in it. Wearily he prises off his battered sandals and slides down further in the chair. Catching a glimpse of his c.v., he realises he has omitted the year spent teaching in Beirut. He shrugs. It seems a long time ago. Bored at university, he had taken a year off.

'Perhaps, Mr Doyle,' says the lieutenant, doggedly, 'we could turn our attention to the activities of your father . . .'

4

Alexia continued to attack the wheel. With each loud crump as the pick-up crashed through a pothole, the headlights soared up into the night. Finding their path blocked by the fog they swirled back down again in a lambent parachute, engulfing hapless villagers who scattered like rabbits from the roadside.

Alexia's control seemed at best precarious; her vision obscured less by the fog than by her hair tumbling over her eyes in long braids that were festooned with beads. The glittering beads reminded Doyle of oxygen bubbles and, indeed, as her feet slapped the pedals it seemed to him that she wasn't so much driving as treading water.

Poor Alexia, he thought, as he wound the window down and tossed the empty whisky bottle out into the night. She expected so much. Yet she knew so little about him. He had slept with her without really allowing her to get close. As a result he remained an enigma to her; a puzzle whose pieces were beginning to multiply . . . Why, she'd wanted to know when the boycott had broken out, hadn't he sent for the police? Why had he stalled, allowing Majogo to make a fool of him? Why had he allowed himself to be questioned without the boys? As for his release, surely that ought to have been something to cheer about? Instead: 'Go back? You want to go back to Ngagabhaleko? But what about Mazeppa? Doyle we should celebrate!'

Alexia Primrose Xolile: petulant, streetwise and brittle. A thorn in the side of the *amaqaba*, who had of course weathered far more and so suffered her scorn with indifference. Loose-hipped and lanky, her very build seemed an harangue; her restlessness a rebuke aimed at the world. But while passionate, her eyes betrayed a confusion which Doyle knew he had done nothing to allay. If anything their love-making had only made matters worse.

He remembered the first time he had seen her. Shortly after moving into his hut he'd gone round scouring the mission compound for a piece of tin to block up the hole which the rats were using to invade his room. And there she had stood, beside a malodorous heap of rubbish that the servants were burning, in bright yellow stockings, matching skirt, sweater, and blue beret. She was pointing angrily to something, remonstrating with the two old crones who were covered in ash. The braided tresses obscured her face, but he could sense the undercurrent. He was about to postpone his search when one of the servants looked his way. Immediately she swung round. As she swept her hair back he found himself staring into her large, frantic eyes.

That evening she knocked on the door of his hut. Twisting her beret between her fingers, she introduced herself as: 'the object of my uncle's shame and vengeance', and straight away launched into her appeal.

'I want to become your student. A private student. I want you to teach me. I only have one more year to finish my matric and then I shall be free to leave this *bundu*. I shall be able to get a proper job in Durban or Johannesburg and be my own boss. I shall be able to look after myself and live as I please.'

Startled – she had been his first visitor – he didn't know what to say. He watched her pull and tear at her beret; the moonlight spilling like rain off the hut's golden thatch, drenching her face and hair, bathing her skin in a fetching glow.

'My uncle doesn't want me to finish school. But I myself am determined. If I do not get my matric at the end of this year then I will end up a housemaid or a slave for some white madam who will pay me only just enough to breathe so that I can be her slave for the rest of my life. I do not want that. I am determined to avoid that slow death which has been responsible for so much useless waste in our country. Please, this is my last chance. My patience will not last another year. I must do it now. I must get my matric this year. That is why I am asking you to help me.'

Her teeth were as white as the moon; her cheeks rising like freshly baked scones in the warm African night.

'I . . . eh . . . don't know,' he stammered. 'Haven't you left it a little late?'

A pink tongue arched itself against the roof of her mouth. 'In our country it's not unusual. There are many students like me in their twenties who are trying to complete their schooling. It all depends on the circumstances at home. Children must wait until their parents can afford to send them. Or else if they are old enough, fifteen or sixteen, they can take a few years away from class in order to earn money for themselves. Then if there are no boycotts they can return to finish their studies.'

Money was the reason she hadn't finished? Given the Reverend's position, he felt it was unlikely. The Reverend had only just returned from the International Conference of Lutherans in Kenya – driving a spanking new car. And what about her own fashionable taste in clothes . . .?

But she'd sensed his scepticism.

'The reason my uncle refuses to let me finish is because I became pregnant in my final year. I was attending school in Soweto. These things happen to the young girls there. But when it happens the authorities throw you out on to the street. I was fortunate because it was near the end of the year and so I got permission to write as a private candidate. But then my uncle refused to allow me to take the examinations. "Vengeance is mine sayeth the Lord." And so sayeth the Reverend Benedict Xolile. It is more than five years now.'

'But why haven't you tried to write before?' he asked.

'Because then my uncle was transferred to Transkei and I was forced to accompany him. So now I have been stuck in this *bundu* place ever since, where there is no one who will help me. These people are backward. The former principal, Mr Mjozi, he was afraid of my uncle. He refused to allow me to enrol at the school.'

'What makes you think your uncle'll change his mind?'

'He will not refuse me permission to study if you talk to him. He will be too embarrassed. It will show the world that he is not a real Christian, that he cannot forgive.'

'The world?'

'You are a white man. Please. You must help me. My uncle cannot refuse you.'

Alexia: avid, chic and unabashed; yet like the *amaqaba* she scorned, seeing the *umlungu* as a miracle worker.

It had all been in vain of course. The Protestant shame, as he could have predicted, had not yet been expunged. When it came to Christianity there wasn't anything remotely isolated or backward about the amaXhosa.

At first Alexia had scorned his efforts, accusing him of not really trying. But then she informed him that she'd registered in any event, secretly, as a private candidate, and began to conceal her books in his room.

The lessons took place at night. She was ardent and punctual. And her handwriting was flawless. Soon she began to pull ahead of his regular pupils. Of course she was older; wasn't burdened with their shyness. If anything she was too direct, too transparent, lacking in objectivity. In their study of *Othello* she grew increasingly frustrated with Desdemona's blind obedience to the ill-tempered Moor. 'The spineless woman! Where is her dignity? To suffer such ill-treatment for nothing. It is asking too much of a wife. He orders her to her room and she goes, blindly, like a dog. She does not even defend herself. Never will I allow a man to use me in such a way; to treat me as though I was his to do with as he pleases.' And then one night, slamming the text down on the table she took her frustration out on him, demanding to know what he, Doyle, was doing in a place like Ngagabhaleko.

'Even the Xhosa teachers don't want to come here. There is nothing for them. It is a *bundu*. The land is poor and the people are backward. They do not speak English. You do not speak Xhosa. How will they trust you? How can they be sure that you are really concerned for their children? They might think you are here for other reasons. Or have you come to taste the freedom of Africa? Look! I am an African. Where is my freedom?'

Freedom? Alexia: bruised, unbowed romantic.

In the murky glow of the dashboard, Doyle watched her pounding the pedals, flattening her palms against the hooter as the haunting silhouettes of cattle floated by in the fog. Part of him saw her as a child beating her fists against his chest. Part saw the luxurious mouth and olive-smooth throat . . . Soon he began to regret his earlier coolness toward her.

'Go back? You want to go back to Ngagabhaleko? But what about Mazeppa? Doyle, we should celebrate!'

However, alarm bells had been ringing even before the brittle 'we' cracked in the oven heat of the bush; and 'curfew' was all he had muttered as they clambered into the pick-up outside the police station.

Earlier that afternoon she had burst into the charge office and demanded to see the commanding officer. Doyle, esconsed with the lieutenant in a cell down the passage, had immediately recognised her voice. Clipped and confident, it struck a note of casual, deadly sharpness.

'Not here? That's too bad. Come with me.'

Followed by the stupefied duty officer, she'd marched into the smoke-filled cell, announcing: '*Mister* Doyle' (at first he wasn't sure whether she was striking one of her imperious poses, or just being streetwise), 'this is my uncle, the Reverend Xolile's younger brother, Colonel Xolile. He has brought the papers for your release. These . . .' She broke off, indicating the startled assembly of policemen in the doorway. 'These monkeys, they don't know what they are supposed to be doing.'

'Just following orders, I expect, *Miss* Xolile.'

'Orders!'

'You know – the organ grinder,' he said, glancing at the lieutenant in the corner. How old and tired he seemed, staring with ragged eyes as he tried to make sense of the ill-timed change of set. No curtain call. No standing ovation. Simply a hostile command to clear the stage.

'Well, their orders were to arrest Majogo and his *tsotsis*,' said Alexia, turning up her nose at the sour smell of props and make-up.

'Whose orders?'

'Where are your shoes?' she demanded, noticing that he stood in his bare feet.

'Your uncle's?' he asked.

She swooped down on his sandals lying under the desk, handed them to him along with the scuffed copy of his c.v. He shook his head at the latter and she crumpled it into a ball, lobbing it across the cell.

'My uncle does not work for the Security Branch,' she announced disdainfully.

'So how could he have brought papers for my release? Besides, I haven't been arrested.'

Ignoring the increasing numbers of policemen arriving at the door, some of whom were armed and had spilled into the cell, Alexia looked haughtily at him. If there was an element of over-dramatisation – the hands on hips, orange-painted fingernails, head flung back – it was because she was determined not be intimidated. An orphan, part of

32

Alexia's charm was that she had learnt to fend for herself. Not for her the helpless dependence on some dull-witted Othello. Indeed she had turned the tables. It was he who was the pathetic Desdemona.

'You were a fool to go with the Security Branch. You! A school principal! And you let these uneducated creatures take you away. What will the people of Ngagabhaleko think?'

'What do you mean?'

'Tsha! You are nearly as stupid as them.'

'I had no choice.'

'They will say you are weak.'

'I was trying to make things easy.'

'They will say you are a police spy.'

'After being *detained*?'

'The Security Branch issued no orders to detain you. These men were merely instructed to question you at school.'

'What about Majogo?'

'It was Majogo they were supposed to detain.'

'Maybe they got it the wrong way round.'

'There are people who will blame you if Majogo is arrested. They will say you pointed the finger.'

'They should know me better than that.'

'Better than what? You do nothing but mark students' books. At the weekends you do not go away but hide inside your *jondolo*, where it is dark and the thatch is rotting and the walls are bare of pictures – not even one to remind you of your home. It is the life of an ox always ploughing the same furrow. Who will believe you are here just for that single purpose?'

A match flared on the far side of the room as Lieutenant Mbanjwa lit another cigarette. Doyle thought he detected an ironic gleam in his eyes, but the lieutenant's expression reflected no more than a tedious air as the cloud of smoke drifted upwards. Alexia's stunning entrance had made a nonsense of his dogged performance.

'To the people of Ngagabhaleko you are free to come and go as you please,' she continued, in her loud, reproachful voice, 'but your car always stands inside the mission like a beast that is chained. They can see you do not visit Umtata or drive to the coast. Why is the *umlungu* here, they ask, living the life of a prisoner? Surely he has not come to die with us, in poverty.'

33

'So you agree with the lieutenant that I should leave?'

'Tsha! You are not frightened by that fool? It is my uncle who is in charge of this district. And if he wishes you to stay then no harm can come to you.'

'But you said the villagers would be suspicious.'

'They will learn that my uncle has ordered your release.'

'Won't they want to know why?'

'Why? Because he's an officer! A general, a . . .'

'Colonel,' croaked a voice in the background.

'General? Colonel? What does it matter? You are all his monkeys.'

Alexia failed to realise the voice was in fact her uncle's. Certainly the colonel, who had slipped in quietly along with everyone else, was a small, rather unobtrusive figure whose dappled fatigues lent him a curious boyishness. His face was smooth and clean-shaven. His eyes large and lucid. Fingering the rim of his cap, he stood with one leg bent, the ankle turned inward as if a thorn were embedded in his foot.

It had been impossible to tell what effect his niece's outspokenness had had on him. Like everyone else he waited patiently for her daemonic performance to end. Perhaps, like the lieutenant, he was reluctant to compete. Or perhaps something he'd seen or heard had intrigued him. Had he begun to read between the lines? It would not be difficult with Alexia. But while she remained transparent, Doyle had no desire to see his own role fleshed out under the colonel's scrutiny. And so in an effort to cut short the proceedings, he held out his hand to him. Surrounded by the ever-growing number of policemen who'd been arriving, red-eyed and slack-jawed, from a nearby shebeen, the colonel ignored it.

◇

Alexia was still sulking when they entered the outskirts of the village. Doyle, who was finding it difficult to keep awake, made little attempt to comfort her. Instead he watched through sleep-filled eyes as she began to brush the dust from her jumpsuit, tugging impulsively at the zip spilling down her front like a trickle of wine. He heard her loud palatal cluck of frustration as the zip jammed, then skidded free, momentarily exposing the velvet outline of her breasts. Deftly she drew it back up again and for a moment her long, quick fingers rested on the flawless curve of her throat before she reached round the back of the seat and threw a sweater over her shoulders. Elasticated at the wrists and ankles, the jumpsuit hugged her hips while a pair of gold earrings danced like puppets behind the perforated screen of beads decorating her hair.

Peering at him through strained eyes, she said: 'I'm not just a shell you picked up on the beach, Doyle.'

5

Ngagabhaleko: a string of huts appear out of the fog like notes on a sheet of music. The pick-up rattles past and they slowly fade . . . saxophone blue. Spilling smoke, a tin shack – the local shebeen – disgorges a crooning figure who lurches down the hill, the strap of her satin dress shimmering like a sliver of moon on the dark, liquid flesh. Jilted lover? Or village whore? Hollow-eyed, she gazes upward. But not for long. The fog's own sadness presses down upon her. Crushed, the crooning ceases as silver earrings slide like tears against her cheeks. In the breast-torn silence she throws out a hand – a flash of light. A shooting star? Or empty bottle flung into the night?

She turns, stumbles, and with a voluptuous moan sinks to the ground. On her knees she dreams . . . of summer rains and the rattle of the honey-guide . . . a child at her breast whose clammy fingers knead the beeswax with which she seasons and polishes the gourds brimming with milk . . . dreams of a kraal soothed by chanting herdsmen who slip like water round the horns of sleek and dusky oxen . . . of moonlit nights, bloodseed, and lovers who must find *lobola*.

On her knees she dreams . . . Until the rough hand on her shoulder startles her. She looks up, feels the hot breath of the mines on her cheek, the steamy Judas kiss of a lover returned – married though he denies it. With a shrug, she hitches up her dress and lies down in the dirt. Dreams slide swiftly into nightmare.

$$\diamond$$

Passing the mud-brick school on their way to the mission, they saw hooded figures dashing across the veld toward them, shouting and waving their arms. Alexia swore and clamped her foot to the accelerator. Blinded by the headlights the hooded figures froze. Alexia's furious hooting failing to scatter them, she swung the wheel round, throwing the pick-up into a violent tailspin. The engine stalled. As Doyle wound his window down there was a relieved cheer.

'Good evening, sir. How are you? We are fine.'

The faces of the four girls, dressed in black tunics and white shirts, beamed at him from beneath the cowls they'd made by pulling the top of their jerseys over their heads to keep out the damp. Lean, stringy adolescents, they held hands and bowed.

Alexia tugged at the handbrake in disgust.

'Please, sir,' squealed Promise, straightening the front of her jersey, 'we are alone.'

'Do you know what time it is?' he asked.

The girls crowded round the window, examining his wristwatch. 'Au! Au! Au!' they chanted.

'I suppose you've been cramming,' said Doyle.

'Oh no, sir,' cried Faith, who was quite bald. 'We have already completed our studying.'

'For all the papers!' Her earlobes were torn and her cheeks bristled with tribal scars, but Constance rolled her eyes with a cheerful innocence.

'Except Physics,' said Lily, carrying her pens and pencils in her hair like knitting needles in a ball of wool. 'Physics is much too difficult.'

Then Promise, the tall, shy leader of the four, gracefully slipping her arms round her companions, and pulling them closer to her, announced nervously: 'Please sir, we have a problem. Elizabeth Jwara. She has become very ill.'

'Have you gone for help?' asked Doyle.

The girls stared uneasily at one another.

'There is no one, sir.'

'At the clinic?'

'It is closed at night.'

'Have you been down to the village?'

'The people have all gone to Elukholweni for the funeral of Chief Mzolisi Gumede who died end of last week.'

'Everyone?'

'Everyone except the Christians,' said Promise, her eyes darting toward Alexia who shifted threateningly in the dark. 'A few like the Reverend Xolile did go, but most of the Christians remained behind.'

'Did you ask any of them to help?'

'We did ask.'

'And?'

Once more the girls stared anxiously at one another before Promise, biting her lip, confessed: 'We are not Christians, sir. We are from the other side, from the village of . . .'

'Tsha!' The massed beads in Alexia's hair rattled against the window as she said scornfully: 'These girls are afraid. They will not have asked the Christians for help.'

'Why not?' Doyle asked.

'Because they are from the other side of the river, from the village of the *amaqaba*. See . . .' She pointed to the ribbon in Lily's hair. 'They are the red blanket ones, the traditionalists who practise circumcision, who live like their forefathers before the white man came.'

'*Amaqaba* don't attend school.'

'Au! sir, we are not *amaqaba*,' Lily protested.

'But we are not Christians either,' said Promise.

'Does it matter? Surely the mission wouldn't have refused.'

'Tsha!' snorted Alexia. 'The *amaqaba* are superstitious. They will not ask anyone who isn't one of them for help.'

The girls meekly bowed their heads. '*Hayi mawetu*. We have asked. Even at the mission. But only the servants are there and there was nothing they could do.'

'And have you sent anyone to the sick girl's home?'

The four nodded.

Alexia eyed them closely. 'And when will her parents come?'

'Early in the morning.'

'Why only in the morning?'

'It is too far, *mawetu*.'

'Hayi!' Alexia jabbed out a hand and her orange-painted nails flashed in the dark. The girls swayed as if mesmerised.

'It's not because it's too far,' she hissed. 'It's because the *amaqaba* are afraid to travel at night. They say it will expose them to the evil spirits. What evil spirits? Where are they now? Tsha! Superstition. You are all superstitious!'

A light breeze shifted the ribbon in Lily's hair, spilling it down the side of her cheek, like a trickle of blood. The girls, clinging to each other, retreated into the fog.

'Please, Mr Doyle,' cried Promise, 'we ask your help. Nomanthando – Elizabeth – she is very much ill.'

Five shiny, plastic suitcases stood at the entrance to the old church. Stepping over them, Doyle pushed open the rickety door and was greeted by the familiar smell of freshly smeared dung. It was as black as a corpse's mouth inside and it took him a while to locate Elizabeth, Nomanthando to her friends. She lay in one of the aisles between the desks, stretched out on her back, her eyes closed, her tongue lolling out of the side of her mouth, her face draped in saliva.

'All evening,' whispered Promise, shielding behind him. 'She has been this way. Sometimes quiet, sometimes kicking and shouting. Always spitting.'

The heavy folds of oily flesh gleamed against the earthen floor.

The fog rolled in through the gaps in the walls where the windows had been, shrouding the desks lurking like rows of vultures in the background. The fog too seemed to smell death, and brought with it a depressingly cold silence, in which Doyle heard the girls shivering. He leaned forward and cautiously touched the damp cheek of Nomanthando.

'Somewhere there is a blanket,' said Promise, 'she must have thrown it off.'

'So someone has been to help.'

'It was the servants at the mission,' the girls chanted hastily; Promise adding: 'They borrowed us the blanket from your room. They said you wouldn't mind because it is an extra one. They said there wasn't any in the mission. Tomorrow we shall wash and return it to you.'

Nomanthando gave a little cough and a bubble popped against her blunt lips. She opened her eyes and they too seemed like transparent bubbles, slowly expanding as she groaned and began to writhe in the dark. Lifting her head, she cracked her fingers on an overturned desk as she struggled to gain some sort of leverage. Doyle noticed she had managed to stab herself in the neck, possibly with the broken pen lodged in the ground nearby. Ordering the girls to move the desks out of the way, he knelt down beside the stricken figure who, with her short, bent arms immediately lashed out catching him in the face. After a brief struggle – she clearly didn't recognise him and was hitting out blindly – he eventually managed to secure her hands and felt the numerous cuts and callouses that were a testimony to village life. However, she soon jerked them powerfully out of his grasp again, leaving him to sink back helplessly on his haunches, thinking of Alexia who had wisely remained in the car outside.

Warm, honey-limbed Alexia. Bold, yet soured with life in the village. Perhaps she had every right to be. Ngagabhaleko, its rolling hills and spectacular sunrises notwithstanding, was no Wordsworthian idyll. Here bit parts were handed out like confetti. Nobody queued except to escape. And many had even given that up. Wasn't that why she created such a storm, sensing the hopelessness of it all, the futility of the villagers' hand-to-mouth existence? Perhaps she lashed out at them because she saw her own fate mirrored in theirs.

Fortunately, Doyle reflected, the strident plays of youth were short. One quickly learned that protest could never be sustained as a way of life. It wasted life, wasted time and energy; the struggle consuming not ones enemies but oneself. Had the villagers survived because of their ability to struggle? They had survived because they'd been stripped of it; just as he, a distraught fifteen-year-old had learned to survive after having his script stolen by those closest to him; by the very people who, until then, had given his life dignity and meaning: his parents. Neither Alexia nor the Security Branch had been able to grasp this one salient fact: namely that his presence in the village stemmed directly from his own state of dispossession.

To Alexia he was rich, educated, above all – free. He could come and go as he pleased, bowing to no one, owing no one anything; being owned by no one. For their part the Security Branch saw him as a threat. He was the liberal hero, living with, identifying with, and, as in the case of his father – or so Mbanjwa claimed – prepared to die with the dispossessed.

Yet what would they have made of his tortured picture of the past, his parents struggling hill-farmers in the north-west of Ireland; isolated and vulnerable; selling their torrid birthright for a place in the sun; rebels – eternal rebels since the English will always be with us – who, in a vain and squalid bid for respite had allowed themselves to become what all their embittered lives they had denounced: members of the ascendancy – in this case not Protestant, but white; forcing him, Seamus Paeder Doyle, an angry teenager with his own fiery script of Catholic frustration, to submit to the alien role of chief –

a colonial *nkozi* feted by the poor, the landless, disenfranchised . . . black Catholics.

Who could find anything redeeming in such a role? From that moment on life had lost all its dignity.

$$\Diamond$$

Squatting beside the delirious figure, Doyle was startled out of his brief reverie by a convulsive roar as suddenly Nomanthando sat up, grabbing him by the throat, sending Promise and her companions screaming into the dark. The girl's sour breath spilling into his face, he tried to pull away but the knotted muscle of her thigh, smeared in a viscous fluid smelling of blood and urine, pinned him against the side of a desk. Struggling to unlock her fingers, he slipped and fell. Her knee smashed against his temple. Dazed, he crouched down like a boxer waiting to be counted out. He knew he couldn't match the girl's ferocious strength. He lacked the speed, the agility, and above all, the will. For this, like Majogo's boycott or Alexia's battle against the self-righteous indignation of her uncle, wasn't his fight. The girl seemed possessed, swaying, wide-eyed and terrified on her feet; her fingers slashing the air, her body wracked with a primeval terror; until, finally, emitting an abortive howl, she collapsed once more to the ground.

Silence. Damp, nauseous. The press of fog and the throb of despair as lovers in the veld scramble to their feet. And part.

'It is better we wait,' warned Promise, emerging from her hiding place behind the old pulpit, 'otherwise it shall end badly.'

Doyle staggered over to the door. 'How long?' he gasped.

'It is difficult to say, but if we interfere it shall end badly for all of us.'

'Interfere?' said Doyle, resting his forehead against the jamb.

Promise eyed him stoically.

'Go on,' he said. 'What do you mean *interfere*?'

Promise, whose tribal scars resembled a piece of lace draped over the edge of her cheeks, glanced nervously at the derelict pulpit. Failing to persuade her companions to come out, she stammered: 'Th . . this is the work of the *liqgira*, sir. He . . he is the only one who can do such things. You can ask anybody in the village. It . . it is his medicine . . . the witch-doctor's.'

Out of the corner of his eye Doyle saw a match flare as Alexia lit a cigarette in the car outside. Illuminated behind the dusty windscreen, her profile – the high forehead, crescent cheeks, long, beaded tresses cascading over hollow eyes – echoed the girl's shamanistic terror.

'It is our way, sir, the way of the amaXhosa. Everyone is taught to respect the witch-doctor and his medicine. Even educated ones like ourselves, we fear him. That is why he is so strong. If we interfere with his medicine he will use it to punish us. It is better for us to wait.'

'Wait?' Doyle muttered as he slumped down on to a bench beside the door. It was the last thing he wanted to hear. For how long? A night? A day? A week. Eight weeks. It was like another blow from Nomanthando. Another round to go before he could retire. Surely this was his final warning. Things could only get worse.

Feeling the bruise that was beginning to swell above his temple, he groaned and said: 'Why don't you take her to the clinic? Nurse Fumba can attend to her in the morning.'

Once again Promise turned to her companions for support, but in spite of the fervent whispering between them, neither Faith, Lily nor Constance could be coaxed out from behind the pulpit.

'Nomanthando might have to go to hospital,' said Doyle.

'Please, sir, we cannot interfere. The witch-doctor has many spies. He will know who is responsible and will punish us.'

'Then get Alexia to take her.'

'Oh no, sir.'

'Why not? You know what she thinks of witch-doctors.'

'But it is not safe.'

'Well, Promise, I don't know how else we can help you. If you want I'll drive her to the clinic now. I may not be here in the morning.'

'Please, sir, it is not a good idea for you to take her.'

'You think he'll punish me too, eh?'

Again Promise looked over her shoulder. 'The witch-doctor is too strong.'

'You really believe that?'

'We do, sir.'

'Did Mr Mjozi?'

'Yes, sir, everyone believes in the witch-doctor.'

'And was the witch-doctor responsible for what happened to the principal?'

'No, sir,' said Promise, flashing her teeth at the hesitant trio who at last emerged at her side. 'That was an angry student from Mr Mjozi's last school. The witch-doctor's medicine is much more powerful than that.'

'Mr Mjozi has a cracked skull.'

'But he is still living. If he wishes the witch-doctor can take your very life.'

'Frankly, he's welcome to it,' sighed Doyle, and watched as the girls threw up their hands in horror. 'Who knows, maybe he's already helping himself.'

'Oh no, sir,' they cried.

'It certainly feels like it.'

'Please, sir,' said Promise, frowning, 'it is dangerous to talk like that.'

'Any more dangerous than talking to the Security Branch?' said Doyle.

'Oh sir,' they chanted, helplessly.

'Or Majogo?'

'Hau, sir! It is!'

Doyle ran his fingers through his hair, as if somehow that would clear his head. What he needed was a drink. If only he could get back to the mission. Would the girls let him go or would he have to rely once more on Alexia to set him free?

'Your belief in the witch-doctor doesn't say much for the school, does it?' he remarked, as they continued to huddle a safe distance away, not only from Nomanthando, but, it seemed, from him also. 'Is there any point in keeping it open?'

The girls eyed him with tearful disapproval.

'Education is important, sir.' Promise gripped the belt of her tunic in both hands, wringing it like a chicken's neck. 'It's just, one cannot escape the power of the witch-doctor. In fact sometimes it is education that leads one into his path. For instance there are people in the village whose children are unable to attend school, or maybe their child is attending but is not doing as well as their neighbour's child. They are the ones who go to the witch-doctor to ask for help; especially when it is exam time. They ask him to frustrate those who are doing well so that their own child will not be embarrassed. Nomanthando's neighbours have asked the witch-doctor for such help because she is beating their child, Sindiswa Skhosana.'

'Sindiswa?'

'Ruth – Sindiswa Ruth.'

'No, I meant . . .' Becoming suspicious of the girls' motives Doyle paused, sniffing the sour air. 'What I meant is, Sindiswa's been absent such a lot and fallen so far behind in her work that you and I and everyone else knows her chances of passing the exams are slim. Surely you aren't suggesting she's set the witch-doctor on Nomanthando simply because Nomanthando – no great scholar herself – is a couple of places above her in the class? Unless, of course . . .'

'Oh no, please, sir,' Promise, moaned, releasing her tunic belt and folding her hands beneath her chin so that her knuckles reminded him of empty candle-holders on a makeshift altar.

'Unless, of course,' he continued, shrugging off the girls' embarrassed plea, 'this is all an elaborate plot to get Nomanthando exempted from the exam, so she can write it later.'

This time the girls with their round, wafer cheeks eyed each other sorrowfully. A rat scurrying across the floor behind them caused them to jump. Joining hands, they huddled together silently in the pain of desecration.

'Tell me, is it realistic to expect the witch-doctor to help Nomanthando pass?' Doyle asked, as the rat vanished into the large hole beneath the pulpit. 'Do you think she can get through without doing any work on her own? Tradition. I know, you'll say it's tradition. But let me tell you, tradition, in so far as the pupils of Ngagabhaleko are concerned, is a ship heading for the breaker's yard. It means you have to choose. Either you stay on board or you transfer to something more modern. You can't sail on both the old and the new simultaneously. They're travelling in opposite directions.'

'But our tradition is too strong, sir,' cried Promise.

'Then stay with it.'

'You mean that we should abandon our education?'

'Education doesn't always know where it's going, Promise. It's a vessel that sometimes sets people down where they don't want to be set down, leaves others stranded, or simply throws them overboard. It offers progress but you never know what the price is until you get there. You might be able to afford it. You might not. Why take the risk?'

Promise stared at Nomanthando's pen impaled in the floor in front of her like the spring of a trap. The top button of her shirt was fastened, her feet placed one behind the other. Tucking her elbows in at her sides, she bent her knees and seemed to pray.

'It's true,' said Constance, massaging her torn earlobe as she took a cautious step forward, 'we, from that side of the river, have not been your best pupils. But we have tried. Even Sindiswa who all year has remained at the bottom of the class has done her best. It has not been easy for her. She lives too far away. For her there are two rivers to cross. That is why she has been absent so many days when it rains. Also her mother is away from home, working in Johannesburg. And her father and brother, they come home just for ploughing, then they must return to work, also in Johannesburg. Sindiswa must do the work around the house. The last-born and the second last-born are still small. Only one old aunt is there helping her. We think it is she who has called the witch-doctor to do this thing to Nomanthando.'

'But how does that help Sindiswa?'

Promise quickly interjected: 'If Sindiswa fails then she will not be embarrassed by her neighbour who also will have failed.'

Doyle's fingers were drawn back to the bruise at his temple. 'Let's be honest,' he said. 'Nomanthando was always going to fail, even without the witch-doctor's intervention. Though,' he added thoughtfully, 'I don't suppose we could expect the aunt to have known that.'

Promise clapped her hands to cheeks. 'But Nomanthando has tried very hard, sir!'

'Sure – on the days she's actually been at school.'

'But her home is far away.'

'And she has two rivers to cross. Yes, I know it isn't easy. But frankly I think Nomanthando's expecting too much. So are a whole lot of others.'

'Sir?'

Painstaking over their appearance – even at this late hour Promise smoothed the front of her tunic with flattened palms while adjusting her socks which somehow had remained as white as the whites of her eyes – they caused him to see his own dishevelled state – the frayed trouser bottoms, the worn sandals, his shirt which Nomanthando had smeared with saliva, sticking to his back as he leaned against the wall.

'Education isn't a miracle cure, Promise,' he said, rising to his feet. Alexia's footsteps could be heard advancing through the fog. He might as well get it over with himself, he thought. Spare the girls the unnecessary drama. 'It can just as easily cripple people, like the witch-doctor's crippled Nomanthando. It's like exchanging one witch-doctor for another. Why go to all that trouble? Why don't you stick to the one you know? What has life in the towns or on the mines got to offer you? If you really knew I doubt you'd still be pouring over your books . . .'

He paused as a suitcase was kicked out of the way; then said rapidly: 'If I were you I'd stay here, in the village, get married, have children, look after the home . . .'

Another suitcase skidded against the door.

'. . . Not because I think you shouldn't try to improve your lives but because it's the safest way of avoiding disappointment. Let others go out to fight, take part in the struggle – a struggle more unequal than yours or Nomanthando's, believe me. Even your witch-doctor would find it difficult to survive out there.'

The door flew open. Alexia marched up to the girls and said: 'Where is your respect? You expect the titsha to stay here all night with you? Tomorrow he must go to school. Come, there is a spare room at the mission. In the morning I shall take your friend to the clinic. Nurse Fumba will know what is the matter with her.'

6

It was shortly after lights-out that Sprinkler appeared at the head of the stairs. Young Doyle, stealing down the darkened corridor, saw him and ducked into the nearest doorway.

'Doyle!'

The upper wing of the hostel rang with electrifying effect as boys, engaged in the usual nightly horse-play, froze beside their beds, silently praying theirs would not be the door that Sprinkler opened.

'Doyle.'

Doyle calmly stepped into the open.

'Where d'you think you're going?' demanded the deputy.

'Naismiths',' said Doyle.

'What's the rule?'

'No moving between rooms after lights-out.'

'So what are you doing?'

'Moving between rooms after lights-out.'

'You know the penalty?'

And so while in the warm, summer's night a goods-train thundered over the bridge behind the school, Doyle bent beneath the deputy headmaster's cane, the train's high-pitched whistle drowning out the three swift swipes that followed over his pyjamas.

'Christ! How'd you get away?' bubbled the unsuspecting Naylor as Doyle returned to his room.

'Leprechauns,' said Doyle, feeling his way in the dark to his locker and taking out a packet of biscuits which he broke in half.

His room-mate, the founder member of the embattled Society for the Prevention of Cruelty to Non-rugby Players, gave a prodigal cheer as the chocolate creams struck him on the shoulder.

'Celebrating your escape?'

'Hungry,' Doyle replied, climbing into bed. 'Soon as Sprinkler's gone I'm going round to Naismiths' to fetch that bloody salami he owes me. Remember the bet? Said I couldn't down a can of Black Label in under seven sec . . .'

The door swung open. The light snapped on. Shouldering his cane, the deputy said: 'Doyle I want to talk to you.'

It was Naylor who immediately sat up. Oblivious to the half-packet of biscuits sticking out from under his sheet, he ostentatiously rubbed his eyes.

'Not you!' growled the deputy.

'I think he's asleep, sir,' Naylor yawned.

'Don't be moronic. His mouth's stuffed with biscuits.'

'Oh?' said Naylor, slipping on his glasses which he kept in a case under his pillow. 'I didn't realise. Doyle you sneak.'

The deputy flicked back Naylor's sheet with the tip of his cane.

'That's not fair, sir,' whined the youth whose marble white legs, protruding from a pair of short pyjamas, failed to hide either the biscuits or the stick of biltong he'd been chewing on when Doyle had returned from his abortive trip to Naismith. 'Especially after you let Doyle off,' he added, quickly covering himself up again. 'Must've been a good excuse to fool you.'

'Excuse?' frowned the deputy. 'I'm pleased to say Doyle hasn't sunk to the level of the SPC or whatever you pooftas call yourselves.'

'Society for the Prevention of . . .'

'Naylor shut up!'

Naylor dauntlessly hoisted up his sheet to ward off the shower of saliva.

'Doyle,' said the deputy, a powerfully-built figure with mountainous fists, a belligerent mouth and eyes that floated in cerise pools, like bloodied egg-yolks. 'Doyle, listen carefully. This is your last year at Saints. It's a pity as you've not been with us all that long. We'd have liked the full five years to drag some of that stubbornness out of you. However, I have to admit that in spite of your disappointing performance on the sports field, you've more or less managed to live up to Saints high academic standards – even if the staff had to force you most of the way. What you're eventually going to do with this talent we've had to fight so hard to rescue I honestly don't know. I do know though that if you want to make a success of your life, you're going to have to get rid of your slack-arsed approach because no one in that dirty big world out there is going to encourage you the way we have. You'll have to dig deep to find the drive and the resources in yourself.'

Unable to restrain himself, Naylor blurted out: 'But Doyle isn't a digger, sir, he's a paddy. Diggers are from . . .'

'Naylor!' The deputy's cane hovered menacingly above the bed.

'Sorry, sir. But Doyle doesn't mind being called a . . .'

'Ag man, belt up,' spluttered the deputy. 'Why must you always butt in? Who am I talking to? Am I talking to you?'

Naylor blinked myopically.

'Look, Doyle,' said the strangely beleaguered figure, brushing aside a thread of spittle from his lips, 'you're in the middle of your mock exam with the finals just eight weeks away. If it had been anyone else I'd have tried to keep this away from them until after they had finished writing.'

'Keep what away, sir?'

'Naylor!'

In a flash the youth pulled his legs up as the cane rapped the foot of the bed, leaving a deep imprint in the fresh white sheet. 'Doyle your mother rang me from the farm at . . . what's the name of that place again? . . . black name . . .?'

'Lusikisiki,' chimed Naylor. 'It's in the Transkei.'

'I know where Lusikisiki is, Naylor. Anyway she rang me earlier this afternoon but I didn't know how to break the news to you. Your father's had an accident, bit of a freak really . . . burst tractor tyre . . . sent the thing crashing on top of him. I'm sorry, Doyle. It killed him. I want you to pack your case first thing in the morning. I've booked you on the Transcoach which leaves at nine. Obviously I'm not setting any time limit on your absence but you don't need me to stress the importance of passing your finals, especially as you've made up your mind to go back overseas. I still think you should consider going to varsity in this country. By the time you've graduated you're unlikely to be as homesick as you are now. I'm willing to bet these pictures on the wall here . . . where are they from? Galway . . Donegal . . well in three years' time I reckon you'd be pinning up photographs of places like the Drakensberg, Kruger Park and . . .'

'Wild Coast, sir. Doyle's always going down to the coast. He's a regular strandloper. Last holiday I saw him wandering along the beach on his own . . . had a great big pack on his back.'

Once more the deputy raised his cane, but it was a sign of helplessness rather than anger or hostility. 'Doyle,' he said, 'the staff have high hopes of you but I have to say we've always been concerned by your failure to do yourself justice. You don't seem to be interested in expanding your horizons at all. It's as if you don't care what happens — to yourself, or in the world in general. You just steal quietly along allowing others, often less intelligent than yourself, to gallop past you. That's why we threw Naylor in here with you. We hoped he'd sort of provoke you, get you to open up. Maybe it hasn't worked as well as we thought it might, but you can't say we didn't try. We get some of the brightest boys in the country at Saints and we give all of them the best attention we can.'

'Sir?' said Naylor with his knees still tucked under him, like a grasshopper, 'don't you think I should go with Doyle on the bus tomorrow? He'll be much too upset to travel on his own.'

'No I do not,' replied the deputy who, with a final exasperated glance at the crest-fallen Naylor, drew his cane up under his arm and turned briskly toward the door. Pausing with his fist above the light-switch, he said: 'I'm sorry Doyle, these things happen. There isn't a lot we can do about it. I know you're not all that religious but it's important to have some sort of faith to draw on, some sort of guiding light to break up the dark's terror as you make your way through life. Faith gives one a sense of purpose; it helps to explain where we're going. It's the difference between seeing your father's death as being a reunion with God or just bad luck.'

The deputy gave an exhausted grunt as his fist slid down the switch. Quietly he shut the door.

7

'*Mhlekazi*?' The shadowy figure leaning over the foot of the bed tapped him lightly with his kierie. 'Forgive me but I saw the candle burning.'

Doyle peered up at the old man as he slipped a woollen hat from his head and sank down heavily on the edge of the bed, resting the stick across his thighs.

'I'm sorry for disturbing you, my friend, but you know every year at Ngagabhaleko a kraal goes up in flames because someone has left a candle unattended.'

For a while Doyle lay motionless on his side, watching the shadows flit across the wall of his hut. The bits of broken furniture – a cane sofa unravelling at the arms, a work table strewn with candle stubs and papers, a cracked chair and a wardrobe propped up on bricks – seemed to expand and fill the room. Dwarfed by this crush of bat-wing shadows, the candle-wax spilled in a frozen cataract over the rim of the battered tin-holder, perched precariously on top of a pile of science fiction books which he kept at his bedside. It was still dark outside and the old man whose brow was illuminated by the candle's flickering light pulled his greatcoat tight around his shoulders.

'Only last summer my sister saw her neighbour's kraal burn down. Two children died in the fire. Hayi! These houses, they are just too vulnerable.'

Doyle struggled up, resting on his elbows.

'You are not afraid, *mhlekazi*, of being burnt alive?'

The candle-flame spluttered, shrank, then steadied itself. Doyle yawned.

'I see you sleep like a mine-worker,' said Abraham Dlamini, patiently, 'with all your clothes on.'

Doyle unbuttoned his shirt, propped up a pillow and leaned back on the unmade bed. The shadows leapt from the walls into the high roof space where the smoke-blackened rafters, overlaid with thatch,

gleamed solidly in the amber light. The conical roof lent a spacious-
ness to the hut whose mud walls remained unpainted, revealing only
a pair of crooked windows, no bigger than the old man's gnarled fists,
tucked away behind makeshift curtains. The roof had lost it's golden
sheen and resembled the ruffled feathers of a fighting cock. Outside a
car tyre slung over the top helped weigh down the broken thatch,
preventing it from being savaged by the violent winds that occasionally stalked the unprotected hills.

The tyre also doubled as an alarm-clock thanks to the family of
starlings nesting in its hollow shell. With polished claws running like
sand along the rubber, beaks probing the dry thatch for insects, they
flexed their crumpled wings in the dawn each day, chattering and
singing before flying off, just as the first rays of the sun slithered over
the horizon.

To Doyle it seemed the starlings saw each day as the beginning of a
whole new life and yet as they flew off noisily to greet it, they left him
with the morbid thought that no dawn chorus, however splendid,
could disguise the fact that there were no 'new beginnings', no 'new
dawns'. Each day started and finished exactly like the one before –
with the dull, whisky-induced hammering in his head.

A smile spreading across his broad, peasant face, Abraham
Dlamini waited while Doyle poured himself a drink from the bottle
beside his bed. Then he said: 'So! They let you out. I wasn't sure
when I passed and saw the candle burning whether I would find you
or an intruder present. One knows your door is never locked. It could
not have been pleasant for you being confined to the cells at Bala.'

Doyle set the bottle down on the floor. 'How d'you know it was
Bala?'

The rusty iron bed rocked on the uneven floor as the bulky figure,
leaning forward, nudged him with his kierie. 'Umtata is too far away
to drag such a small fish.'

'You mean monkey.'

The old man winked slyly. 'I hope you did not tell them the name
of the organ-grinder.'

'Didn't have to,' said Doyle, his eye on the whisky floating in the
unwashed glass. 'They knew. Or rather thought they knew.'

'There is one?' The old man's silver brows arched in amusement.

'Seamus Doyle.'

'Ah!'

'Senior,' said Doyle, as the whisky slipped like molten wax over the rim of his glass and on to his tongue. For a moment the fumes billowed up until the dull hammering, gathering a suddenly violent momentum, caused his hand to shake and he dropped the glass into his lap where it lay, the stain spreading across the sheet. Quickly he gathered it up again and poured himself another drink.

The old man looked questioningly at him.

Doyle leaned back, pulled the sheet up and shrugged: 'Well you know what the Security Branch are like, always chasing after phantoms.'

'Your father?'

'He died years ago.'

'Then what is the connection?'

'There is no connection, Abraham. You know how their minds work; leave no stone – or tombstone – unturned.'

The old man nodded. 'It's true. The Security Branch never tire looking for conspirators. Even a young boy living far away in the *bundu* cannot express his frustration without these people suspecting he belongs to an international conspiracy. There must always be a plot behind everything. Who knows, Mbanjwa is to this day probably still looking for Vladimir Ilyanov.'

The whisky rapidly clearing his head, Doyle said watchfully: 'How sure are you Majogo is on his own?'

Abraham Dlamini frowned. At seventy the furrows massed across his brow, colliding with the grey fuzz at his temples, which he scratched with the stump of his right index finger – severed at work when he was a young man. Large earlobes dangled like pieces of coral, torn from his bald pate. Deep lines sliced through the folds in his cheeks while heavy rolls of flesh gathered in an oily heap at his neck. Beneath this sagging swathe was a strong and powerful jaw keeping the tide of infirmity at bay. For this the old man also had his kierie, a stout stick with a head as round and shiny as a cricket ball, which he leaned on as he shuffled between kraals; a quiet, genial figure, always quick to use his breathlessness as an excuse to stop and talk.

Now he raised the kierie upright on the bed, and for Doyle it's shadow on the wall took the shape of a question mark. 'I am sure, *mhlekazi*, the boy is acting on his own initiative. It was what you yourself suggested just a few days ago when you defended your decision before the committee not to take immediate action against him. Have you forgotten?'

'No,' said Doyle, 'I haven't. But I've been thinking. There *could* be a hidden hand behind this.'

Abraham continued to balance the kierie on the bed. 'It seems the Security Branch are not the only ones chasing after phantoms.'

'Not chasing,' said Doyle. 'I'm not interested in catching whoever's responsible.'

'May be,' said Abraham. 'Whoever *may* be responsible.'

'I don't think it's a phantom,' said Doyle. 'Nor do I believe the motives are political, whatever Mbanjwa and the Security Branch say.'

Abraham's frown deepened as he rubbed his eyes with the back of his thumb. Swollen, they revealed that he too, like Doyle, had been up most of the night. 'So what does the lieutenant think? Just now you mentioned something about your father. Is there a connection?'

'Never mind the lieutenant,' said Doyle, sensing that he would never be able to explain to the old man why he really had to leave Ngagabhaleko, or indeed why he had ever come. 'The whole idea of a boycott, so close to the exams is just ludicrous. Whoever thought it up must have other, non-political motives.'

'Majogo is from the townships, *mhlekazi*, where the cost and the timing of these things is measured differently.'

'The cost we are talking about here is to a man's pride. I don't think it was intended to seriously disrupt the school. Someone hoped that by showing me up in a bad light the boycott would force the department to reconsider my position.'

'And since when,' said the old man, pointing without ceremony to the bottle on the floor, 'have you ever worried about being shown up in a bad light? In any case, and I mean no disrespect, even if the department disapproved of your handling of the situation, who will they find to take your place? No one will come to this *bundu*. Even Pilot Mjozi's was not a voluntary appointment. As you know he got into serious difficulties with a pupil at his previous school and the department had to hide him somewhere in a hurry. It was not for his career that he came but for his personal safety.'

'My safety's the reason I have to leave,' said Doyle.

'But you are in no danger.'

Doyle pulled his feet up under the sheet which smelled of Nomanthando's sour wretching. 'I may be,' he said.

'I do not think so, *mhlekazi*.'

'The villagers' smiles are not always what they seem, Abraham, you know that.'

'Yes I know, you speak often of the weight of History. But now you have to be more specific.'

'History is a blunt instrument.'

'Names, *mhlekazi*. You have yet to name any names.'

A stirring in the thatch caused Doyle to look up. As a tiny russet feather floated down on to the bed, the first cold light appeared in the cracks round the door and windows, like mould around cheese. The air felt damp. The iron frame of the bed groaned. 'Well . . .' Doyle hesitated. It wasn't Nomanthando's wretching the sheet smelled of, but Alexia. He wondered how much Abraham knew. How secret had his affair with the Reverend's niece really been? He looked into the old man's tired eyes where the light ebbed and flowed as he swayed forward on his kierie. Then in a moment of cowardliness said: 'The chief's always been afraid of the school. If you remember he withdrew his daughter because her slowness was becoming an embarrassment to him.'

Abraham Dlamini seemed to slump over his kierie. 'The chief, *mhlekazi*?'

'Yes,' said Doyle. 'His daughter could hardly write her name.'

'But the chief is dead, my friend. You may forget about him. I have just this night come from his funeral.'

'The boycott started before he was taken ill.'

Abraham gave a long and crushing sigh.

Doyle said: 'What about the witch-doctor? Tonight I saw the kind of power he wields. These kids have had five years secondary education. They know that Einstein worked out $e = mc$ squared, that Newton discovered the law of gravity and man has walked on the moon. And yet when it comes to exams they're terrified of what the witch-doctors may do to them.'

'The witch-doctor has no motive,' said Abraham.

'The school's a perfect motive. It threatens his power the way it threatened the chief's.'

'The school is well protected.'

'By?'

'The mission of course.'

'Am I?'

'You mean because you are not a Christian?'

'The witch-doctor may see it as an opportunity.'

'I do not think so.'

'Did you ever talk to Mjozi about the attack on him?'

'That had nothing to do with the witch-doctor, *mhlekazi*.'

'It may have everything to do with him. If you consider the influence he has. Even the village footballers go to him before a match. His medicine gives them courage. The kid who had a grievance against Mjozi may have needed a little of the witch-doctor's *muti* to give him the nerve to attack the principal.'

'*Hayi*,' said the old man who, having sat patiently staring at the spluttering candle, now leaned wearily forward and blew it out with an unhappy sigh. Illuminated in the grey-blue light as if under X-ray, a crooked finger of smoke pointed upwards to where particles of dust, bits of grass and broken feathers, dislodged by the starling's beaks began tumbling out of the thatch into the grasp of mergent spiders' webs, tautly spun between the rafters. '*Hayi, mhlekazi*, I cannot believe what I am hearing. All this talk of the witch-doctor? You are here to help educate our children. The customs of the amaXhosa are nothing you need fear. Many people may still follow them, but they do not do so blindly. That is why our children come to you for their second initiation. When they are ill they go to the witch-doctor. When they are healthy they go to school.'

Releasing a steady shower of dust, the starlings pursued each other across the thatch. It would only be a matter of minutes before they took to the sky. Already the mission dog sniffed at his door, while cocks from the village below began their rusty tintinnabulation.

As the light strengthened, revealing numerous cracks in the mud wall, Abraham planted his kierie firmly on the floor. Emitting a series of strenuous grunts, he rose slowly to his feet, his greatcoat unfolding like a crumpled wing which he smoothed down with his fist.

'Really, it is not like you to be troubled by these things. But then I see I have come at the wrong time. The lack of sleep, as our friends in the Security Branch will know, can play harsh tricks on the mind. I'm truly sorry, my friend. I did not mean to disturb you, but it was important for me to see that you had not come to any harm.'

Doyle blew into his glass before pouring himself another drink. 'Nothing you could have done anyway,' he said.

'One can always do something.'

'You sound like Mbanjwa,' said Doyle as the hungry face of the mission ridgeback squeezed through the door. 'He also seemed disappointed I didn't put up more of a fight. I suppose you think I should have refused to go to the station? They'd only have come back later. Besides it would have looked as though I'd something to hide.'

Abraham lifted a piece of three-day-old bread from among the books and papers on the table and tossed it through the narrow crack in the door. The ridgeback missed it and they heard the foggy clunk as it struck the fender of the pick-up outside. The old man shoved his hand into the pocket of his greatcoat and shuffled across the room.

'As far as the police are concerned, I do not think you need worry. It is their job to be suspicious. Fortunately for you and for all of us who are concerned for the future of the school, you have nothing they want.'

'How can you be so sure?'

'I am sure, *mhlekazi*.'

'Aren't you suspicious?'

Abraham looked back over his shoulder and chuckled. 'I am over seventy. What is there left to be suspicious of?'

'South African History. You're a product of it, after all.'

'A product, not just a pawn,' replied the old man, bent doggedly over his stick. 'No, my friend, I am not suspicious, except for just one thing. Something is telling me you are looking for a reason to leave us. You are a man who likes to linger in the shadows of life and now that the police are shining their light in your face you may join the *intshiyani* here in your roof and take to the sky. That would be a pity. A terrible pity. It would be a sad loss for us all, including yourself.'

A furious scampering on the roof and the starlings were off, skimming like pegs along the thin washline of dawn. With a final wave of his kierie, Abraham Dlamini announced cheerfully: 'In the

57

meantime, now that you are back, we shall keep our regular date for dominoes,' and hobbled out into the yard.

Doyle waited a while before slipping out of bed. Realising there was little to choose between Abraham's innocent perception – 'you are here to help educate our children' – and the Security Branch's view of him as a hero, (both insisted on reading more than was healthy into his sojourn in the village) he began searching for his car keys, unaware that Alexia had left them in the ignition.

Half an hour later the ridgeback returned to find him lying, blind drunk, on the floor.

$$\Diamond$$

'It is noted in point number three of the minutes to the previous meeting, that I brought to the committee's attention the absence of morning worship at our school. To which Mr Doyle replied that since half of the students attending classes were not Christians, he thought common worship once a week on Friday mornings sufficient. He also added that as this was the system he had inherited from Mr Mjozi, he saw no reason to change it. However, following a discussion on the matter, Mr Doyle conceded that as daily worship is provided for by the department in its instructions to all school principals, it would henceforth be the policy of our school to hold such worship in the mornings before the start of normal classes. Well, I'm pleased to be able to inform you that that policy is now in operation, although not under the supervision of the principal who has left it to the mission.

'But now before a vote is taken on the accurate recording of these minutes, I wish it to be noted that our previous discussion, which was forthright and honest, was not intended in any way to undermine Mr Doyle's authority as the principal of our school. As chairman of the committee, I merely felt it my duty to clarify a certain matter of which Mr Doyle was unaware, or maybe misinformed. I feel, Madam Secretary, that your recording of the minutes of that meeting does not reflect this fact and therefore I wish to make my position clear. And I am sure I speak for all of us when I say it is our duty to give the principal whatever assistance he needs in carrying out his job in this isolated and largely uneducated community.'

$$\Diamond$$

Like a family of egrets stealing through the grass, the committee members tiptoed into the round hut that served as the principal's office and staffroom, gracefully ducking under the cotton sheet Pilot Mjozi used as a partition and which Doyle had left hanging for some weeks now so that it crackled like old paper as they bowed under it. They were followed by two sombre-faced girls whose spotless school uniform, ironed to a metallic crispness, seemed to reassure everyone present, especially Nurse Fumba who, while the others took up their usual positions on the bench against the wall, managed a wan smile of appreciation as she squeezed in behind the wooden desk where the minutes of the previous meeting lay waiting to be read.

The first girl, a shy, dimpled creature who never lifted her eyes from the floor, carried an enamel dish filled with water, while her companion, strong and broad-shouldered, followed with a bar of soap and a fresh towel draped over her arm. Curtsying, the girls presented the soap and water to the Reverend.

A tall, elegant figure whose streamlined features reminded Doyle of a racing yacht with the grey temples as ballast, he dipped his hands into the tepid water. The long fingers glistened like oiled rope. The wrists swivelled, smooth and subtle, causing hardly a ripple. A wedding ring sparkled as it bobbed to the surface, a gold watch-chain gleaming at anchor among the folds of his black silk shirt. Then, with a slow, painstaking grace, he dried his hands and returned the towel to the overawed girls who once more curtsied before gliding round to serve the rest of the committee.

There were seven members on the school committee. One was a village headman who spoke no English; another a primary school teacher long past retirement age but who was forced to carry on working because of the inadequacy of his pension. The third was Abraham Dlamini, a former dock worker. The fourth, a Mr Churchill Mulilo, had spent twenty years on the mines before being laid off because of ill-health and then 'repatriated' by the authorities on the grounds that he no longer held a steady job and was therefore an itinerant. The final member, apart from Doyle and the Reverend, was 'Madam Secretary', as the Reverend Xolile referred to Mrs Margaret Fumba, a qualified nurse who ran the Tsindi Clinic serving, among others, the villagers of Ngagabhaleko.

The washing ritual over, the girls took up their positions in the doorway. The Reverend cleared his throat and the committee, of which only Nurse Fumba, a Catholic, and the Reverend were practising Christians, duly bowed their heads.

8

From its isolated position high on a hill the derelict church looked out over the crowded village of Ngagabhaleko, over a throng of grim, blighted hills shrunken in the fine drizzle. Inundated with kraals, these low-lying hills swarmed at the church's feet like exhausted pilgrims, the whole countryside resembling a vast, open-air mass with supplicants jostling in a silver sea that stretched as far as the horizon, dwarfing both the altar and the 'priest' who, although spared the momentous crush, seemed startled by it. Would the body of Christ be enough to go round?

The blood of Christ wasn't a problem. Ripped open by traditional cattle tracks, the earth's jagged wounds ran red in the rain. Vestments were spattered. Crowns of thorns donned in stoic silence. A smell of death pervaded. This was a mass held not in hope but despair since the land was clearly spent, rubbed to the bone. It was land that could not be forgiven. A land – caught in the blind grip of eternity – that would never forgive.

But what's eternity to youth? Eternity's the present and what you make of it. For Majogo and his disciples it was time to break the host.

And yet . . .? Doyle who'd been called away from the committee meeting to clarify one of the trial exam questions and who now stood watching the placard-waving youths through the classroom window saw little to separate Majogo's New Testament fervour from the tenacity of the pupils currently bowed at their desks. For both groups sought to replace the Holy Trinity – of past, present and future – with a presidency of the immediate. Both wanted hope to be the new constitution; daring, its spirit. They called for a new republic, a new land with new laws, free of prejudice and constant humiliation. Both saw in their new vision an escape from the old dogma, not only for themselves (contrary to popular belief youth is not always selfish), but for all their peers, even their elders – an escape from the iniquitous rule of the past.

Being true revolutionaries, however, they had fallen out as soon as it had become clear each despised the other's strategy; Majogo's being to march around the school's perimeter fence, chanting slogans that were echoed by five khaki-clad figures trudging barefoot through the mud after him. Together with their more elegantly-attired leader, they constituted the school's Bolshevik wing.

Inside, the Mensheviks were doing their best to ignore them. There were enough other distractions. Rain dripping through the iron roof formed puddles round the desks which had constantly to be moved. Rats scurried out from the hole beneath the pulpit where the young teacher who was invigilating threw pieces of chalk at them. Papers fluttered in the cold draught from the uncovered windows and the open door which flapped listlessly at the back but could not be closed because of the poor light. Yet with a single-mindedness that was as moving as it was fraught with danger, the bowed figures, shivering in their pristine uniforms, refused to look up from their work.

'NO-TO BAN-TU EDU-CATION! NO-TO BAN-TU EDU-CATION!'

The chanting grew louder as Doyle emerged from the classroom and made his way back to the meeting.

'NO-TO BAN-TU EDU-CATION! NO-TO BAN-TU EDU-CATION!'

He paused outside the staffroom.

'. . . items remaining on today's agenda? Oh dear, they are too many. And I must be at the clinic by one o'clock.'

'And what are these items concerning, sister?'

Doyle recognised Abraham's coal-shuttle voice. The old man was having one of his little digs at the punctilious Nurse Fumba.

'In short, sir,' she replied, 'absenteeism, pregnancy, and the current boycott.'

'NO-TO BAN-TU EDU-CATION! NO-TO BAN-TU EDU-CATION!'

'. . . the absenteeism concerns two particular students. Their names are Nomanthando Jwara and Sidiswa Jama. The teachers have suggested we do not permit them to write the external examination next month as they are bound to fail.'

'Bound to?'

'Yes, *mhlekazi*. And their failure will lower the overall pass rate of the school.'

'But is it not their right to sit the exam?'

'It is so, but my feeling and indeed the feeling of our teachers is that by failing to attend classes regularly these two girls have forfeited that right. Besides, we must think of the name of the school. When the results are published and it is found we are low down on the league table we shall all be ashamed of ourselves.'

'But how can we compete with those schools in the towns which are never short of books, are always having qualified teachers . . .?'

'There is nothing we can do, *mhlekazi*. We must compete. It is the way of our Government.'

'What does the principal say?'

'Well, I do not know. And since the Reverend has also just a few moments ago been summoned to the deceased chief's kraal, I think that we must do as we have done in the past, that is, decide the matter among ourselves. The principal will always oblige us with the necessary rubber stamp.'

'The principal is most accommodating.'

With the chant of 'NO-TO BAN-TU NO-TO BAN-TU' ringing across the veld, Doyle continued to hang back in the doorway. He could hear faint laughter in the distance but otherwise the village remained curiously silent, as though holding its breath while the long awaited rain stalked the hills.

'Then let us proceed,' declared Nurse Fumba.

'First with the issue of pregnancy, if you do not mind, sister, since the rules are clear on this matter and it can be dealt with quickest. Who is the student who has submitted herself for a gynaecological instead of academic examination?'

'NO-TO BAN-TU! NO-TO BAN-TU! NO-TO BAN-TU!'

Doyle glanced hurriedly across the empty yard but the boys remained hidden by the church; the whitewashed building protruding like a splintered bone out of the earth's skin.

'Well, sister?' said Abraham.

'Well, brother Dlamini,' replied Nurse Fumba after a lengthy silence, 'the one who was so bold as to report to the clinic at Tsindi while I myself was on duty, is in fact the niece of our chairman.'

'But he has many. Many daughters, nieces. He has truly gone forth and multiplied.'

'*Hau mhlekazi*. This is serious. The one I am referring to is . . .'

'Primrose . . . Alexia?'

'You, old man. Is there nothing in this village you do not know?'

'*Hayi, inkosikazi*, I was just guessing.'

'Ha!'

'Truly. But now how does this concern us? The young lady is not a pupil at the school.'

'She has been registered as a candidate for the final exam. And you know that the department expressly forbids such registration.'

'And who has permitted this?'

Doyle turned quietly away from the door.

'NO-TO BAN-TU EDU-CATION! NO-TO BAN-TU . . .'

The Majogo militants noticing that he was about to leave the schoolyard hurried over to cut him off at the gate.

9

'Go back? You want to go back to Ngagabhaleko tonight? What about Mazeppa? Remember Mazeppa? Doyle, we should celebrate!'

Oh Alexia! And the spell of Mazeppa.

Now Doyle had never actually been to Mazeppa, while Alexia had managed less than an hour there, in the company of her uncle who had taken her along to a church conference on the coast. It was the first time she had been down to the sea – an experience very nearly ruined by the conference secretary's failure to mention when booking by phone that the attending members would all be Xhosa. Turfed out by the white management they had retreated northwards, to Shark Bay, once a popular holiday resort on Transkei's Wild Coast, now left with a solitary, run-down hotel.

But for Alexia no indignity could rob her of that first magical glimpse of the Indian Ocean, a glimpse that had instantly made her realise how small and tame her dreams had been until then. And so twelve hours later, bumping into Doyle on the beach at Shark Bay, she expressed her delight by throwing out her arms and shouting above the din of the waves: 'Doyle! What a surprise! You have followed us all the way to Mazeppa. Isn't it beautiful? I can't believe my eyes. I have never seen such magnificent scenery!'

Doyle pointed coolly to the hotel verandah where numerous church officials stood gazing at the wind-whipped bay and its cauldron of white water. 'Your uncle,' he said, 'tells me the hotel at Mazeppa wouldn't let you stay.'

'Tsha! Those monkeys think they can keep us prisoner in the bush forever. Look! Look around you. It makes me feel dizzy. All this space! All this freedom! It feels like I'm standing in the doorway of a small, dark house. The door is open. There's the way. There's the road to freedom. It makes me want to run into the water, to throw myself into its arms. But look how strong and terrible – those waves will crush me. Tomorrow, the workers at the hotel say, the wind will disappear and the water will be calm. Then it will take me – I shall march into the arms of the new witch-doctor. I shall be afraid but such fear will not hold me back. I shall throw away everything and let the water take me. Oh Doyle, I can't wait for tomorrow. I want to go now. Let's go together, you and I. Let's run into the wild water. Look, here's the door. I want to go. Doyle, why didn't you tell me? You have been all over the world. Why didn't you say, "Alexia, you must go to Mazeppa". Truly Mazeppa is the happiest moment in my life. And the happiest moment must last for ever. No more Ngagabhaleko. No more Transkei or Soweto, or Durban or Johannesburg. Just the sea. And now it has brought you here too! Oh I want to run. Come, let us be just as wild and terrible as these waves. Let us run. Let us leave the old men to their fate. They do not listen to their own voices. They do not really know why they are here. I know – because the trembling earth tells me. We are alive. We are not caged animals. We are like the wind – free to express our joy. Doyle, why didn't you tell me? Did you think I wouldn't believe you? Come, throw away your shoes. You must swim – tomorrow you will teach me to swim. I want to go out there – beyond the land's claws. I want to see the blue sky shining in the blue water. They say there are sharks. I'm not afraid. Freedom is bigger than fear. But look! See how strong those waves are! They'll crush the hotel in the night. We'll all be swept away while we're dreaming. Doyle, the sea will sweep us away together. You can't prevent it. Tonight we'll see your courage. Come, let's run. The wind is too cold – though inside I'm not cold. Inside there's a big, big fire no one can put out. The waves are logs rolling on to the fire. Come, we must run. We cannot stop the wind fanning the flames. Welcome the wind. Welcome Mazeppa. They greet us – we are long lost lovers. Come, give me your hand. I'll pull you. I've strength for two. For twenty. Come, run, Doyle. Please, run with me!'

◇

'Your bit of nookie?' asked Naylor, pointing to the beach where Alexia stood feverishly waving her arms in an effort to attract their attention. 'A little black meat on the side, hey?'

Having just waded out from the shore, Doyle grunted as he grabbed hold of the launch's starboard ladder and hauled himself up out of the water. 'It's a little early in the morning for bar-room jokes, Naylor. You got a towel? Water's bloody freezing.'

Naylor threw him a towel, along with a dry pair of trunks. 'Bladdy kaffir! What's she screaming about anyway? Sounds hysterical.'

Doyle, whose glance rapidly took in the launch's size and sumptuousness, rubbed his legs vigorously. 'You might've picked me up later. It isn't as if there's not enough barracuda to go round.'

Naylor slapped him reassuringly on the back. 'The earlier the better. That way . . .' He broke off as Alexia's voice floated plaintively over the rose-coloured water.

'Doyle I want to come too. Please, Doyle, take me with you.'

Doyle threw the wet towel back at Naylor. 'What are you waiting for? Let's go.'

But Naylor seemed to hesitate; thirteen years lying between them like a calm yet treacherous sea. There'd been no attempt to shake hands. That would have heightened the feeling of estrangement. A capricious gleam in his eyes, a bit of schoolboy banter: these had always been Naylor's stock in trade. But how did you laugh with someone you hadn't seen for years? Someone you felt you no longer really knew? Or perhaps, to your horror, had become everything you despised?

In the end Naylor's reaction was to spread the wet towel disconsolately over the back of one of the deck's leather seats. 'Shit, Doyle, I might have known it'd take a woman to drag you down here. But Christ – a goff! Where's your pride man?' And with that he swept up the short flight of stairs to the cockpit and switched on the engines.

'Doyle please take me . . with . . .' Alexia's voice sank among the dunes as an angry whirlpool rocked the launch's stern and they lurched thunderously out to sea.

◇

Doyle couldn't bring himself to look back. As the launch thrust its bow out of the water, pinning him to his seat, he watched the sun shake itself free of the horizon, tossing burning embers among the feathered cloud that flared up – scarlet, gold, then pearly white, before dissolving against the bone-hard sky. A flock of shearwaters traced an unerring line overhead, that suddenly snapped as they dived. Then with long, stiff wings they rose again and the delicate line resumed until finally it grew faint in the distance and gulls and petrels took over, like infants with their own tactless scrawl; the hungry birds darting so close in the wind it felt as though they were clawing at his beard.

Mercifully the *G*-forces crushing him against the soft leather and making him feel distinctly bilious eventually relinquished its rampant grip; Naylor, as soon as they were out of the bay, eased back on the launch's engines, allowing the wind to drop to a pleasant breeze and the deep, sapphire water to lap gently against the hull. Immediately the smell of diesel gave way to the stench of rotting fish, itself overpowered by the unmistakable scent of leather and suntan oil.

Yet all Doyle could smell was the furtive scent of a night stolen from under the Reverend's nose; the warm and heady fragrance of Alexia's lissom body. For he had run along the shore with her, or rather, splashed a few yards through the wind-driven surf before the whisky and the years of sloth had caught up with him, by which time she was away, sprinting the length of the beach and back again, like a cheetah in pursuit of its prey. He could still see the hunger in her feline eyes, in the lean silky flanks uncovered by the sheets as he slipped out of bed in the morning, anxious not to waken her. It was a hunger that shamed him, made him feel less and not more of a man. Watching her sleep, a hand curled at her mouth, a knee pressed against her belly, he'd begun to pull the sheet over her, then stopped. It was his shame he was trying to cover. Shame because he had nothing to offer her. How could he repay her trust? Her brave transparency? She was young and spirited – 'alive' as the Xhosa would say; while all he longed for was to get the unwanted reunion with Naylor out of the way so that he could return to the quiet backwater of Ngagabhaleko.

$$\Diamond$$

'Some choice,' Naylor complained, after they had drifted down the coast, anchoring a mile or so off shore at a spot he pointed out to Doyle on the chart. 'Shark Bay, I mean. Bladdy useless for diving.'

'Sorry,' said Doyle. 'I wasn't thinking of the diving when I chose it.'

'So I noticed,' Naylor replied, folding the chart with a smirk.

'That's not what I meant,' said Doyle.

Naylor returned the chart to a drawer in the wood-panelled cockpit from where he looked down out of the sun at Doyle.

'You can't fool an oke like me,' he remarked. 'That place went to the dogs soon as we gave Transkei independence. No white business left, just darkies, those that can afford it. It's a riff-raff place, ideal for the sort-a-thing you got in mind. Screw all the black meat you like. Nobody gives a damn. So long as you got the money to pay for it.'

Doyle struggled up out of the elegant bucket seat at the rear of the deck and with a resigned gesture – he held up his empty glass – stumbled below. With the sun lancing through the portholes on to the polished mahogany and brass surfaces, he poured himself another drink from the well-stocked cabinet Naylor had shown him earlier. Gulping down the expensive whisky, he idly jabbed on the video while his eyes ran over the plush furnishings – yet more leather interspersed with hardwoods and ivory, brown velvet curtains, satin sheets on the bed in the next room, a surfeit of lamps, switches, and an exquisite Turkish rug on the floor beside the hi-fi. A library of forty or fifty videos was stacked beside the mounted screen on which two naked women with shaven crotches appeared, writhing sinuously toward each other over a dead tree trunk in sparse savanna. Refilling his glass with ice from the freezer, Doyle threw the remote control down on the bar, picked up the bottle and staggered back up the stairs, collapsing into the leather seat which he swivelled round so that he had his back to the sea.

'Do you mind if we leave the girl out of this, Naylor?' he said, squinting through a pair of cheap sunglasses. 'I didn't come all this way to be lectured on screwing in the Homelands.'

Naylor lifted a military bush-hat from a shelf above the wheel. 'Suppose you know everything about it, hey?'

Doyle ignored the remark by putting his feet up and pouring himself another drink.

'So why did you come?' Naylor growled, slapping the camouflage hat on his head.

'You're asking me?' said Doyle. 'After the trouble you took tracking me down?'

'Wasn't any trouble. I explained in my letter. I was in Ireland on a business trip and got the hotel switchboard to trace your mother. She told me where you were. I have to admit I was bladdy surprised. After all the stuff you spouted when we were kids at Saints, I didn't ever expect to see you set foot in this country again. But I suppose it only goes to show, when you're a kid you'll say anything to be different.'

'What else did the old girl tell you?'

Naylor glanced over the side of the launch at the sun-filled water and began unbuttoning his shirt. 'Ah, now I didn't organise this little reunion just so we could chat about your mother.'

'Why did you organise it?' asked Doyle as he watched the bronzed figure strip down to his bathing trunks and begin hauling out diving gear from the storage boxes lining the perimeter of the deck. 'As for all this stuff, Christ, if I remember you couldn't even swim at school.'

'There was lots I couldn't do at school, Doyle. But you're looking at what I've become, not what I was then.'

'What have you become? The new Rambo?'

Naylor swooped down over the mounting pile of gear, lifted up a diving suit and shook it out, like a rag doll. 'We all change, Doyle. Some of us more than others.'

Change? thought Doyle, who found it hard to associate the rugged physique in front of him with his former boarding school room-mate – the pale and emaciated chairman of the 'Society for the Prevention of Cruelty to Non-rugby Players'. How had Naylor done it? With weights or anabolic steroids? By pumping iron all these years? Or had it been military service? The hat appeared to be a favourite.

Maybe the question wasn't how, but why? Why the bleached hair? The over-developed chest, bristling biceps and strapping thighs? Why the vanity that had never been the scrawny youth's at school? Naylor had always been brash, frantic and above all disorderly. Now he looked like someone who would kick a farmhouse door down; who would be happy stalking narrow country lanes in a camouflage uniform; someone who could terrorise with his cold-sore eyes. What was the reason for this violent metamorphosis? Indeed for this potentially violent reunion?

'Look around you, Doyle,' said Naylor, adjusting the valve of an oxygen tank that gave a quiet hiss before he shut it off and tossed it on top of another, the metal cylinders rattling like glasses in a bar, which was precisely where Doyle at that moment would have preferred to be. 'Go on, look around. You want to know why we're here? The answer's staring you in the face.'

'You mean the boat?'

Naylor picked up a snorkel and peered theatrically down it at Doyle, who saluted wryly with his glass.

'You could have sent a few photographs. Wife at the wheel. Kids staring through their goggles at Table Mountain. Bloodied shark on the deck . . .'

Naylor continued to peer down the snorkel at him.

'Would've been cheaper,' Doyle continued, cradling the bottle in his lap; 'though I suppose money isn't a problem, is it? Not with an expense account. What're you charging this venture to? Advertising? It isn't really worth it. Not for one of the riff-raff. I'm afraid your rich, maritime fare's lost on me, Naylor. The only thing you could sell me out of this little lot is the drinks cabinet.'

Naylor threw the snorkel aside. 'Bladdy hell, Doyle. Forget the launch. I didn't bring you down here to brag. I just want you to look around. Check the scenery. See those huge cliffs over there? Africa's own Notre Dame. And you don't have to pay to get in, nor leave donations.'

Doyle swivelled round in his chair. 'You ever been inside Notre Dame, Naylor?'

'Oh screw Notre Dame!' cried Naylor, yanking a speargun from the tangled heap of equipment and brandishing it against the sun. 'This is Africa, Doyle, remember? The Africa you always swore you'd never come back to. So you've been around. But have you ever been back to any of those places you taught in? South America? Solomon Islands? I bet you haven't. Why did you come back here then? Because it's something else? Am I right? Something special. OK so maybe . . .'

Still brandishing the speargun, he jammed a foot against the edge of Doyle's seat, a broad, bare foot, like a brass lock, preventing the seat from moving. 'Maybe you figure I'm coming on a little strong hey, what with the launch and all the gear and that. You're probably thinking I arranged this meeting so I could brag to you about the success I made of my life – Naylor the little runt, now a first-rate farmer, building contractor, businessman . . . You're feeling

71

intimidated. All right, I can understand that. After all you're used to a different way of life. A different set of values. You're used to slumming it in villages. Used to mud huts and brak water. Well the way you choose to live is your own affair. Far be it from me to interfere. But then we were at school together. And since we shared the same room, I like to think we were close. We broke the same rules, bunking study, sneaking into town. And we fought the same fights, against bullies in the playground and all those rugger-buggers. It's because of that I got in touch with you. And now we're here, I want to share things again with you. Chew the fat, as they say. If it doesn't work out that's OK. But at least I tried. And at least we can talk, spend a bit of time diving, fishing, just relaxing, like old buddies. The Wild Coast – remember how you used to spend your holidays hiking along the beach? – it's the perfect setting. Sure, it looks pretty tame right now, sea-birds floating on a light swell, cool breeze. But we got to watch out for later on. Weather forecast is for a strong easterly. I expect you still come down here a lot so you'll know what that means.'

'No,' Doyle said, 'I don't.'

Naylor stared at him through cold blue eyes. 'No you don't know what that means? Or you don't come down here all that often?'

'I don't come down.'

Naylor continued to jam his foot against the edge of the seat. 'I don't believe you,' he said.

'Hardly matters.'

'What about your dirty weekends?'

'What dirty weekends?'

'The ones with the goff.'

'There haven't been any,' said Doyle, pouring himself another drink. 'This is the first time I've been out of the village.'

Naylor lifted his foot from the seat. Throwing the speargun down on the deck, he said: 'So why the bladdy hell did you pick Shark Bay for our reunion? Why not somewhere civilised? With a bit of life, like Durban or East London. At least you could have got yourself a decent hotel. Mzamba's just up the coast. You could've booked a room; fabulous casino.'

'That where you're staying?'

Naylor nodded. 'Why don't you join me? I'll bring you back in the morning. After that I got to fly to Johannesburg.'

'What about the boat?'

'Ag, I've hired someone to take it down to P.E. for me.'

'Expensive weekend.'

'You must be worth a buck or two yourself,' said Naylor, returning like a magpie to investigate the gleaming nest of diving equipment. 'Expatriates don't come cheap . . . what with lucrative contracts, free flights, subsidised rents . . .'

'I doubt I could afford the casino,' said Doyle.

'Jesus, man. If that's all that's stopping you, you don't have to worry. I'll take care of that side of things. We could have a swell time. Two blokes on their own.'

Doyle felt something soft and fleshy against his foot. 'Thanks for the offer,' he said, realising it was part of the speargun, 'but I think I'll stick with Shark Bay.'

'Yeah,' said Naylor, 'so you can screw your black meat. That why you chose the place, because of the goff?'

Doyle leaned over and picked up the gun. It felt surprisingly light. 'I chose Shark Bay because it's on the Lusikisiki road. I had to drive past the farm to get here.'

Naylor looked up from the diving belt he'd been examining, its lead weights clustered together like startled fish eyes. 'I didn't realise,' he said. 'Jeez, why didn't you tell me?'

'Nothing you could do.'

'What about the goff?'

'She doesn't come into it.'

'Oh yeah?'

The sun flashed along the shaft as Doyle raised the gun against the stainless steel sky.

Naylor said: 'Man, when I saw your mother and she told me you still hadn't been to your father's grave, I couldn't believe it. Course I knew you refused to go to the funeral but that was a long time ago. You were just a stroppy teenager then. After all these years – and she said you still hadn't been! Christ you'd better write and tell her you finally made it, hey. Halle-bladdy-lulya!'

Doyle wiped the sweat from the rubber grip on his T-shirt.

'Actually, I saw the grave you know,' Naylor grinned. 'Your mother showed me a photograph of it. It's like one of those things you sometimes see on the top of a mountain. What do you call it . . .? A cone . . . cairn. That's it a cairn. No marble or anything like that; just a pile of stones, ordinary stones collected by the farm-workers. She said it took them half a day to . . . well, I suppose you know all that now. What did you do with the goff when you were there? Leave her in the car?'

Doyle swung round sharply in his chair as a Cape gannet swooped down over the boat.

'The gun isn't loaded,' said Naylor.

'Give me a minute,' said Doyle.

'Careful or it'll tear your head off.'

But by the time Doyle had pulled the rubber spring back along the shaft, the gannet had dived, resurfaced with a maasbanker in its beak and taken off, its wings unbending as it skimmed over the surface of the water. Doyle threw the gun down at Naylor's feet.

'I didn't stop at the farm,' he confessed. 'I'd planned to, but I drove past.'

Naylor leaned over and carefully unloaded the gun.

Doyle said: 'It's the only reason I came back to Africa – to visit the grave. Sorry to disappoint you, Naylor, but it wasn't the scenery that brought me back. Scenery's never been high on my list of priorities.'

'Africa isn't just scenery, Doyle, it's all kinds of things.'

'Like money and fine living.'

'You know what I mean.'

'All those things beginning with b . . . braaivleis, biltong, boerewors . . . and black.'

'You've had your share of the fine . . .'

'Not forgetting blood,' Doyle added.

'It's easy to mock.'

'Yeah, well, Africa doesn't speak to me the way it does to you. I'm only here to pay my respects to the dead.'

'You might be a while then.'

Doyle waved his empty glass. 'Time doesn't mean anything in the village. One day, week, month – it's like any other. That's the real beauty of Africa. Time can't touch its desolation.'

'You know what I think, Doyle?' said Naylor as he began stashing away the surplus gear – the masks, flippers, knives, weights, air-tanks and wet suits, enough it seemed to equip an entire diving team. 'I think your living in the village is a form of revenge. You always blamed your parents for behaving like lords on the land – the *fat* land you used to call it. Now you're getting your own back.'

'We can't avenge ourselves on the dead, Naylor.'

'Maybe it's a kind of penance then.'

'Sack cloth and ashes?' said Doyle, squinting through the empty glass. 'You must be joking.'

Naylor slammed down the top of a storage box. 'At least I'd understand it if it was. I could even understand revenge. But something tells me you're living with those kaffirs out of spite, which is cheaper and nastier than revenge. What's more, it's childish. I also suspect the spite is aimed not just at your parents, but at the rest of us – the white tribe you've always despised. Living in a mud hut is a slap in our faces. And the longer you put off the visit to your father's grave, the bigger the kick you get out of seeing people like me squirm with embarrassment. After all, it's nice to have someone else's pain take your mind of your own, especially when that someone is an old school friend because it involves all the old grudges. School grudges always last the longest, Doyle. Remember how you would have nothing to do with any kid whose father owned a Merc? How you refused your classmates' holiday invitations because you thought all they wanted to do was show off the country to you. You even kept leaving your blazer at the dry-cleaners so you wouldn't have to go on school outings. Jeez, you haven't changed, you know that? If you had, you would have called me the minute you landed at Jan Smuts. And I'd have picked you up, taken you home to meet the wife and kids. You could have stayed – as long as you liked. When you were ready, we'd have driven you to the grave, or lent you the car so's you could go by yourself if that's what you wanted. But no. What do we get? The cold shoulder. The leper treatment. The sort of thing our critics in the media like to advocate. Why, Doyle? We'd have looked after you. Why'd you turn your back on us? Now listen you sour bastard. There's something I want you to think about.'

Having packed away everything except his own personal gear, Naylor leaned over and lifted the empty whisky bottle from Doyle's seat. Perching on the armrest, he put his hand on his former room-mate's shoulder. 'Doyle, what I'd really like is for you to come back with me tonight to the casino. We'll have us a good time, man. Tomorrow I'll cancel my trip to Johannesburg. We'll fly straight down to my place. The wife and kids will be over the moon. They know everything about you. And Saints. I even told them how you helped me pass my matric. Christ I was thick in those days. I don't know what I would have done without you. They'd really like to see you, Doyle, the family. They feel they owe you something. What can those people in the *bundu* offer that we can't? You'll never be able to trust them. And they'll never trust you. No hard feelings. That's just the way it is. They're peasants. They live by their hands. You're an intellectual. You'll always be alone up there. Hey, Doyle? What do you say? I'm serious, man. I've never been more serious in my life.'

The muscle-bound Naylor stood up. Without taking his eyes off Doyle, who sprawled haphazardly in the large leather seat, he began climbing into his wet suit. His face was hard, almost statuesque. As he pulled the zip up over his flattened stomach, his chest seemed to expand and the fair hair stuck out like a sea-anemone waving in the current. He bent over and strapped a diving knife to his calf, patting it reassuringly. Expertly he slung the lead belt round his waist. Then he said: 'I'll be gone about an hour. I'd take you down but you've had too much to drink. It wouldn't be safe. Never mind. Drink as much as you like. Help yourself to anything else you want – some good videos there. Only do me one small favour . . .' The broad feet were sucked into a pair of enormous flippers, goggles strapped to the blonde head. 'Think about what I've said. Think seriously about it. If there's anything you're not sure about, let me know soon as I get back. And Doyle . . .' Naylor swung the yellow oxygen canister over his shoulder, like a rucksack, 'skip the petty details, OK? Car, job, rent – the woman at the hotel. All that can be taken care of. No sweat, man.'

10

'NO-TO BAN-TU! NO-TO BAN-TU! NO-TO BAN-TU!'

With Majogo and his cubs pawing at the gate, Doyle crossed the
school yard. He could see his car parked in the distance, outside the
mission compound. The rain had only just begun. The roads would
still be passable.

'NO-TO BAN-TU! NO-TO BAN-TU!'

Doyle felt like a hunter being pursued by a dangerously wounded
animal.

'NO-TO BAN-TU! NO-TO BAN-TU!'

Drumming the base of his placard on the gate-post, Majogo led the
angry chant. A lean, testing figure – 'E string' to his friends – in some
ways he reminded Doyle of Alexia. For he was tall and swaggered
with a natural arrogance. His lips were curled in a permanent sneer
and the dimple in his chin masqueraded as a *tsotsi*'s scar. Like
Alexia's, the sneer was softened by idyllically fine features; the
prominent cheekbones, scimitar curve of the jaw, the clear eyes,
slender nose and gentle brow, forming a natural elegance which
seemed to make anything hurtful they said or did, somehow
forgivable. A prince dropping ash on ones sofa would always be
forgiven. And in village terms Majogo certainly dressed as a prince.

In contrast to the drab khaki of his followers he sported a blue-
striped, monogrammed shirt, flared trousers with blue socks, white
leather shoes and a tie whose knot was just sufficiently loose to
suggest a jaunty aloofness. His shirt was buttoned at the wrists, his
navy trousers pressed. A steel comb jutted out of the back pocket. In
spite of the large placard which he wielded, he was able to shelter
beneath the umbrella that was held for him by one of his companions.

In a climate where pupils ducked beneath their desks for fear of
punishment when asked a question they couldn't answer, Jackson
Dzumele Majogo had won a reputation for turning questions back on

teachers. It was perhaps not quite the reputation he thought it was, for, like Nomanthando, he wasn't one of Ngagabhaleko's most gifted: his challenges, unknown to himself, were usually fatuous, producing loud clicks of frustration among his peers who, though wary of the disdainful figure encamped in a desk by himself at the back of the room, were nonetheless anxious to get on with their work.

Yet Majogo never gave up; not even when facing the unresponsive Doyle who more than any other teacher seemed to trigger the youth's impetuous behaviour, his rash scepticism. Majogo saw in Doyle a blindness he couldn't understand, or indeed believe. He felt it was contrived. It was far too thorough. Nothing he said or did could move the *umlungu*. He never blew his top; never seemed to expect anything better. The *umlungu* saw or wanted for nothing. And yet where, this razor-lipped refugee from the townships wanted to know, had anyone ever seen a white man who wanted nothing?

As Doyle entered the V-shaped gateway, designed to keep out village livestock, the boys crowded round in front of him.

'So why you didn't stay with the police?'

'Accommodation was too crowded?'

'Bad food?'

'Such things never trouble you at Ngagabhaleko!'

Doyle felt a tug as his shirt caught on a bent nail.

'Why you go with them, come back, act like nothing is happening?'

'What *is* happening, Majogo?' said Doyle, pointing to their placards. 'It's raining. The ink's running. And no one can read what you've written. Why don't you go home and wait for the sun to come out, hey?'

Majogo's narrowed eyes flared in the grey light. Doyle unhooked his shirt and squeezed through the gate. Immediately the youths took up positions along the path to the mission, balancing on stools of sandstone, like lions in a circus act.

'It may interest you to know,' said Doyle, sliding up to them, 'the police thought I started this. That's why they picked me up. They took me for the organiser, or ringleader. I hope you can see the funny side of it. I wouldn't want you to think I was trying to steal your thunder.'

Majogo shot out an arm as a sudden squall tore the umbrella from the grasp of the boy beside him, a surly faced youth with clawed cheeks, black, broken teeth and a vicious weal over his jugular. Together they wrestled with the flapping wing, struggling to bring it under control. Finally the squall passed and they stood looking rather sheepishly at the inanimate object lying in the mud at their feet.

Majogo was the first to recover his composure. Turning his back on his companion, he strutted across to another stone. 'What ringleader?' he growled. 'You think we depend on others to organise us?'

'It's none of my business,' replied Doyle in a jaded voice that seemed to take its cue from the monotonous roll of the rain on the drum-shaped hills.

'Nothing is ever your business,' Majogo snarled.

Doyle picked up the bent umbrella. 'It *is* the police's though and you can be sure they'll want to know more. I'm assuming . . .' he shook the mud from the handle, 'this isn't another half-cocked idea, like Nomanthando's, to get out of the exams. Seems like it's that time of year, when witch-doctors get anxious calls from unprepared students who hope to avoid writing.'

'You think Nomanthando is acting?'

'What do you think?'

'We saw Promise this morning. She says her friend is seriously ill.'

'She may be.'

'You don't believe?'

'I don't know.'

Majogo took the umbrella which Doyle held out, studied it curiously for a second, then opened it. Like his lips it was slightly buckled. 'Well I can tell you we have no witch-doctor behind us. We are not afraid of writing exams.'

'Then drop your feeble boycott and write for Jesus' sake. You're not going to achieve anything like this.'

'Tsha! We are refusing to write those Bantu examinations.'

'Then you leave the school committee, which is meeting at this very moment, with no option but to expel you.'

Majogo swiped the air with the bent umbrella. 'Tsha! They can expel no one without the principal's authority. And you are afraid to expel us so you put the blame on them. If you were not afraid then you would have expelled us yourself before now. Why did you not do it? We know what is written in the department's circular. Troublemakers must be expelled and reported to the police. But you did not do this. Maybe because you were looking for the ringleaders? Always you say nothing is your business but maybe everything is your business.'

'What are you trying to say Majogo?'

'I say you only pretend to be blind. Really you are the eyes and ears of the police.'

'Teacher?' roared a youth in the background. 'Tsha! You look and listen for the police!'

'How much the police pay you?' roared another.

'Detention, ha! They take you to Umtata Holiday Inn.'

'You watch television.'

'Get drunk.'

'Sleep with Umtata ladies.'

Snapping and snarling they slid down from their perches under the watchful eye of Majogo. Soon they were brushing resentfully against him, a sluggish steam rising from their wet clothes. He could see their scars, township scars, livid in the rain; their mouths quivering, their eyes dull and contemptuous as they circled round, trying to provoke him . . .

'You can expel us!'

'We not afraid!'

'Of you. Or the committee. Police? Tsha!'

'We know you afraid.'

'You afraid of committee.'

'Of the Reverend.'

'You afraid of the witch-doctor.'

'Why you only visit the old man?'

'Hide in your *jondolo*?'

'Why you teach without punishing students? Mjozi always punished students, made them work, wear school uniform, come to class on time.'

'He was strict. He beat the students. And they respect him.'

'You beat no one; punish no one.'

'No one is afraid of you.'

Like a horrified audience the hills began to slip away under the torn sky and he found himself trapped against the fence with the gnawing heat of their bodies driving out the chilliness of his drenched clothes. He was aware that Majogo hung back but he wondered how much control the aristocratic figure, calmly wiping the mud from his shoes, had over his enraged pride. Driven by the pain of past wounds, they guarded the future's carcass with more than just a flunkey's snarl.

'Why you come to Ngagabhaleko?'

'No white man ever come here.'

'Who has sent you? Who you work for?'

'How much money they pay? You want money, why you not work on the mines?'

'You afraid to go underground?'

'Black man just a shadow underground.'

'Bantu education send us there.'

'*You* send us there.'

Doyle watched as at last Majogo descended from his perch. Meticulously avoiding the glutinous puddles he advanced toward them, grasping the handle of the umbrella with sharp fingers that spat out from the wrist like razors. A high forehead glowed with a sanguine elegance; the taut, hollow cheeks inflated with hostility.

'Go! Tell the committee they can expel us! We are not afraid!'

Doyle shook his head wearily. 'Look, in six weeks all of this'll have blown over. Your classmates will have matriculated and gone off to look for work. Where will you be? Left kicking your heels in the village. Is it worth it? Why not call it off? Write the exams . . . I'll have a word with the committee. Afterwards you can do whatever you want. You can use the qualification to find a decent job. Or you can throw it in the bin. It's up to you. At least get the certificate.'

Majogo's answer was to leap with a ferocious scowl on to a rock which was already occupied by one of his acolytes, whom he sent spinning into the mud.

'Tsha! You are making a mockery of us. What do you think we are fighting for? Standing here all these days, even when the police have been to our homes to question us.'

'So they've spoken to you?'

'They came to the front door of our homes! How did they know where we live? People in the village would not tell them such a thing. You can see how long we strike for before the police know what is happening. But now they know everything.'

'I expect the chief's *indunas* must have . . .'

'Tsha! What need have they of the police? The chief has his own court. If he thinks we do wrong, he sends for us to that court. But the *indunas* know we have done nothing wrong. They know we are quarrelling with the Boers because this is education to make us into slaves. Transkei is cradle and grave of the Boer slaves. So expel us. But then you must also expel yourself from Ngagabhaleko because it will no longer be safe for you to be here. People will become suspicious. They will ask how the police found out about this thing.'

'The villagers are equally suspicious of you,' Doyle countered. 'How many students have joined your boycott? You're an outsider like myself, Majogo.'

The regal figure sneered beneath his umbrella. 'I am a Xhosa. Here we are all Xhosa. Even that one who is your neighbour at the mission; who is ashamed to speak like a Xhosa. She too is one. And was once made pregnant by one.'

'I doubt,' said Doyle hurriedly, 'whether Miss Xolile would try to hide the fact she's a Xhosa. Anyway, you of all people should know it isn't easy when you've grown up in the city to adapt to life in a village like Ngagabhaleko. Not that that excuses Alexia's . . . eh . . . Miss Xolile's behaviour. After all Transkei's full of migrants, broken families . . . It is itself part of a broken family.'

'Tsha! The woman is a whore. She sleeps with men in the village.'

'That's none of my business – or yours for that matter.'

'If nothing is your business then why you come to Transkei?'

Doyle, studying the livid figure, recalled Mbanjwa's more measured restraint. For both Majogo and the lieutenant – still struggling with the historic failure of the Xhosa to withstand successive onslaughts by Boer and Brit – appeared determined to hide their pain behind highly stylised performances – performances restricted to deserted theatres in the bush, where the public needed no reminding of the pain, however well disguised – by the lieutenant as cool, unflappable cop, Majogo the urban firebrand.

'So why you come this country?' Majogo demanded.

'I thought it was my leaving that concerned you,' said Doyle.

'It is for your own safety.'

'Where's the angry horde calling for my blood? Is this it? The five of you? What about all the pupils who are writing, who want the school to remain open? Or their parents who depend on the jobs their children will get? Are you going to threaten all of *them*?'

'Writing will not help them.'

'Will marching in the rain?'

'It can teach them to fight. They must learn to fight, not just hide their heads in books.'

'And what happens to them after the revolution, when they are all illiterate? What use will they be to anyone then? They'll end up sweeping the streets, like their parents do now for the Boers. So may you.'

Majogo swore as his foot slipped from the rock he was perched on. 'I shall finish school,' he yelped, leaping over a pool of burgundy mud.

'And when will that be?' Doyle asked.

The youth carefully wiped the toe of his shoe with a handkerchief. 'It will not be long. The revolution is coming. It is here now!'

'Here?' Doyle flung out an arm, indicating the grey wilderness, where the hundreds of tiny, whitewashed huts that dotted the hills appeared to be dissolving like Aspros in the rain.

Majogo shook his umbrella. 'It is here. This is the first boycott in Transkei. Soon there will be many. You cannot defeat us.'

'It's never been my intention to try,' said Doyle.

'Then why the police came to our homes after they spoken with you?'

Doyle shivered as the damp began to penetrate through to his bones.

'Beware we shall deal with informers!' Majogo warned. 'We are not afraid of our teachers. In the townships some have died.'

'No doubt Mr Mjozi was lucky then.'

'He was not beaten up for informing.'

'Some consolation,' said Doyle.

'Students here respected Mr Mjozi.'

'Yes, I get the message, Majogo.'

'Then go!' screamed the youth. 'We not want you in our village. Go! Go now!'

But Doyle's feet were trapped in the dark, bruised earth, like corks in a bottle. 'The Security Branch's sentiments exactly,' he shrugged.

'Obviously one of you's jumped to the wrong conclusion. Or you're both just paranoid.'

The youth's sneer seemed to mellow momentarily, becoming a bleak, almost wistful smile, until with two loud popping noises, Doyle broke free of the mud and began to walk away, whereupon Majogo leapt out angrily in front of him.

Immediately the rest of the pack encircled him, their eyes bobbing in their streaming skulls, their teeth chattering as they trembled with fury and excitement in their wet clothes.

Yet even in their ferocious scrutiny, Doyle saw the familiar hopelessness of it all. As the cold poured into his bones, so despair filled theirs – just as it filled the bones of their classmates, scratching away in the crumbling church, like insects at the poisoned bark of life. The tree was dead. The dereliction of the church proved it, signalling the villagers' rejection of all the false prophets who passed their way and to whom, like Doyle, they remained polite in their quiet and inner disillusion.

'Titsha!'

Yet still the scratching and gnawing went on.

'You say we may write the examination if we give up our boycott?'

'I'm sure I could persuade the committee,' said Doyle.

'Then,' Majogo replied with a scornful grin, 'let us also give you a choice. You have not said why you came to Ngagabhaleko. But one cannot come to such a poor place without a reason. If you are not an informer or collaborator then what is your business here? If it is to help these uneducated people then you will not be afraid to help us. Together we can get rid of this Bantu education. We can make our own system, find our own books, choose our own teachers. There are many who are qualified but have been banned by the government. The people here will support you in all of this. They will help to build proper classrooms. We shall be serious about this thing. And we shall want to see that you are also serious . . .'

The earth, giving way beneath the steady onslaught of the rain, felt as if it had clamped its icy teeth on his ankle and was about to drag him down the hill in its powerful jaws. It hissed and growled as water streamed from its flanks, exposing its bones through the thin flesh. Emaciated at best in the winter, it would not be long before the summer rains ripped the skin off the mangy animal.

The boys, themselves taut and trembling, as if having to hold on to the rabid creature's leash, waited expectantly for his reply. As their hungry eyes met his it seemed for one brief moment that he was united with them in their struggle; that their isolation was his, their desperation a spark that could light up the dark days ahead. However, reflected in their eager anticipation, Doyle saw his own adolescent anger – shrivelled and spent, and knew that Majogo's offer had come more than twenty years too late.

And so as the rain suddenly eased and the earth began to breathe again, he shrugged and stepped past the youth who, in a last, forlorn act of defiance spat at his feet then turned, and pursued by his comforters, sped off down the hill.

Just then Abraham Dlamini and the rest of the committee filed out into the schoolyard.

11

The chug-chug of the fisherman's tiny outboard had been with him all afternoon, like a faithful dog at his heels. He had grown so used to it that as they dragged the old boat up on to the beach and he saw its patched hull, he felt a slight sadness, tinged with guilt. Yet he hadn't asked to be ferried through the storm. In fact more than once when they'd been swamped by a large wave and seemed about to sink he'd urged Manku to give up their perilous journey.

'Shark Bay! Shark Bay!' came the fisherman's rebuff, above the roar of the wind and the booming waves. 'I take you. I take you.'

Now less than thirty yards away the hotel's coloured lanterns danced wildly in the wind and as the thin, heron-like figure secured his boat in the sand, Doyle tried to get him to accept a meal and a room for the night. But Manku who had earlier seen Naylor's luxurious launch driven on to the rocks and had helped rescue the two men from the surf, wanted nothing to do with what smacked of a reward. Muttering through broken teeth, 'Too many big shots, I stay at village,' he set off stiffly across the sand, carrying his pride like a broken wing.

$\diamondsuit$

Manku's 'big shots' – check-out girls, clerks, civil servants, nurses, teachers – had been driven indoors by the stormy conditions. Misted windows and a black moonless night whipped by a frenzied wind concealed the desolation they had escaped, leaving behind over-turned chairs and tables, an uprooted sun-umbrella, empty beer cans bobbing in the swollen tide, a whisky glass filled with blue-bottles and a wall of sand piling up in the car park.

None of this deterred Shark Bay's regular weekend revellers. In the bar, the 'Captain's Table' and the ladies lounge, they gathered like gulls round a ferry, the sound of their laughter ebbing and flowing between breaks in the juke-box.

Doyle was certain that by now Alexia would have thrown herself into the licentious euphoria. Crossing the verandah in his bare feet, his body bruised, his shirt torn, he pushed open the foyer door and was relieved to find no one paid him the slightest bit of attention. Struck by an overpowering wave of perfume he staggered up the stairs to his room where, a few hours later, he awoke with a raging thirst, and the distinct impression that someone had just closed the door on their way out.

As he lay quietly in the dark he listened for the sound of footsteps echoing down the corridor. But all he heard was the muffled thumping of the juke-box, the subdued sigh of the wind and voices fading in the salt air.

Then, slowly, like instruments being tuned before a concert, the discordant notes of the previous day's aborted symphony began to resurface – the sad and unrequited, 'Doyle, wait. Doyle, please take me with you,' answered by the ruthless explosion of the launch's engines . . . the siren whisper of the sea, the tinkling of ice, muted time, and the patter of a breeze as light as a bird's foot – until it was savagely stamped on and the splintering of wood against rock made a mockery of the conductor's baton . . . 'Doyle you bastard, you drunken bastard! I should have known I couldn't trust you.'

Gently exploring the bruises appearing across his body, Doyle wondered whether he should get dressed and go down to the bar or finish the bottle he had saved in his cupboard. If he stayed in his room he faced a certain showdown with Alexia – he felt sure it was she who had just tiptoed out of the door. On the other hand it seemed unlikely he would be any safer hiding in the bar. For who was to say Alexia wouldn't burst into the all-male enclave and with those orange-painted nails flashing under his nose demand to know why, if she was good enough for his bed, she wasn't good enough to be taken out on Naylor's launch?

He could see the bar rising to her defence, their judgement influenced not so much by the bitter aftertaste of History as by the pain of a proud lover betrayed. He could expect little sympathy. That she was bold and cavalier would count for nothing. It was the pain of betrayal, a pain many of those with wives and lovers knew all about and hated themselves for. As they would hate him.

He must have dropped off to sleep again because the next time he awoke the juke-box was silent though a noisy hub-bub continued to colonise the verandah and the car park outside, where he could still hear cars arriving, fresh bottles of beer being opened. Here too, as at Ngagabhaleko, breaking the curfew was a way of life; not one of lawlessness or sedition but temporary amnesia, one which Doyle himself recognised and embraced as a lover.

It was the only lover he cared for. One who asked no questions and delivered no ultimatums; who ran no risks yet always returned. It was a lover he could depend on; who travelled easily, never balked at rivals or ridiculed them. A brazen lover yet easily discrete, unlike the couple haggling over their price outside in the corridor . . .

'I give you thirty rand. That's how much they ask in Umtata. But if you want more, I give you more. There is no need to fight over money.'

No need at all, thought Doyle, unless it was a matter of pride, though in a sleazy hotel corridor . . .?

'Let me tell you, my car is an XG. I work for the government. A certain somebody in the Department of Agriculture. I travel all over. Cape Town. Durban. Pretoria. Sometimes I stay behind and look after the office. Then I am my own boss.'

Take your chance, Doyle whispered softly to himself in the dark. Isn't this what you came for?

'I have my own house in Lauderdale. All mod-cons. I live by myself. You can see it if you want. Now what you say, we jive hey? I make you rich. Fifty rand.'

Jive, for Christ sake, woman. No need to be ashamed. Just name your price. We're all whores in the end.

'. . . think I not good enough for you, hey? Maybe you come looking for the *umlungu*. You want white sugar-daddy? White treat you like shit, man. Money is money. But I not treat you like shit. Come, the night is running away from us. Do not let us waste this opportunity. I give you sixty rand. It's worth it. You are young and beautiful. I treat you nice. Not like white shit. Forget white shit. His money is blood money. Come, I give you seventy rand. Here is my room . . .'

Doyle sat up abruptly as light from the corridor splashed over the cracked plaster on the wall opposite his bed.

'*Hau*! I do not understand. Now you hold back. Look, here is a room. Why you so . . .?'

Coy? thought Doyle, for it dawned on him that price wasn't the issue here at all. Alexia had allowed herself to be followed up to his room. It was her way of getting back at him. This was the 'expensive boat' she would pretend to sail away on, naively thinking he would come after her. If only she knew. Nobody came to the rescue when your plans, those fraught, balsa wood dreams, got smashed on the rocks. Nobody. Least of all Doyle.

'Ag now, where is your courage? There's no need to run away. You will not make such an easy money. Here, see, the door is open. I put forty rand on the table. Later I shall give you the rest.'

Doyle waited in silence as the money was counted out.

'There, it is yours. Take it.'

Doyle watched her shadow retreat in the doorway.

'If you continue to resist I shall . . . hmph?'

There was a startled grunt as Doyle flicked on the bedside lamp. A bull-necked figure bursting out of a silver suit swivelled round, knocking over the three-legged table he'd set his money on.

'Eh! B.b . . but how is this?'

Doyle took his eye off the door though he was sure Alexia was hiding just behind it.

'Au! I am t . . truly sorry . . I . . I did not realise,' stammered his astonished guest, 'I thought this room was unoccupied. You see, sometimes . . .' he paused, mopping his brow with a handkerchief while his large, raw eyes darted between the bed and the door. 'No. I . . . I do not think you will wish to know such details.'

Doyle pointed to the money on the floor. 'I suggest you try next door,' he said.

The stocky figure scooped up the notes, crumpling them in his fist. The corner of a pleated mauve shirt stuck out of the waistband of his trousers which sagged beneath a large quivering belly. He tucked the shirt back in along with the end of his white tie before ceremoniously removing his hat, a black fedora with a silk band which he juggled disconsolately. He was almost bald.

So this, thought Doyle, ruefully watching him set the table back on its feet, this was the rival Alexia was presenting him with: a balding, pot-bellied philanderer.

'Y-yes, I think I shall take your advice. In any case I am very sorry for disturbing you. Here . . .' with some effort he pulled a half-jack from his pocket and held it up. A gold cuff-link tinkled against the bottle. 'If I may leave this by way of apology. Sorry. I'm most sorry. Goodnight.'

Doyle leapt out of bed. 'Wait,' he cried, 'there's no need to apologise.'

'Eh?'

He pointed to the whisky on the table. 'There's enough for both of us. Why don't we share it?'

The startled figure gaped at him, his eyes rolling in a red mist of confusion.

'There's more in the cupboard,' said Doyle. 'I'll get the glasses.'

'*Hayi*, no friend. I would not dream of imposing myself.'

'The bar's closed isn't it?' said Doyle.

'Eh . . . that is so, but . . .'

'Then be my guest.'

His cheeks were round and bloated like washed-up jellyfish. His jaw, shrouded in stubble, moved spasmodically, throwing up beads of sweat that caught the light and made his skin seem oily. He waved his hands in a plea for mercy.

'Really, I see that you are alone; and that you are also too kind. But I cannot stay. It is late and I . . . well, I have someone who is waiting. In fact I hope she has not abandoned me.'

'I'm sure she hasn't,' said Doyle.

'Please, you must excuse me.'

The words were an apology but Doyle thought he detected a deeper note of resentment. It did not bode well for Alexia. Lowering his voice, he said: 'It's none of my business but I think you made a mistake not picking one of the regulars; someone who understands the rules of the house. You see, she . . .' he gestured toward the door; he still hadn't caught sight of her but he was sure she was waiting outside, a smouldering taper of innocence. 'She's with the church . . . you know, the conference in the Ocean Lounge? Her uncle's the chairman. The tall man, looks like a soapstone carving. That's his room across the corridor. I know it's a bit late to find someone else, but there's always the whisky. And you look like you could do with a drink. I know I could. Why don't you help me look for the glasses?'

A burst of laughter from the bar below saw Alexia's ungainly knight crush his hat under his arm and with a frightened, almost tearful grimace, lurch out of the room, the floorboards echoing as he stamped down the corridor, charged through the glass doors and down the stairs. Like sparring partners the doors swung briefly at each other before the upper floor of the hotel returned to a muffled torpor.

Doyle picked up the discarded half-jack and examined the label. As he unscrewed the cap he heard a faint click and knew that Alexia had just closed the door. Before he could turn she'd swept across the room and flung her arms around his neck.

'Oh Doyle!' she cried, 'What a relief! That man, he was so drunk. First he was calling me outside the lounge. Then he was tricking me to go with him upstairs. And no one saw anything. They are too busy drinking. Even the women are drunk. What for? Why don't they just dance and enjoy themselves? Look how smart are their clothes! How beautiful they make themselves. Why do they need to get drunk? When I go to live in a civilised place, like Johannesburg, or London or Paris, I'll get a job and save all my money, not waste it on drink. A person drinks when they are unhappy. But why should they be unhappy those who have jobs, a house and money for food? They are free!'

Doyle noticed an empty glass lying on the floor and slipped out of Alexia's arms. After his hazardous journey in the storm, his body felt stiff and sore while the monotonous chug-chug of the outboard, previously only following him at a distance in his sleep, now returned with a dogged insistence that made him feel sea-sick. Was the real danger of that journey through the tumultuous waves only now becoming apparent to him? Or was it the recollection of Naylor's horror, the sickening realisation on the blonde face that he had been betrayed, followed by the crunch of his friend's bloody fist which Doyle had seen coming though he had made no effort to avoid it.

Alexia noticed the discoloration below his eye. She waited until he'd poured himself a drink. Then as he settled on the edge of the bed she began tracing her fingers inquisitively over the bruised flesh. But Doyle pulled his head away.

'If you were in trouble you should have called your uncle,' he remarked tersely.

Undaunted, Alexia squatted down in front of him, resting her elbows on his knees. 'Would you wish that I embarrass him in front of so many people?'

'I didn't know you cared,' he said.

Alexia's glance was audacious. 'If you are referring to last night, then my uncle was not here. Because the noise from the juke-box was too much the church members decided to hold their meeting at a village nearby. So you see there wasn't any chance of us embarrassing them.'

'What about just now?' said Doyle, gulping down his drink. 'Don't you think he might have heard you being propositioned in the corridor?'

Alexia turned up her nose at the smell of the whisky. 'His room is no longer on this side of the building. He wanted one where he could look out over the sea.'

'The Reverend . . . a romantic?'

'He is in love with God because God gives him the rooms which are usually reserved for the white man.'

'Not in Mazeppa.'

'One cannot divide the sea, Doyle.'

'If you can divide God you can divide anything.'

'But you do not believe in Him.'

'No, but we all live in the hell created by those who do.'

The floorboards creaked as Alexia sat back thoughtfully on her haunches. She was wearing a yellow polo-neck sweater with high, cut-away sleeves, white culottes and leather sandals which exposed her painted toe-nails. The bleak light of the bedroom took some of the shine out of her hair, but he could detect bright, ox-blood streaks streaming down over her shoulders. From beneath the immaculate fringe hanging over her pencilled brow she peered up at him, and said: 'One day I shall save you, Doyle, as you have saved me tonight. It would have been unbearable to be forced by that big-head to go with him. Ugh! How terrible, it's too sick. My stomach is like a stone. I want to vomit . . . Really if you had not frightened him, he would now be pulling me round all the rooms until he found one . . . one that was . . . No it's too painful for me to think about it. Doyle, when we return to Ngagabhaleko I shall tell my uncle. It's not like my studies with you, which is our secret. This kindness he must know about. I shall tell him.'

'Alexia!' Doyle said sharply, unaware that she flinched as he dug his fingers into her shoulder. 'You deliberately brought him upstairs, didn't you? You saw he was drunk and you let him follow you – not to your room but to mine. You knew I was here. You'd been to check.'

But he was wrong. And Doyle knew it the moment she lowered her head like a guilty child. For guilt was a stranger to Alexia, a burden she had never taken up. Adversity she wrestled with, as fiercely as any hot-blooded woman. Pain, anger, desire . . . she suffered all of these and probably more. But never guilt. That too was part of her charm. Guilt was a brake that stopped life in its tracks. And he had yet to see anything that would stop Alexia . . . '*Come, Doyle, let us run, let us be as wild and terrible as these waves. Leave the old men to their fate. They do not really know why they are here. I know . . . because we are alive . . . We are not caged animals. We are free. We are lovers!*'

No, not for her the anxiety of looking over her shoulder. Of seeing her uncle and the church committee staring disapprovingly from the hotel verandah. Not for her the embarrassment of having a 'sugar-daddy', of 'white shit' or 'blood money' . . .

Instead she threw her head back and said resolutely: 'Doyle you cannot humiliate me. Please do not even try. Curse me. Spit on me. Kick me like a dog. We Xhosas are used to such things. Even when you ran off this morning on that rich man's boat and pretended not to hear me calling you, I was not humiliated. You know, I wanted so badly to go with you. I have never seen such a luxurious boat. But I knew it was too smart for you. A man who lives in a hut has no use for such luxury. I said to myself, he'll be back. In any case his car is here and his clothes. I must just be patient and wait.'

'Wait?' said Doyle, brushing the exotic fringe from her eyes. 'What for?'

Alexia frowned. The answer seemed obvious.

Doyle said: 'Only yesterday you were celebrating. You said the sea had brought you freedom. Being free means not being left behind. It means you don't have to wait. You musn't wait, Alexia. There isn't time. Your first day at the sea is already over. How will you remember it? Did you get someone to teach you to swim? Did you explore the rocks? See the porpoises? The sharks? You've had your

93

hair done. You must have attracted a few 'sharks' yourself. But then, what the hell, they only want what you want. The freedom to forget, to eat and dance, to live it up with a bit of style. No guilt, no shame or humiliation. They're the ones you should be with, the young, Xhosa avant-garde; not some pot-bellied drunk.'

Dabbing at her fringe, Alexia continued to frown. 'I did not dance with that fat creature. I only saw him when he followed me up the stairs to my room. Then I became afraid.'

'I wasn't referring to him,' said Doyle. 'You need someone to rescue you from *this* pot-belly; someone who'll give you hope. A rich young Xhosa with courage; who dreams and has the energy to make those dreams come true. All I want is to go back to Ngagabhaleko.'

Ngagabhaleko! The word seemed to strike at her like a sjambok. Incensed, Alexia pulled away, knocking the glass out of Doyle's hand.

'Tsha! You only think you want to go back. But what will you do there? Become a prisoner of your *jondolo* again! When will you spend another day sailing on such a boat . . . enjoying yourself so much that you return late, even when a storm is blowing? Such recklessness! It is the real liquor, Doyle. The liquor we humans cannot give up. See how quickly you took it when it was offered to you. Yesterday was the first time I saw you run. And I didn't see, what you call, that 'pot-belly'. I saw the wind and those giant waves put colour into your cheeks. And your voice was on fire. You shouted above the waves. 'Alexia, look out!' I heard it. I heard the voice of a passionate man; one who cared. Oh I know you say you don't care about anything. But *then*, you cared. For that brief moment you escaped from your prison. You were free and you were concerned. So forget about Ngagabhaleko, OK! It's Death Row. For you and me both. But tonight we are still at large and I want it to be like last night when we ran across the sand. I want to run again. I want to feel the salt burning my throat as we drink the liquor of the sea. I want to hear your voice: 'Alexia look out!' The real voice. Of the real man! Oh Doyle, what are we waiting for? You said it yourself, one mustn't wait. There isn't time. Let's go. We must go – now!'

But Doyle, who still had visions of the tiny fishing boat ploughing through the storm, raised his hands in protest. 'At three in the morning! Are you crazy? Don't you remember what those waves almost did to you? They could have crushed the life out of you. They'd have swept you away, like a piece of seaweed.'

'But you were there.'

'You were lucky.'

'Lucky? Tsha! It's because you shouted.'

'Lucky the wave broke.'

'Come, you are wasting time.'

Doyle groaned and sank to his knees, groping for the glass which had rolled under the bed.

Snorting, Alexia pulled him to his feet. Suddenly he saw in those wide, tempestuous eyes an even greater storm, a storm of dreams, a hurricane he couldn't duck. The sea had changed her, had pushed her horizons dramatically further back, beyond her studies, beyond mere matric, even beyond Durban and Johannesburg. *London? Paris?* It seemed to have opened up all sorts of possibilities in her mind, all sorts of wild improbabilities . . . He was the 'Moor' from across the sea, who'd 'marry' Desdemona; the 'Moor' she'd always sworn she would never submit to. And yet here she was, the curve of her cheeks knifing through the room's shadows, leaning over the foot of the bed and from among the sheets flushing out his shirt which she skilfully slipped over his head. Bursting into laughter as his arm became caught in the sleeve, she leapt joyfully on his back and they collapsed like children on to the bare floor.

◇

By morning the storm had blown itself out. The sky was flat and grey and the sea calm. Dawn had come and gone without so much as a blush over the dunes where Alexia lay stretched out beside him in her bra and pants, using the rest of her clothes as a pillow.

Doyle sat up and pulled on his sweater. He noticed the fisherman's boat had gone. Except for the hotel at the far end, the long beach lay empty and windswept. It looked as though it had just rolled off a steel press. After the waves' relentless thunder an exhausted silence hung over its smoothed surface. There were no cries from gulls or harassed sandpipers. The smell of salt had evaporated. The air had been thoroughly cleansed. Perhaps too thoroughly. For the natural colours of the bay appeared bleached, matching the worn woodwork of the ramshackle hotel which from a distance reminded him of a crumbling sand-castle . . .

He nudged Alexia, alerting her to the incoming tide. Moaning softly, she folded her arms and curled up into a ball.

'We'd better be getting back to the hotel,' he warned.

Her feet dug feebly into the sand.

'Alexia?'

Opening her sleep-filled eyes, she murmured: 'I don't want to leave Mazeppa.'

Doyle shook his head. He no longer bothered to correct her. Alexia had lived her dream, ducking and weaving with him in the rapid gunfire waves which she'd hoped would somehow flatten reality. But they hadn't and now that it was over all she had to look forward to was the long drive back to the village.

Doyle stood up and began brushing the sand from his legs. Suddenly he heard her sobbing. She held her hand against her mouth and as the tears slid down her cheeks they melted the sand on her gold-encrusted fingers. Doyle knelt down beside her, gathering the sticky strands of her hair together on the makeshift pillow.

'Alexia, don't,' he whispered.

She swatted his hand aside. 'I don't want your pity, Doyle.'

'It's all there is,' he shrugged, 'apart from your uncle's impatience to get back to Ngagabhaleko. I can see him from here. He's standing on the verandah. He obviously thinks you've gone for a walk along the beach.'

'Tsha! It's not his impatience you see, but your own. It's you who wants to go back.'

'Alexia,' he sighed as she lay curled up in the hollow of the dune, like a newly hatched egg, 'I *have* to go back. So do you. You depend on your uncle. We both do. Is it worth the risk, letting him find us here, like this?'

'What are you ashamed of, Doyle?'

'I'm not ashamed.'

'Then why are you in such a hurry to go back?'

'I told you, we can't afford to embarrass the Reverend.'

'You care so much for your job? You can get a job anywhere you like.'

'I like Ngagabhaleko,' said Doyle.

Alexia sat up and blew her nose in the sand. 'Ngagabhaleko. Ngagabhaleko. It's all you think of. There are many schools by the sea. Why do you not teach down here? Why do you not teach at home in Ireland – where it is civilised? Why do you want to go back to that barren place? What scheme are you dreaming up? You and Dlamini have become good friends. Are you plotting something?'

Doyle sank back on to the wet sand. 'We play dominoes,' he said. 'It passes the time.'

'Tsha! That is what you wish me to think. What you wish everyone to believe.'

'It's the truth,' said Doyle, 'boring as that may sound to you.'

Alexia leaned forward, rubbing the salt between her toes. 'Maybe the truth is, you are an activist.'

Doyle looked sharply at her. Her drawn face was matted with strands of hair, like a dried-out cocoon. Her wretched expression mirrored the grey sea creeping toward them. He wondered whether it would make things any easier if he suggested she travel back with him. It would give her time to reorientate herself. Perhaps the Reverend wouldn't mind. He and his stewards would be keen to discuss issues raised by the conference while Alexia's presence, as she babbled on about freedom and the sea and the hopelessness of anyone trying to achieve anything at Ngagabhaleko, would almost certainly drive them to distraction. The road into the interior was long, hot and dusty. He couldn't imagine the churchmen's composure holding.

'You see!' cried Alexia, clawing back her hair. 'You don't deny it.'

'Don't be absurd,' said Doyle. 'You know I'm not an activist.'

'But you're going back to Ngagabhaleko.'

'Of course. So are you. What does that prove?'

'I am forced to go back.'

'And I've told you, I've a job to go to.'

'No, Doyle. You do not depend on your job – unless it is for another purpose altogether. For instance to hide the fact you are a member of the ANC.'

'Surely you mean the Security Branch?' said Doyle.

'No, because you would not live in the poverty you are living in now. Only someone who has a guilty conscience would put up with

97

your conditions. Someone who is an activist, who wishes to rescue the poor from their oppression.'

Doyle scooped up a handful of sand which he allowed to trickle over his lacerated knee. One or two of the cuts would leave scars – a small price to pay for getting off Naylor's launch in time. He couldn't help wondering what deep, inner sense had woken him from his alcoholic stupor and so prevented him from being smashed with the boat against the rocks. It couldn't have been a sense of self-preservation – not with a time-bomb like Alexia ticking away by his side.

He watched as she swept up her culottes and cotton top and shook them out vigorously. 'One of these days I shall find out the truth,' she warned, 'believe me, Doyle. I have been through it before. Only my father did not lie to me. There was no need to. He knew what he was and what he wanted his children to be. You are still playing games with me. But I will find out. I will learn the truth.'

Doyle brushed the sand from his knees. 'What are you talking about? Your father was a policeman.'

'It was my uncle who told you that.'

'You never denied it.'

'I never talk about it,' Alexia mumbled as she examined the creases in her clothes with a crestfallen air.

'The Reverend said your father was shot during an armed robbery.'

'You believe him?'

'Why shouldn't I?'

'He's a Christian, that's why. A Christian who chooses to live among the poor but who is himself rich. You believe such a man? Such a hero? The world is full of these heroes all trying to save the weak. And do the weak grow any fewer? No. Our heroes just keep multiplying. First one then another and another. And so it goes on and on.'

Doyle put his hand on her shoulder. 'Tell me about your father,' he said.

Alexia dropped her crumpled garments in her lap. Her body seemed to slump beneath the weight of her long, hennaed hair and the burden of the yellow sand clinging to it. From behind her broken fringe she looked up at him with large, still eyes. 'He wasn't a policeman. That's just a story my uncle uses to impress certain visitors. My father was in the ANC. He was an activist hanged by the Boer government. My mother died a few weeks later in prison giving birth to her fourth child. It would have been her first boy. My parents wanted sons but they were cursed with three daughters. My father was a fighter and wanted his children to be fighters also, not just to live like zombies in the townships. He wanted all of us to take part in the war against the Boers. Our women, my father used to say, must produce fighters. They must be the factories of the revolution. To me, a six-year-old child, he said one day, "Alex you must bear me grandchildren, many as you can . . . boys who will feed the white dragon until its stomach bursts." How he would scorn me now. Childless and unmarried. But what did he do? He gave his life away – for what? Human factories! It was because of him my mother died in prison. Because of his influence she did not trust the prison authorities and so she refused to let anyone help her with the child. It was born dead. The next day she too died. She was a brave woman but she should have thought for herself, not let my father tell her what to think. Maybe you will say he was also brave. But he was a fool to give up his life. He should have stayed at home and looked after his family. What has the struggle done for his children? It has made them all into orphans. Soon all of us in this country shall be orphans. No, not all. Not the Reverend's children. Not the Boer's children. Just the children of those who answer guns with guns. We are the heroes' forgotten children. The ones for whom everything is sacrificed. But what do we get from this "sacrifice"? Nothing. Sorrow and pity do not fill the belly. We must teach ourselves to walk. We must go out into the streets on our own and fight the *tsotsis*. We must become like the *tsotsis*, lying and stealing. We must become cleverer than everyone. We must learn to make the most out of every opportunity, no matter how small. And when we fail, when we grow weak with hunger, we must swallow what little pride we have in order to eat the scraps from our uncle's tables. Heroes and activists! Tsha! This is the life they give us. The life of an orphan. Who would wish it on anyone? Who would wish such a life on their child? No, Doyle, I do not want to go back to Ngagabhaleko, back to the life of an orphan. I don't want to study just to get a matric so I can become some white secretary's secretary. I want to leave this place. I want to leave this country. I want to go away, somewhere far, far away . . . across the ocean.'

12

'*Mhlekazi*! One moment, please!'

Having watched Majogo and his friends disappear down the hill, Doyle set off for the mission.

'Hello, sir!'

Feeling the cold, clammy grip of his hair on the back of his neck, he splashed on determinedly through the rain.

'Hello, *mhlekazi*?'

Washed of its coat of dust the pick-up gleamed in the distance, like a bright new chrysalis.

'*Mhlekazi* wait. Wait one moment please!'

He stopped as he saw the outline of a woman's head through the steamed-up rear window. He recognised the tresses, the dark, shamanistic silhouette. Was this what Alexia had been waiting for? Was this where she announced the price of his release?

'Mr Doyle!' The commanding voice of Nurse Fumba suddenly rang out across the leaden grey veld.

Doyle immediately turned around. Sweeping the hair back off his face, he saw the figure in white uniform and scarlet-lined cape pointing to Abraham who was struggling across the school yard.

'Please, Mr Doyle, you must help your friend. I am late for the clinic.'

As the old man negotiated his way over the muddied terrain, leaning heavily on his stick, the other members of the committee dispersed over the stile on the far side, except for the tall and dedicated Nurse Fumba who set off at an alacritous pace in the opposite direction along the well-trodden path leading to the Tsindi Clinic, thirteen kilometres away. Balancing a large carrier bag on her head, she swept through the open veld with a self-assurance that contrasted sharply with the old man's diffident progress. Soon she was out of view, vanishing like a great she-elephant in pursuit of her threatened calf.

'So!' the umbelliferous figure exclaimed with a triumphant wave of his stick as he squeezed through the gate in his buttoned-up greatcoat. 'Nurse Fumba stopped you in your tracks. A good thing too as you were not able to hear me calling. Come, help me to my kraal. I have much news to pass on to you from the committee.'

Wheezing like a paraffin stove, Abraham Dlamini took him by the arm. Together the two men made their way down the hill to where the retired dock-worker lived alone, 'just some few inches', as he put it, 'above the Plimsoll line'.

The 'line' was a donga which the rains had gouged out of the steep slope, dragging Abraham's kraal steadily nearer to destruction. Others had already sunk below it and lay with their cylindrical shells melting, like chocolate cones on a hot day. Abraham's kraal consisted of three huts: two round and one rectangular. The last had been built at Rebecca's insistence. With a galvanised iron roof and bright blue walls it was a sign of how buildings in the village were changing. But Abraham only used it for visitors and were it not for his sister, the furniture would have lain under a thick layer of dust. The two round huts, one served as a storeroom, the other as Abraham's living quarters, were Spartanly decorated, their mud walls outlined at the base with a single stripe of green paint. The same paint had been applied around the edges of the door and two side windows and from a distance the huts resembled faces sheltering beneath straw bonnets – grey bonnets that were losing their shape, though it was unlikely Abraham would replace them.

By contrast, the yard between the huts was regularly raked. A tiny garden, dug over and ready for sowing, was bisected by a path neatly lined with white stones. It led to a wooden privy. More flat stones were set into the hard ground around the privy which was kept clear, being constantly swept by Rebecca. Although the kraal remained unfenced there was no sign of litter, none of the old tyres, stripped-down cars or broken bedsteads that cluttered similar outlying yards. Even the handful of chickens that Abraham kept seemed ultra-cautious about setting their feet down on the fragile soil.

'There, we have made it!' the old man gasped, collapsing on to a bench in the doorway of the smaller, front hut.

The curtains remained drawn and at first glance the hut's interior seemed gloomy. But as with the yard everything inside was kept spotlessly clean and packed away, the dark wood furniture melting into the shadows where brass handles gleamed and a Victorian chamberpot remained partially concealed behind a large counter-pane spilling over the edge of the iron bedstead – the twin of the one in Doyle's hut. Overhead the smoke-blackened rafters helped to sustain an atmosphere of old world tranquillity, smelling of polish and Brasso and echoing to the steady drip of rain from the watertight thatch.

'I shall rest,' said Abraham, puffing as he threw off his greatcoat, 'while you, my friend, prepare the coffee. You may use plenty of milk. Later, after we have first discussed the morning's events, I shall change out of this old suit and, if I can find where my sister has hidden the dominoes, we'll begin the next round of our interrupted battle. How long is it . . . two, three days? Perhaps Mbanjwa has taught you a trick or two. That at least would make up for any discomfort you may have experienced.'

With a fist that had moulded itself round the ball of his kierie, he shepherded Doyle toward the primus stove. Then pausing, as if remembering something important, he frowned and said: 'You will find a towel at the foot of the bed which you may use to dry your hair.'

$$\diamondsuit$$

The rain had stopped. In the yard large pools of water shrank rapidly, leaving behind silver threads to stretch and snap, exposing the worn fabric of the soil. There was a chill in the air and a fusty smell emanated from the dripping thatch. Grey cloud continued to hang low over the hills, while sounds from the village remained muted.

As they sat on the bench in the doorway, sipping their scalding coffee out of enamel mugs, the old man gave Doyle a cautious nudge.

'Supposing, *mhlekazi*,' he said, 'just supposing, you are invigilating in the final exams and you see a pupil cheating. Tell me, what would you do?'

Following the progress of a few mangey-looking goats plodding past the door, their hooves clipping the rock through the mud, Doyle answered impassively: 'They know what to expect if they're caught.'

'Indeed,' said Abraham, blowing the steam over his cupped hands. 'But here in Africa the children also know the consequences of failing.

These are severe. Would you report such a pupil, knowing that in effect you condemn him or her to a life in the *bundu*?'

Doyle set his mug down on the floor to cool. 'Are you asking me why I didn't report Majogo to the police?'

The steam seemed to clog the old man's throat. 'Something like that,' he croaked.

'You think it's because I was being . . . charitable?'

Abraham hesitated.

Doyle said: 'Is that the reason no one complained? Why the committee held off until three days ago? You were waiting to see whose side I was on.'

Abraham's crooked hand slipped round the bottom of the mug, cradling it as though it were an egg that had been cracked and the yolk had begun to seep out of its shell. 'One cannot always remain on the fence, *mhlekazi*. If you turn a blind eye to the one who is cheating it is assumed you take their side.'

'And steer them toward a life in the townships instead of the *bundu*? What's the difference?'

'You do not see any?'

'I can see you're making the same mistake as Lieutenant Mbanjwa,' said Doyle.

Abraham swatted a fly away from Doyle's mug with his stick which he kept propped up beside him on the bench. 'I am not suggesting that you are in league with the boy. Of course not. That would be absurd. As absurd as thinking that the chief or the witch-doctor were involved. No, all I'm saying is that you have been able to understand the difficult situation Majogo has landed himself in, an understanding which is much to be appreciated around here. It shows that you are willing, even at some risk to yourself, to give those who have transgressed the opportunity to redeem themselves.'

Doyle retrieved his mug from the floor, lifted the skin that had formed on the surface and flicked it through the doorway where it was seized by a scrawny hen patrolling the yard. 'Look,' he said, wiping his fingers on his trousers, 'I left Majogo alone because I didn't want to escalate things, that's all. He enjoys no popular support. I felt, and still feel, time would be a better teacher, would show him he couldn't buck the system, that it's futile to try. We all get squeezed in the end. Of course if the committee wanted to take any disciplinary measures, well, as you know I've always left those decisions up to you. You see I'm not the hero you or the lieutenant are looking for. I only play bit parts, which is why Ngagabhaleko suits me. It only has bit parts to offer. That's something Majogo still has to learn.'

Abraham stuck out a foot to bar the path of the hen clucking greedily in the doorway. 'It's to you that our people bring their young, *mhlekazi*. Is the stick you discipline them with such a pessimistic one?'

'I know it isn't the iron rod Pilot Mjozi used. But look where that got him.'

'He did not end up in a police cell.'

'If it's a choice between a cracked skull and prison,' said Doyle, 'I'll settle for prison.'

Abraham withdrew his foot from the doorway causing the hen to raise its eyes suspiciously. 'Let us hope it does not come to that, though Majogo may still wish to have something to say about it.'

Doyle swirled his coffee round in the enamel mug, but did not reply. Instead he watched the scrawny hen's cautious advance over the threshold; its ruffed neck outstretched, recoiling, edging tentatively nearer. It made a soft defenceless noise, like a child whimpering. Its limpid eyes closed then opened wide, begging for reassurance.

Abraham said softly over the rim of his mug: 'Actually you no longer need to worry about Majogo. The committee has taken the decision to expel him. With the final examinations approaching we felt it best to get this matter out of the way. If the boy wishes to take it any further then he will have to deal with the committee. It is no longer in your hands.'

'Everyone knows the principal is the final arbiter.'

'In most schools, yes,' said Abraham, hurriedly swallowing a mouthful of coffee, 'but that is not how it works here at Ngagabhaleko. You are blessed with a group of people who are not only able but willing to make important decisions, decisions which as you yourself just now admitted, you have been reluctant to take.'

'Yes, but does anyone else know that?' said Doyle.

'Do they need to? As the Reverend himself has pointed out, one does not wish to see your authority undermined.'

'It might have helped to convince the Security Branch.'

'That you were not their organ-grinder?' said the old man with a wry smile.

'Convinced them I was not a star actor in their paranoid play,' Doyle replied.

Showing a surprising freedom of movement the old man swivelled round on the bench. While the rust-coloured hen looked on in confusion he gripped Doyle firmly by the knee. 'Please, *mhlekazi*, you must not let this business with the Security Branch frighten you. You are much too valuable to us. Our children need your expertise. They have already lost one headmaster this year.'

Doyle threw the rest of his coffee out over the startled hen. 'Sorry, Abraham,' he said. 'The committee can't help me now. The Security Branch are too suspicious. And so is Majogo. Who knows what the villagers will think. It's a morass of dogma and suspicion.'

'People are simply interested to know whose side you are on,' said Abraham, patiently. 'These days it is a difficult thing to be sure of.'

'Whose side am I on?' said Doyle setting the empty mug down on the bench between them. 'The Security Branch says Majogo's side. Majogo says the Security Branch's.'

'Are you afraid to choose?' asked the wizened figure, retaining his powerful grip on Doyle's knee.

'I'm an outsider. Why should I become involved?'

'You would not be so exposed.'

'I'd be even more exposed.'

'But then you would have friends. People to advise you. You would not be so scared of the likes of Mbanjwa.'

'It suits me to be alone,' said Doyle.

'*Hayi, mhlekazi*, that is a stop-gap. No doubt a reaction to an old wound. In the long run it suits no man to be alone. It is not how we have been made. It doesn't matter where we live, whether in the village or in the city. We cannot cut ourselves off. We are part of a common body.'

'I've grown used to living on my own,' said Doyle, 'just as your hand has got used to the shape of your kierie.'

'My hand?' said Abraham Dlamini, releasing his hold on Doyle's knee. 'It has gone numb with old age. But never mind . . .' The crumpled figure broke off as he grabbed his stick and began levering himself up from the bench. 'I can see you are determined to remain

. . . out on a limb so to speak. It doesn't matter. I understand your fears.'

'Do you?' said Doyle.

Abraham prodded him in the belly with his kierie, his eyes hazy and sunken, yet, like the eyes of the gaunt hen in the doorway, sizing up all the options.

'Look, *mhlekazi*, you just carry on teaching. And the children will carry on learning. Next year pupils will come from all over the area to enrol at Ngagabhaleko. And the government will extend your contract. In the meantime . . .' The old man dragged his feet across the lino floor, his head bobbing and weaving – again, like the hen following him intrepidly to the glass-fronted sideboard which he drummed with his iron fingers. 'In the meantime let me escape out of this suit and then we can get on with the serious business. Now where do you think my sister has hidden those dominoes? Last time it was in here, tucked behind the photograph of my late wife.'

◇

As he sat astride the bench, setting out the dominoes which Abraham had located behind the old typewriter, Doyle wondered what it would take to disturb the old man's inimitable composure. Outwardly agitated – he frequently waved his kierie, swatted flies, frowned, made restless gargling noises in his throat – he remained distinctly calm on the inside, leaving people like Nurse Fumba to worry about school standards or Rebecca to fuss over matters such as the encroaching 'Plimsoll line', the dust on the furniture, or the state of his clothes which no longer fitted him – his shirts always losing their buttons, his trousers requiring a belt as well as braces.

It was this indomitable equanimity which had drawn Doyle to the retired dock-worker, who on most afternoons could be found dozing on his bench in the doorway; his wrinkled face, at peace in the shadows, as much a feature of the static landscape as the huts whose pointed roofs reminded him of oriental bonnets in a paddy field. Indeed over the year Abraham's hut had seemed to him to take on the atmosphere of an oriental shrine with the endless games of dominoes developing into an elaborate ritual over which neither of them any longer appeared to have control.

It would be difficult, Doyle realised, to leave this all behind. Yet he knew the shrine – this dark hut on a remote hillside – and the ritual, both lay under threat, not only from Majogo, Alexia, and the Security Branch, but from Abraham himself. For in spite of the constant reassurances – 'You are much too valuable to us', 'You must not let this business with the Security Branch frighten you'; or, 'I understand your fears' – it was surely only a matter of time before the old man, too, scrambled up on to the stage and, along with the rest of the cast, insisted that he play the role assigned to him. Liberal hero was all there was. The drunk and incompetent made no sense to people fighting for survival; it was a luxury. So was the reckless lover. Only, prodding him in the belly with his kierie before scurrying away in search of the dominoes, Abraham had remained too polite to point it out. To have done so, he must have sensed, would have brought their ritual to a premature end. But then he too was merely an actor in the play; with History retaining its firm hold on the script.

◇

'So, how many doubles have you dealt yourself?' The old man's creased face glowed with affection. Waving his arms about in order to shoo the hen out of the hut, he gave Doyle's beard a light tweak before taking up his position on the opposite end of the bench.

He had changed out of his shiny, black suit into a pair of workman's overalls which he tucked into his unlaced boots. The boots' leather was cracked though the steel caps still shone, like bent coins. A wide leather belt sagged beneath his enormous girth while his shirt collar lay entangled in the heavy folds around his neck. He kept his woolly hat pulled down over his ears.

'No, there's no need to check, *mhlekazi*. My daughter returned to Johannesburg while you were away. She has taken her mischievous goats with her.'

The 'goats' were two of Abraham's grandchildren who, one morning discovering a bottle of Tippex beside the old typewriter, had amused themselves by painting dots on all the dominoes, forging an entire set of what were no doubt to them aesthetically pleasing doubles.

Doyle knew such visits by his children were rare. Yet Abraham did not feel abandoned or forgotten. On the contrary, he feared it was the younger generation having gone off to work in the city, who were being neglected. So he did what he could to help them, by fending for himself; performing odd jobs in the village in order to maintain a degree of financial independence, though his broad, muscular back had begun to buckle like a strata of rock beneath his sagging shoulders, and Rebecca, his sister, continually urged him to 'stop behaving like a donkey'.

Clearing his throat the stubborn figure threw down the double-six.

'Looks genuine,' remarked Doyle, sliding the six and four in beside it.

'And that one too,' Abraham chortled.

'Let's hope it . . .'

He broke off as Abraham pointed to a footpath in the distance where Majogo and his rejuvenated pride were marching back to school; fresh placards swaying above their heads, as bright as traffic lights in the gloom.

'What do they say, *mhlekazi*? My eyes are not so good.'

Doyle stared into the grey light.

'*Mhlekazi?*'

Stamping their feet and chanting, the boys wound their way noisily up the hill.

'Well?'

As they vanished over the crest, Doyle turned and studied the piece in his hand. '"Students betrayed", "Teacher collaborator", "Teacher spy",' he said, and dropped the double-four into place though he knew he wouldn't be able to build on it.

Abraham scratched his stubbled jaw, then purred as he set out the blank-four. 'There is no cause for alarm, my friend. The people of Ngagabhaleko will soon be rallying to your side. I can tell you many in the village have been unhappy with the boys' behaviour and have reported them to the chief's court. Unfortunately, as you know, it has not been sitting because the chief was unwell. But when it reconvenes under the new chief the whole matter will be carefully looked at. Any accusations the boys make, they will have to back up with hard evidence. Now as you and I know, no such evidence exists to support their slander.'

'It can always be manufactured,' said Doyle, with a resigned wave of his hand to indicate that he passed.

'By?'

'Find out who is behind the boys.'

'The witch-doctor?' said Abraham gleefully, as he slid another carefully chosen piece across the bench.

'Why not?' Doyle countered.

Abraham answered with a blank-three.

Doyle stared at the wretched hand he had dealt himself. Already two behind he was on the verge of passing again when he saw his opportunity and dropped the double-three into the middle.

'Have you thought of the Reverend as a possible organ-grinder?' he asked, then sat back and watched as Abraham struggled to reply.

After a lengthy pause the old man passed.

Doyle said: 'I was told when he heard I'd been appointed, he drove all the way to Umtata to try and get the department to change their minds.'

Abraham frowned. 'Who told you?'

This time it was Doyle who passed.

Abraham said: 'The Reverend has grown used to you, *mhlekazi*. He no longer sees you as a threat. Like the chief and the witch-doctor he may initially have been wary of your presence but that is no longer so. He has seen that you have no wish to challenge his or anyone's authority and it has put his mind at rest.'

'He still isn't happy with the way the school is run,' Doyle argued.

'It doesn't mean he would wish to see you in trouble with the authorities.'

'He'd be a lot happier if I left.'

'He has told you?'

'No, but . . .'

'*Hayi, mhlekazi*. You are being unfair. Naturally he was upset when you failed to enforce religious worship but he got his way in the end and the matter was resolved without much opposition from you. So now he is satisfied. Besides, my feeling is he enjoys having you for his neighbour. It encourages him to believe in his own tolerance whenever he remembers that he has a non-Christian staying at the mission.

'My feeling is it hurts him,' said Doyle, trying to anticipate Abraham's next move.

But the wily figure, noticing his agitation, paused. 'I do not understand why you see the Reverend as a threat. You have not embarrassed him in any way. And even if you had it would be a matter between him and God. The Reverend is not a hypocrite. He is a very devout man.'

Doyle, aware of Abraham's hesitation, tried to recover the piece he'd begun to play. But Abraham had seen it. Nonchalantly the old man changed his strategy.

'Anyway there is no one behind the boys. No chief. No Reverend. No witch-doctor. Majogo is, as he has always been, quite alone.'

Doyle stared uneasily at the bench.

'You do not believe me, *mhlekazi*?'

Looking up into the worn face whose lines seemed to crackle like kindling, Doyle once more found himself wondering how much the old man really knew. Surely the committee meeting and the news of Alexia's pregnancy must have warned him . . . could he not see the danger? See why the Reverend had become a threat? For Alexia had not always been discrete. And though 'Mazeppa' seemed a long way off, there was no denying the unfortunate timing that had forced her to turn to the Reverend's estranged brother for help. Whatever hold Alexia had over the colonel – perhaps it was simply the antagonism between two brothers – she had used it to get him out of the cells at Bala. By now everyone in the village must have know it. Surely these were connections, pieces Abraham could see as easily as if Doyle, resigning a game, had knocked them over in front of him.

But as the old man slipped a double-one into place, to which Doyle again had no reply, he stretched out a reassuring hand and said: 'Believe me, *mhlekazi*, the boy is on his own. He has no family even to speak of. He and his sister are the last. They were on their own long before they were old enough to pay full fare on the buses. Their father, a councillor in one of the townships around Johannesburg, was shot on his way to the toilet at the bottom of the garden by the very policeman who was supposed to be guarding their house. Their mother then tried to run a shebeen which was burned down. It is not known by whom. The next morning her body was found in the ashes. Majogo's elder brothers, all teenagers, disappeared. Some say the eldest went to Zambia, for training; another to Tanzania. Majogo himself ended up in reform school. Oh the trouble he was said to have caused! But what can you expect when a child is left to fight for himself in the city? Eventually our late chief sent for the boy – Majogo's line is distantly related – and offered to take care of him. But now the chief, as you know, was a simple man, misguided by the government some will say, though who is not nowadays?'

With a cunning smile Abraham shifted the one and four across the bench, once more leaving Doyle unable to respond.

'The chief didn't understand what he was letting himself in for. Majogo had become a *tsotsi* and showed little respect for village custom. Soon the chief lost patience, gave him a hut and a piece of land and told him to look after himself. Somehow, do not ask me how, for I have seldom seen him in that field of his though it is ploughed each year like everybody else's, somehow the boy has managed to survive.'

'Help from a secret backer?' suggested Doyle who finally was presented with an opening as Abraham shed his third last domino.

'Other than that piece of land, the chief has not helped him,' Abraham replied.

'I wasn't thinking of the chief,' said Doyle.

Abraham knocked over his second last domino. 'You are becoming predictable, my friend.'

'Nevertheless,' Doyle persisted, though he could see the game was lost, 'he could not have survived without help from somewhere . . . from someone who has either nursed his bitterness or become a victim of it.'

'*Hayi*, we must not judge, *mhlekazi*. It's true the hearts of the young today are hardened, but we must remember the terrible things they have seen, not only in the townships but throughout the country. They have been forced to drink from the cup of sorrow at an early age and not surprisingly they have found the taste not to their liking. And we too, my friend, did we not also pull a sour face at it in our youth?'

Doyle, waiting for the coup de grâce, stared in silence at the muddy prints their shoes had left on the lino floor.

Abraham lifted the final domino but then clutched it to his chest. 'As you are haunting Lieutenant Mbanjwa, so Majogo is haunting you. I am telling you, there is no one behind this angry display of his. And believe me, we too know its insignificance – as we know our own. What are we after all to the people of America or Europe but the helpless creatures of a continent that cannot feed itself? We are no longer even exotic as in the past. We have become a burden . . . a skeleton in the cupboard. But we must survive, until we can discover our own worth. And your presence, whatever its motives, encourages us. It makes us feel less like lepers. That is why I say you have nothing to fear from anyone here. And that is also why I say you must stay. Only put these unwarranted suspicions out of your mind.'

'Abraham,' said Doyle, impatiently knocking over the pieces he was left with, 'I've already made up my mind to leave.'

The light in the narrowed eyes faded, like burnt seeds in the furrows of exhausted flesh.

'On my way back from the classroom to the committee meeting, I overheard the members discussing . . .'

He broke off as Abraham raised his hand, dangling the winning domino forlornly over the game Doyle had conceded.

'There,' said the weary figure as the wooden piece slipped from his fingers and landed in the middle of the bench. 'You lose!'

'There!' screamed a shrill voice in the back of his mind. 'Are you satisfied? Is that what you wanted? We have lost. Everything! Your own flesh and blood – gone! Dead! That your idea of justice? There is no justice in this world, Seamus Paeder. Didn't the Brits teach you that? Play that high-moral game and God's my witness you will lose. You may think you can win. But you'll lose. Do you hear me? Lose!'

'I'm sorry, *mhlekazi* . . .' Doyle felt Abraham's hand brush his own. 'I'm sorry, I did not mean to gloat.'

Doyle looked up into the lugubrious folds of flesh, glowing dully like broken clay. 'No need to apologise,' he said. 'It's only a game.' But his words, as Rebecca came bursting joyfully upon them, sounded distinctly hollow.

With a swish of her long skirts beneath which the yellow soles of her bare feet gleamed, like slabs of Edam, she swept past the bench in the doorway, gathering up in the same buoyant movement the enamel mugs which she laughingly banged together.

'*Molo, titsha,*' she sang.

'*Molo, inkosikazi,*' Doyle replied.

'*Unjani?*'

'*Ndipelile. Unjani wena?*'

Rebecca dropped the mugs with a clang into an enamel basin. 'No complaints, *titsha*. No complaints.'

113

She filled the basin with water from an iron kettle which she then replenished from a large plastic butt – her ample body crouching low over it, robust and trembling, as if the water was gurgling out of the parabola of her bosom. Looking across the room at her brother she said: 'And you, old man, any complaints?'

Abraham gave a lukewarm grunt.

Rebecca was in her early sixties. Staunch and jocular, she appeared unburdened by years of childbearing – of the eleven she'd brought into the world, no fewer than nine survived. The eldest who was in his mid-forties and lived outside Pretoria, had five children of his own, while her last-born, a tall, resolute figure with bandy legs and crushing forearms, and who was Alexia's age, had two.

Like her brother, she was broad across the back and shoulders, though patently free of his rustiness as she swept round the hut with her wide hips and rough peasant hands, lifting, tugging and shifting, like a matron who was impatient with her staff. Neither her badly scarred cheeks, her leaden brow, wrapped in a workaday scarf, the flabby wrists or pendulous, lower lip could detract from her alacrity. Her laughter remained quick and artless, while among the banging of mugs and the purring of the primus, she hummed and sang to herself.

Rebecca, in Doyle's view, was the archetypal village woman: one who knew her place and order in the world. She might not have understood or cared to understand the plot and all its machinations, but her faith in the script was supreme. So, when Abraham informed her that Doyle was leaving at the end of the year her reaction, as she whipped the boiling kettle from the primus, was: 'But of course, *buti*. The school closes for the holiday. Why must he stay? He needs holiday just same as students. Not so, *titsha*? You go for holiday.'

Doyle began packing the dominoes away in their sticky-taped box.

'Is a long way to Ireland, *titsha*? You fly? How much money it cost to go and come back?'

'No *sisi*,' said Abraham, tapping the floor with his kierie, 'the *mhlekazi* is not going just for a holiday. He is leaving us for good.'

'*Hayi!*' exclaimed Rebecca, as she blew on her scalded hands. '*Hayi! Hayi! Hayi*! Is not true. Is too short time he's here. One year, *titsha*. How you can go so soon?'

Doyle leaned forward over the bench and felt round blindly for the domino which had fallen on to the floor.

'You tell joke to my brother, *titsha*? He too old man to know you joke.'

'*Hayi, sisi*, I cannot be so old. I have just beaten the *titsha* at dominoes.'

'Dominoes!' Rebecca darted toward them. 'Oh *titsha*! You and my brother play too much. Such a foolish game. You lucky, then you win. You bad luck, you lose. Everything in hand of God. We poor people, nothing we can do. Trust in God.'

Handing Doyle the domino which she'd retrieved from under the bench, she returned to fetch their mugs of fresh coffee, stooping solicitously over them to blow the steam away.

Abraham continued to tap the floor with his kierie. 'Luck? God? Trust? These are the words of a woman who has learned nothing, only obedience. You see, *mhlekazi*, how tradition demands unconditional surrender? One gives up the future for a secure past. No, *sisi*, we cannot leave God to hold the baby for us.'

'Ha! Old man. God punish you, you talk that way.'

'And the *mhlekazi*? Will God punish him for deserting us?'

Rebecca clapped her hands together. 'Au! *Buti*!' she exclaimed. 'I forget. We cook late today, 'cos we back from chief's kraal. I will bring food tonight, but now we have no bread, no biscuits for the *titsha*. I run quick to my home to fetch some.'

Doyle scrambled to his feet but Rebecca ignored his protests. Only an adamant command from her brother in Xhosa stopped her from running half-way across the village. With the air of a scolded child, she retreated to fetch their coffee, placing the mugs on a cheap metal tray which she left on the bench. Removing the box of dominoes she bustled over to the desk by the window, placed them in a drawer from which she pulled a cloth and began assiduously dusting the keys of the typewriter.

'You see, *titsha*,' Rebecca would often say, pointing proudly to the old Remington, 'my brother work in the harbour from when he just a boy, sixteen years old. He work, doing this donkey job for fifty years, but meantime he study for matric and then he study for Bachelor's degree and he write using this machine because his hand not good for holding his pen. He do it by correspondence and nobody know. He tell no one. My brother, he foolish. Why he not become a *titsha*, like his late wife? Like you? But also he smart. He learn to use this

115

machine. Now he type letters for people in the village. He depend on no one. He make enough money for hiself.'

But now all the unhappy woman mumbled was: 'You foolish man. God punish you. He punish us all if we too big for our shoes.'

13

The rosy light rapidly turned grey as it slid across the face of the window. Stripped of their glamour the clouds began to drag their feet across the sky which sank black and moodily into the armchair of the horizon. Like household pets sensing a family feud in the air the hills of Ngagabhaleko slunk away under the cover of darkness. An African crow cawed derisively on the roof.

Doyle crawled out of bed and drew the curtains. A fly buzzing in the empty whisky bottle beside his pillow fell silent as he stumbled back across the room in search of a candle, the phosphorescent flare of the match lighting up the frozen wax, the mud walls and the silver webs in the rafters where, now that the rains had arrived, mosquitoes lurked in ominous gangs. He gathered up the empty bottle, dropped it in the cardboard box that served as a bin, then dug out another from his wardrobe. He poured himself a drink while he dressed and tried hard not to think of Alexia.

A knock at the door startled him. It was urgent and unapologetic, not the knock of a penitent come to explain why she had lied to him. It sounded more like Abraham, banging the door with his kierie. Had he found out about the Reverend's expedition the night before? Perhaps the guns really were his. No, the knocking sounded too imperious, almost careless in its self-confidence. It was probably the Reverend anxious to discover the effects of his warning.

Doyle could still see the elegant figure of the Reverend Benedict Xolile standing with his head bowed at the edge of the shallow 'grave'. It was some time after midnight and the narrow beam of a torch rested on a white, nylon bundle that had been uncovered by the stewards. Doyle tried to read the factory imprint on the side but the red soil had stained the lettering.

'We are very sorry for dragging you out of bed,' the Reverend explained. 'But we felt it was necessary to show you this. You see it is your safety we have in mind, Mr Doyle.'

117

The pained expression, the inevitable Christ-like weariness, had made Doyle suspect that the Reverend had guessed the truth behind his niece's pregnancy. Or else Alexia had confessed, had played her final card: revenge! It had seemed obvious. The secret expedition had nothing to do with Abraham Dlamini's supposed gun-running. It was a veiled threat to get him to leave Ngagabhaleko.

But the Reverend had been determined to put on a show. Climbing down into the hole he picked up a stone and tapped it lightly against the soiled bundle. At the muffled ring of metal he shook his head disconsolately. He tossed the stone aside and wiped the oxidised soil from his hands.

'You must understand, Mr Doyle, we are not showing you these buried weapons in order to embarrass you. It's because we know the Security Branch have become suspicious of your presence in the village and the slightest misunderstanding, such as over Majogo's boycott, or your friendship with Mr Dlamini, may be enough to lead to your arrest. All they need is an excuse. Majogo's boycott shows they are looking for one. After all, they did not take the boys away. You were the one they detained in the cells at Bala.'

This reference – yet another veiled threat? – to the police cells at Bala had caused Doyle to enquire whether the warning had originated with Colonel Xolile. But the Reverend not only dismissed the idea, he seemed to be genuinely taken aback by it.

'My brother? Oh no, Mr Doyle. I was not even aware that you had met him. Surely he was not present at your questioning? He is just an ordinary policeman. He has nothing to do with the Security Branch. No, no. I can assure you this is not his doing. Besides, my brother and I do not see eye to eye on many matters these days. So he is unlikely to have issued any warning through me. No, this is just a few humble stewards and myself trying to impress upon you the need for extreme caution. You have already been held once by the Security Branch. And whilst your position as principal ensured a rapid release, I do not think they will be quite so generous the next time.'

So Alexia hadn't told the Reverend everything. In which case he'd underestimated her. Far from seeking revenge, it appeared she remained determined to keep their relationship a secret.

This was borne out by the Reverend's remarks when, after filling in the hole again and marching the four or five miles back to the mission in the dark, he confided in Doyle that his niece would finally be getting married.

'If you will forgive all this talk tonight of guns, Mr Doyle, but I believe this will be what is called a shot-gun wedding. Alexia has told me she slept with the son of one of the late chief's *indunas*, though whether we can persuade the young man to honour his obligations is of course another matter. These things have happened so often in our migrant society that some people now feel there is no stain or dishonour attached any more. One would not like to judge. Circumstances are too trying. Nevertheless, in God's eyes it remains a great sadness that we treat each other so disinterestedly.'

Alexia had not only lied, she had clearly taken the burden of secrecy upon herself. And yet, he wondered uncertainly, was she really trying to protect him? If so what did she expect in return . . . *'No Doyle, I do not want to go back to Ngagabhaleko . . . I want to leave this place, this country. I want to go far, far away, across the ocean . . .'* Perhaps that insistent knocking was her after all.

Swallowing his drink, he kicked his shoes under the bed, their soles still clogged with red earth.

'Good evening, sir,' chanted Promise as he opened the door. 'How are you? I am fine.'

Doyle felt the whisky sear his empty stomach.

'But my friend, Elizabeth – Nomanthando – she is not so good. She is very ill.'

'Again?'

'Yes, sir. This time she is too sick. Her life may be in danger.'

Doyle leaned unsteadily against the door. 'What about the witch-doctor? Can't he do anything?'

'Sir?'

'You said the witch-doctor is the only one who can save her. You said we shouldn't interfere.'

'Oh please, sir,' Promise cried. 'We need your help.'

'Mine? You need *my* help?'

'There is no one else, sir.'

'I'm sorry. I'm not a witch-doctor, Promise. Find the witch-doctor.'

'But he can do nothing for Nomanthando.'

'What do you mean? That's not what you told me while your friend

119

was lying on the classroom floor. The witch-doctor's medicine is too strong, you said.'

'It's true sir.'

'Well then? Take her to the witch-doctor. Or don't you have enough money?'

Promise lowered her head despondently. 'We have no money, sir.'

Doyle studied the tiny drop of whisky remaining in his glass with a mixture of sadness and relief. Not only had life lost its dignity, but also its capacity to surprise. 'How much does the witch-doctor want?' he asked.

'Sir?'

'How much money does he want to treat Nomanthando?'

'I don't know, sir.'

'But isn't that why you came, to ask for money? So how much do you need?'

Stealing through the open door the night locked its cool fingers round Promise's throat. She gave a rusty squeal. 'Oh no, sir. I did not come for money.'

'Why did you come then?'

Promise rocked back on the balls of her feet, her knees bent, as though she were about to cross herself. But she couldn't seem to disentangle her fingers from the belt of her school tunic. In her nervous state she had twisted it into a small tight knot. There was a tear in the black material where her white shirt shone through, like her moon-white teeth as she bit her lip. She stared at him with wide, despairing eyes.

Doyle staggered away to pour himself another drink. Even on the far side of the room he could smell the girl's soapy freshness. The lines where the melanin flesh vanished – her white shirtsleeves, the starched collar, ankle socks – were like the lines of the glass in his hands, hard and clean-cut, yet liquid smooth.

'Nomanthando is at the clinic, sir. I have just come from there now,' Promise announced hoarsely.

'Is Nurse Fumba on duty? What does she say is wrong with your friend?'

'She says Nomanthando is too ill. She must go to the hospital at Bala.'

'Now?'

'Now, sir,' said Promise.

'Can't it wait till tomorrow?'

'Nurse Fumba says she must go to hospital tonight or she can die.'

Doyle watched through a dull haze as the neat, slender figure of Promise Mhlongo continued to sway sorrowfully in the doorway.

'There is a curfew,' he said.

'Sir?'

'A curfew, Promise.'

Freeing her fingers from the twisted belt Promise rubbed them gingerly to restore their circulation. 'Please, sir, Nurse Fumba said to tell you it is most urgent.'

'Did she give you a note?'

Promise edged back into the night. Doyle, thinking she was about to flee, grabbed her by the arm. The sound of glass smashing saw her eyes widen with terror. Doyle stared in a drunken stupor at the floor. There was no damp stain, no whisky seeping into the dry dung. The glass remained intact in his hand.

Then they both saw the curtain resettle against the window. Below it lay a rough-edged stone rocking on the uneven surface among the gleaming shards. Promise screamed. In the distance the drums of the Zionist sect began throbbing. Doyle shoved Promise inside and heard her catch her breath as her back slammed against the wall. Bits of mud fell like dandruff on her shoulders. The terror in her eyes matched the frenzied drumming. He felt her hot breath on his neck as they sheltered behind the door, saw the pinkness of her tongue illuminated against the dark flesh. Trembling she held on to his arm, her fingers piercing his skin, while her eyes stared directly into his.

For a while the drumming seemed to entwine them in a sterile passion. And then when it stopped it flung them apart again and he saw the marks her fingers had made. Panting he slipped outside, but found the yard deserted. At the far end the mission house squatted like a drugged guard dog in the night. A large, brick building with sprawling verandahs it would not have disgraced one of the richer Johannesburg suburbs – except for the weak glow of a paraffin lamp through its shuttered windows and the distinctly tinny sound of a transistor radio blaring in one of the rooms.

Doyle wandered briefly along the perimeter fence, faint laughter echoing up the hill from the village suggesting that if it had been

121

Majogo and his friends they were probably already back at their kraal. The air felt cool and the croaking of frogs sounded rueful. He traced the call of one to the back of his pick-up and lifted it out. Its clammy flesh skidded out of his hand like a ball of soap as it fell back with a dull thump on to the cold metal. He left it and stood listening for a moment to the rats scurrying along the top of the crumbling outhouse walls. Then as the Zionist drumming started up again he returned to his room where he found Promise dutifully sweeping up the broken glass.

He said: 'I suppose we'd better see about Nomanthando.'

14

At the clinic – a tiny, raised Portakabin boasting two beds, with a flagpole prominent in the drive – Nurse Fumba marched briskly down the wooden steps, a foam mattress tucked under her arm. Tossing the mattress into the back of the pick-up, she called out in her familiar crisp tone: 'What took you so long, Mr Doyle? We were beginning to give up hope.'

Doyle stumbled out from behind the wheel.

Tall, well-groomed, with radiant cheeks and perfect teeth, Nurse Fumba paused briefly to eye the shabby state of his clothes before hurriedly beckoning over her shoulder to Promise who followed her into the gas-lit interior. Immediately the white, scrubbed walls swallowed up her white uniform, Promise's white shirt and socks and the whites of their seemingly hollow eyes . . . a world of such dazzling intensity that Doyle felt threatened by it and quickly turned away, preferring to wait outside while they hauled a drugged-looking Nomanthando to the door and down the short flight of steps.

Having succeeded in lowering the bulky figure on to the mattress, Nurse Fumba took a deep breath. 'Truly you were our only hope, sir. We are very happy that you could make it.'

Doyle could detect no sign of happiness in the inscrutable gaze. This did not surprise him. She used the words 'hope' and 'happy' as though they were instruments – a spatula or disposable syringe – devoid of personal connotation. Not that the proficient Nurse Fumba hid behind her professionalism. Rather he felt it was her way of proving herself to the world – a world in which the African continent had become almost invisible to its northern neighbours so that people like Margaret Fumba, a mother of two, secretary of the school committee, a fully trained and qualified nurse, had to excel at their jobs in order to gain any sort of recognition whatsoever; had to be better to be regarded as equal.

'As you can see, Mr Doyle . . .' the tailboard clanked and left a

123

trail of rust across her starched bosom. 'This is an emergency, otherwise we would not have dragged you from your *jondolo*. The girl is very ill. Now here is a letter of authorisation. Should you be stopped by an army patrol it will serve as your passport. Take care you do not lose it. We do not want you to spend any more time behind bars.'

Doyle did not bother to read the typed page but shoved it into his shirt pocket.

Brushing the front of her uniform, Nurse Fumba suddenly looked up over her shoulder. 'Oh and this one . . .' she pointed to the figure emerging at the top of the steps. 'She is also to visit the hospital. She is experiencing some early problems with her pregnancy and needs to be examined by a qualified doctor. I am sure we can count on you, Mr Doyle, to see that she is taken care of.'

Still feeling the effects of the afternoon's whisky, Doyle slunk back into the car allowing the chastened-looking Alexia to shuffle in beside him. In the back, wrapped in a blanket, Promise sat cross-legged, cradling Nomanthando's head in her lap. He heard Nurse Fumba give the girl last minute instructions on the care of her friend before turning away. As they drove off into the night she waved, shouting after them, 'God be your driver, Mr Doyle.'

$$\diamond$$

Not God but Alexia who, as soon as they were out of sight of the clinic, ordered him to stop.

'You are too drunk to drive,' she complained and forced herself in behind the wheel.

Doyle did not argue but got out and took the opportunity to relieve himself, smelling the sour vapour rising from the hard grass where emaciated cattle grazed in the heat of the day.

Back in the car he said, 'I hope you know what you're doing.'

Alexia's foot pressed down lightly on the accelerator, mocking him. 'Why shouldn't I know?'

Doyle sank back in the seat. 'Nurse Fumba said you were ill.'

'Pregnant,' she corrected him. 'Are you afraid?'

'You might have told me.'

'I meant are you afraid of my driving? You have nothing to fear otherwise.'

'Why did you lie to your uncle then?'

Alexia rolled up the sleeves of her jumpsuit. 'Will you tell Nurse Fumba I saw the doctor?'

'Who are you going to see?'

'An old friend.'

'At this time of night?'

'She is not at home during the day.'

'What about the weekend?'

There was a loud bang on the roof of the cabin. Alexia glanced briefly in the rearview mirror, the light from her rings vanishing into the dark, deep sockets of her eyes.

'There is no need to wait until the weekend. Promise told me you had been drinking. She knew that if she asked to borrow your car and got a driver from the village it might be awkward with the soldiers at a roadblock. So I offered to drive.'

The banging on the roof sounded urgent. Alexia wound her window down.

'*Au mawethu*!' Promise shouted through the rushing wind. 'We must drive fast. Nomanthando is in too much pain.'

Alexia slipped her sandals from her feet and wound the window back up while steadying the steering wheel with her knees. She threw her head back and the long, beaded plaits drummed against the upturned collar of her jumpsuit. As she changed gear the headlights slashed recklessly through the night's voluptuous flesh. Hollows in the dirt road promptly spurted out at them as though blood gushing from a severed artery; tangled scrub lay exposed like fragments of bone. Soon the whisky in Doyle's stomach began to sour.

'*Au mawethu*, be careful please!' he heard Promise shout in vain as Alexia attacked the wheel.

'You haven't answered my question,' he said.

Alexia flung him a contemptuous glance. 'You think I was lying to protect you? Why should I protect you when you do not care for your own safety. You should have left Ngagabhaleko as soon as the Security Branch let you go.'

'Left for Mazeppa, you mean – to celebrate. Remember?'

'Tsha! Mazeppa is a forgotten dream. It came to nothing.'

'Even so, you went to a lot of trouble getting me out of jail.'

'It was no trouble.'

'You took a risk. And risks always carry a price. What's yours Alexia?'

The engine screamed as she missed a gear.

'Honestly, I don't know what you want from me,' he said loudly. 'I can help you with your studies. But other than that I've nothing more to give you. If it's a question of money . . .? But what would you do with it? And how will you support yourself when the money runs out? It's the same in London as in Soweto . . . No qualifications, no money. No money, no hope. And no friends! Just the *tsotsis* hanging about like vultures.'

They swept past an eroded kopje silhouetted against the sky like an ancient burial mound or the tailings of an exhausted mine. The headlights panned the empty countryside – empty of gold, if there had ever been any; empty of hope of which there had certainly once been plenty. But that was a long time ago and now the villages had retreated so far from the road that their fires failed to throw out any spark or light upon the world at all, the night echoing like an empty vault. If there was any hope left, nurtured by the Protestant or Catholic missions whose numerous makeshift signs they passed along the way, Alexia did not share any of it.

'You men think all women are whores! You use us for your pleasure and then when you are tired of us you walk away. All you offer is money. Money stops you from facing the truth. But we must face it. Every day we must face it while you hide. You think it's easy? You think it's because we are used to it? You say you don't know what we women want. But you lie because you know. You lie because it's easy to lie. It costs nothing. It costs only money.'

Like the stones rattling against the underside of the vehicle, Alexia's voice seemed to ricochet around the cabin. As she flicked her hair back over her shoulders he thought he detected an angry tear sliding down her cheek, but with the vehicle's frenetic swaying the beaded tresses quickly fell back over her face and she shouted above the noise of the engine.

'Your suspicion has poisoned everything, Doyle. My uncle set you free but you cannot enjoy your freedom because you suspect there is a plot against you. What should have been a celebration has become an embarrassment to you, a source of fear and mistrust.'

'The colonel didn't have to get involved,' Doyle replied. 'I want to know why he did. What made him risk an argument with Mbanjwa?'

'Risk? There was no risk. He is a colonel. He has the power.'

'Not that kind of power.'

'Why not?'

'To take on the Security Branch?'

'Tsha! You think the Security Branch is all our people fear? You think there is nothing else in their lives but Boers and police, nothing but . . .?'

Her voice trailed away as she swerved round a gaping pothole, the vehicle skidding off the road into the goat-depleted scrub, where a group of heavily blanketed women appeared, marching in single file, bags, pots and bundles of firewood finely balanced upon their heads. Alexia swerved again and like long-term patients in an asylum bundled out of view by attendants when visiting dignitaries appear, they were mysteriously ushered away into the night, the pick-up crashing through a series of crumbling dongas before returning to the road. As Alexia wiped the sweat from her palms she left dull orange streaks down the front of her jumpsuit.

'Let me tell you something about the person who freed you Doyle because, like Mbanjwa, he is not just a policeman. He is also a man and men like him are to be feared even before they put on their uniform. Of course their uniform gives them power. But it is not the only power they have. Once when I was a little girl, my uncle – the colonel, although he was just an ordinary policeman then – came to our house in Soweto. It was late at night. He told his brother, the Reverend – himself then also a policeman – that his wife had refused to allow him in their house because he was drunk. He asked if he could stay the night. There was not much space in our tiny matchbox but we found somewhere for him to lay his head. Later, when everyone was asleep, I heard him creep into the room where I and my two sisters lay. He lay down with Revival – she was the eldest – and he satisfied himself. I did not dare to open my eyes. I held my breath. I remember it was quiet in the house and also outside in the streets. I was afraid he would hear my heart beating. It seemed that we were the only two awake in the whole world. The shebeens had all closed. People had gone home to bed. Or else they just slept where they fell, drunk in the street where the *tsotsis* would find them and rob them of everything. In that terrible silence my uncle grunted quietly like a pig while my sister lay without moving beneath him. It was as if she was dead. Even after he had left, she said nothing. She did not cry out but lay there like a corpse in the dark while we tried to comfort her. The following week he came back. Again he was drunk and said he had been thrown out of his house. Again he came in to our room and lay down with our sister, who still did not cry out. When he left we once more tried to comfort her but it was useless. The next day we did not see her. She ran away. To where, I don't know. Maybe overseas. To this day I do not know whether she is alive or dead. She was fourteen. She was the one we looked up to. She was the strongest of us all, Revival. But she ran away.'

Doyle wound his window down, allowing the dust to swirl around the cabin while the wind roared in his ears and the cold numbed his face.

'Why didn't you tell me before?' he asked, and spat the sour after-taste of whisky into their slipstream. 'Have you told anyone?'

Alexia did not answer. Nor did she slow down as they approached a fork in the road – the left leading to Umtata, the right, a local route which wasn't signposted, to Bala and St Augustine's Hospital. As they shot past the bent thorn tree marking the jumping off point for bus or 'taxi' passengers travelling to Ngagabhaleko, Doyle jerked a thumb in the direction of the main road. 'It's tarred. There'll be less dust . . .'

But Alexia had already made up her mind. 'This way is shorter.'

'What about the army?'

'What about them? We are not terrorists or dagga smugglers so there is nothing for us to fear.'

'The main road would be easier on Nomanthando,' Doyle suggested hopefully.

'This one may save her life.'

'It may also kill her.'

'What is that to you?' Alexia retorted.

Doyle slumped back in his seat, thankful for the dust that continued to swirl like an ether between them.

For thirty kilometres they raced along an unerringly straight road with a hard flat surface which brought a steady sizzle from the tyres. But then all too soon the stones and the potholes reappeared, made worse this time by treacherous sand drifts; thin, white sand retreating across the barren veld like an old skin being peeled back.

Doyle turned to Alexia. 'So you blackmailed him! Your own uncle?'

Alexia kept her eyes on the road. 'Sometimes it is the only weapon a woman has.'

'You should have told me before. Why didn't you?'

She glanced accusingly at him. 'If I'd told you, you would have thought I was making it up.'

'Why should I have thought that?'

'Because you are always suspicious.'

'And your parents – how come you told me about them?'

'Tsha! I knew you would not feel sorry for them. They just threw away their lives. But if I had told you about the colonel, do you think you would have believed me? You would have thought I was asking for your sympathy. That way you would have felt obliged to return to Mazeppa. You would have indulged me like a child.'

'Shark Bay,' he corrected her and then wondered, belatedly, why? Was it a feeling of guilt? Was this the emotion she sought to evoke in him, not pity, but guilt? 'Who wouldn't have been suspicious. The colonel's intervention didn't make sense. Why help me – an *umlungu*? History . . .'

'Tsha! It wasn't the colonel, it was me you did not trust.'

'*You* might have been setting me up.'

Alexia's glance was a brief as it was withering. 'You're a fool, Doyle. Sooner or later you will have to trust someone. And who is there besides me? You think you can trust Dlamini? Well I have seen his type before.'

'Type?' said Doyle, wearily winding the window up. But as this only intensified the jarring of the potholes which Alexia recklessly ploughed through, he opened it again. A rattling noise in the engine punctuated the even more ominous groans from Nomanthando in the back.

'Dlamini,' said Alexia, spitting into her palms and rubbing them over the wheel, 'reminds me of my father. He had the same foolish dreams.'

'I don't think you can accuse the old man of being an idealist,' said Doyle.

'Why not? Last night you saw with your own eyes the weapons he has secretly buried.'

'There's no proof they're his.'

'They belong to Dlamini. Many years ago, when they were young, he and my father were friends. They worked together in the harbour at Durban. Then my father returned to Transkei in order to organise labourers on the white farms. They both belonged to the ANC. In Ngagabhaleko, Dlamini is still the organisation's eyes and ears – unofficially of course, because he is getting old.'

'Why haven't the police picked him up before then?' Doyle enquired sceptically.

Alexia threw her head back in disgust. 'Ha! So he hasn't told you? Maybe it's because he's ashamed. Or maybe he feels he cannot trust you – you who pour scorn on the hopes of others. Why hasn't he told you about the police? Everyone knows that sometimes they come and take him away. He spends a few nights in a cell. But they get nothing from him. So they let him go.'

'And the guns?'

'Perhaps they are waiting for him to do something foolish in his old age. They can afford to wait. There is no hurry in the *bundu*.'

'Sounds improbable,' said Doyle, with mounting unease. It wasn't only the thought that the old man may have deceived him, but everyone's determination to cast him in their wretched play; casting him in so many different and contradictory roles: that of lover and confidant, opportunist, activist, collaborator; all determined to tie him to a production he had walked out on a long time ago. They refused to leave him alone, refused to listen. He simply had to take part. Had to be what they wanted. Well he wasn't going to let them force him. Nurse Fumba's 'passport' would see him safely in the airport by morning.

'It is not so improbable as all that,' said Alexia. 'After all, Dlamini has a past that is badly scarred and one day he and all the others like him may take revenge on those who have given him his scars. If it seems improbable to you, it is because you have isolated yourself from the world for so long. You say you are against the suffering of the poor, yet you do nothing to help them. You teach but then you despair, not only at the foolishness of Majogo, but also at the determination of those students who persevere with their studies.

You say you see no future for them. Nothing for Majogo. Nothing for Promise and her friends. You always talk of History. History is our harsh cradle, Doyle, but you have made it your grave. You have buried yourself in it before you are even dead.'

In spite of its discomfort, Doyle didn't mind the dust. The dust was a shroud, a tingling shroud that dried and deadened the flesh. It was like whisky, or the *tsotsis'* infamous bicycle-spoke in the spine . . . resulting in a painless paralysis. Even when Alexia, uttering a startled cry, appeared to lose control of the vehicle and they slewed into a bank of sand, he failed to react. Instead while the tyres spun ever deeper into the loose surface, throwing out a stench of burning rubber, he continued to watch impassively as she tried to accelerate, flaying the gears which jarred, wrenching her left arm while she tenaciously gripped the wheel with her right and pumped the pedals furiously, until eventually, the beads in her hair rapping like rain against the window, she succeeded in spinning the pick-up back on to the road. Only then did he realise she had completely lost control of the vehicle and that it was only the bank of sand that had prevented them from overturning.

As Nomanthando's distressed groans began to reach them she slumped back exhausted in the seat with the dust gathered like badly applied rouge on her cheeks. Her lips were cracked and trembling, her eyes sunken.

'You'd better let me drive,' he said.

Alexia shook her head fiercely.

'You're in no condition to carry on.'

'I'm all right!' she hissed.

'Are you sure?'

She slid a hand feebly through her hair and the coloured beads sounded like teeth chattering in the cold. 'Always suspicious, Doyle. You and the Security Branch deserve each other. You are no different. You are both the same, trusting no one yet expecting everyone to trust you.'

'I expect nothing of the kind,' he said.

'Tsha! Your very presence shows that you expect it. And yet what right have you to expect anything from these people? What right have you to come to this backward place and think that everyone will ignore you, will leave you alone, allow you to live like a hermit in your *jondolo*? Here we do not live like that. We do not live alone . . . isolated and unprotected. We fight for each other!'

'I don't understand,' he demurred, 'why anyone should fight to protect me.'

'Anyone!' Alexia exclaimed.

'Well then, why *you* should fight. I don't understand why *you* should have lied to protect me.'

'Tsha! You understand. That is why any day now you will run away – because you don't want the responsibility; you don't want to fight, to make things better for yourself.'

'Better? Is that what you're trying to do? Isn't that why you hated your father – because he tried to make things *better*? There's no such thing, Alexia, no such animal. Better and best are like gooder and goodest – signs of betrayal, of grammar breaking its own rules . . .'

'*Mawethu*?' Promise's voice betrayed her own increasing despair.

Alexia sat up, tugging at her sweat-stained jumpsuit.

Doyle said: 'Shift over. I'll drive.'

As Alexia slammed the pick-up into gear, he shrugged and turned away. Yet even as he did so, he felt he could not help but admire her tenacity. It was the one thing that would drag her through not only her matric examinations, but the inevitable bleakness thereafter.

15

'Perhaps, Mr Doyle, we could turn our attention to the activities of your father.'

'*Late* father.'

'Of course.'

And so, in his mind, the play continues, even though the props have been kicked over . . . '*Mr* Doyle, this is my uncle, the Reverend Xolile's younger brother, Colonel Xolile. He has brought the papers for your release . . .'

In any case they are no longer essential to the plot. All that is required is a smattering of History and the rest can be filled in. A sort of painting by numbers.

'I understand he was a farmer. Cattle or was it . . .?'

'A hill farmer.'

Lieutenant Mbanjwa tilts his head with the prescribed air of curiosity. 'I am not familiar with this type. What is a hill farmer?'

'Someone who grows poorer as they move up in the world.'

'Not richer?'

'Angrier – as they look out over the valleys and see newcomers farming the land that once belonged to them. In their anger they turn to building walls, endless dry-stone walls that perpetuate the memories of a lost golden age. You see, Lieutenant, the high land is barren land. It's isolated and useless. But it's wrapped in a romantic mist that soothes the pain of its victims. One day they hope the valleys will be returned to them – a forlorn hope since the past is irretrievable.'

'Who are these people who have lost their land?'

'The Esaus, those who have been tricked out of their inheritance, who are forced to feed on the scraps from the tables of Jacob's descendants.'

'Ah!' exclaims the lieutenant. 'You mean the Xhosas of this world.'

Doyle does not reply.

The lieutenant is immediately suspicious. 'But surely your father was a wealthy man? The farm at Lusikisiki was quite a big one.'

'He died a hill farmer.'

'And Lusikisiki?'

'He never owned it. He managed it for some company.'

'That was unfortunate for you and your mother.'

'It was an illusion to think they could ever own it. Like so many migrants they became the victims of a desperate romanticism. Reclaiming the land from Jacob's descendants turned into a passion. They failed to recognise that it was their own kind – Esau's line – they were robbing. It killed them in the end, just as it killed earlier settlers. The moment they set foot on African soil something in them died. Oh, these settlers were all reborn all right, but as caricatures. They became pioneers, cattle ranchers, gold prospectors, preachers, councillors . . . all the things they could never have become in their own country.'

Lighting up a fresh cigarette with the stub of the old, the lieutenant waves the smoke away from his face as if disentangling himself from a spider's web. 'So, we are back with History,' he coughs. As the smoke clears, he hurries on. 'I believe that as soon as you finished school, you and your mother returned to Ireland. It must have been very difficult for both of you. Of course that is quite some time ago and I do not know what might have transpired since. Indeed I cannot say whether or not your mother is even still . . .' He waits for Doyle to colour in the allotted number.

'Alive? Your guess is as good as mine.'

Lieutenant Mbanjwa is anxious to hide his surprise. 'But it's only a week . . . I beg your pardon . . . a month ago that you sent her money through the bank.'

'I send her something every year.'

'For her birthday?'

'That's in June.'

'Oh I see, a Christmas present then.'

'No need to be coy, Lieutenant. You know when my father was killed.'

'Yes, yes. It was a most unfortunate time, coming up to the festive season. But now the fact that you send her something, surely this must mean she is still alive. Why then do you say, "my guess is as

134

good as yours"? One assumes that you visit her from time to time. If I may be so bold as to ask, when was the last occasion?'

Doyle gives a disinterested shrug.

'A year? Two? Three?' the lieutenant ventures.

Doyle stares blindly at the floor.

'Four? Six?'

'Sixteen – I think.'

'Months?'

'Years. I haven't seen nor heard from her since my university days.'

The lieutenant inhales a large ball of smoke. 'Yet you send her money. How do you know she has received any of it?'

'It's never come back.'

'You are never in one place long enough.'

'The amounts are modest.'

'Are they sufficient?'

'I send whatever I can afford.'

'But even our own migrant workers who are not so well paid as you, they manage to return home at least once a year to see how their families are getting on. You do not appear to share this sense of duty . . .' He pauses, frowning uncertainly. 'Forgive me, Mr Doyle, but you will not find such indifference toward ones parents among the Xhosa people. When we are young our parents take care of us and then when they are old it is we who take care of them.'

'The Xhosa are still poor. Wait until they are rich. Until Africa is *developed*. Then we shall see.'

'I do not think our people will ever lose their respect for their elders.'

'Nothing lasts forever, Lieutenant.'

'Of course the country will develop.'

'And what will development bring? Will it bring more over-ambitious playwrights? More actors, desperate for their brief moment of fame. More caricatures? Take Soweto. Any Third World slum. Take Europe's urban dormitories . . . everyone fighting to get above the crowd. But what about *society*? Social conscience? What about the collective imagination? The shared hopes of people? Where are they? If you ask me, you'll find those hopes buried beneath the corrugated iron roofs, mocked by billboards and glass towers; by a market place that can find no use for them, attaches no value to . . .'

Doyle's soliloquy is interrupted by the lieutenant waving his arms frantically through a cloud of smoke. 'Please! Please, Mr Doyle. I think we are going off the topic. Besides, an individual cannot take responsibility for all these things. All one can do is answer ones conscience. Now for the time being if we can restrict ourselves to your own attitude . . . to your apparent indifference. I say "apparent" because I have some reservations about it. After all, your father was killed by terrorists, leaving your mother a young widow. Surely as an only child you must have realised you would be expected to step into your father's shoes?'

'My father sold out, Lieutenant. He threw away everything he'd ever stood for when he came to South Africa. And he paid the price. I'd say that landmine was a case of divine retribution, wouldn't you?'

'I'm sure that was not the sentiment expressed at his funeral.'

'I wouldn't know. I didn't go to it.'

'You remained at school?'

'Oh they let me out. I just didn't attend. In fact I never went back to Lusikisiki after that.'

'You never visited the grave? But surely at some time in these past sixteen years you must have returned. Why then do we have no . . .'

'Record? Because this is the first time I've been back to your country.'

'Then you have been to the grave?'

'Not yet.'

'Naturally you are planning to visit it?'

'You know what they say, Lieutenant. The best laid plans of mice and men.'

'We could go now.'

'Now?'

'Why not?'

Doyle shrugs. He knows he has been taken by surprise. For this isn't in the script. It is a piece of ad-libbing and shows that he has underestimated the lieutenant.'

'It would be part of our investigation.'

'Into?'

'Surely you are not afraid, Mr Doyle? They say it is better to pull a plaster off in one fell swoop.'

'We've been admirably disciplined up to now, Lieutenant. Why spoil it?'

'Are you really . . .?'

'Afraid that after all these years I might have been wrong?'

'None of us is infallible, Mr Doyle.'

'Then why are you punishing *me*?'

'Please, if we were to leave now for Lusikisiki then by tomorrow I am sure everything would be clear.'

'If I refused?'

'I am only trying to help you.'

'Help?'

'I wish to see you exorcise your father's ghost. Sixteen years is too long.'

'My ghost or yours, Lieutenant?'

'I do not think there can be any misunderstanding, Mr Doyle.'

'Oh no? Then tell me, who do you work for? Who do the Transkei Security Branch take their orders from? Isn't it the Boers . . . the Boers who created this bastardised state . . . who have ursurped the role of parent? Isn't your loyalty to this ostracised regime a source of shame – a ghost you'd prefer to lay to rest?'

Five . . . ten minutes pass. As the lieutenant remains strangely silent Doyle thumbs anxiously through the script. But he can make no sense of it at all and so, bluffing, says: 'I know why you want to go to Lusikisiki. You want to see me throw myself on my father's grave and beg for forgiveness – mine as well as yours since we've both transgressed a common sense of decency. Well, in that case let's go and get it over with. Let's exorcise our ghosts together.'

The bluff seems to work as the lieutenant backs off. 'Perhaps we should first prepare ourselves a little.'

'I've already had sixteen years.'

'Eh . . . yes. But . . .'

'Changing your mind already, Lieutenant?'

'Maybe it would not be right for me to accompany you.'

'Oh?'

'I have to tell you that at the time of your father's death things did not happen quite the way they were reported.'

'They seldom do.'

'The truth was distorted.'

'Who believes the truth any more?'

'Nevertheless you will have read the news reports.'

'Which said my father had been killed by an ANC landmine. It had been intended for a Boer government minister who'd arrived in Lusikisiki to open a new tea-processing factory. My father drove over the mine in his tractor.'

'That was the story given to the newspapers.'

'And to us, his family.'

'Yes. In fact . . .' The lieutenant hesitates. He cannot predict Doyle's reaction. Is the school teacher really as uninvolved as he appears? Alone, without friends. Indifferent? He takes a breath and says: 'Your father was not the innocent victim the media portrayed at the time, Mr Doyle. That was simply a piece of Boer propaganda. You see the mine went off while he was planting it.'

16

'Wake up, Doyle! Wake up!' Alexia shook him by the arm. 'What shall we do?'

Doyle opened his eyes into a powerful light that surged over the windscreen.

'What shall we do? They may detain us!' Alexia cried.

He pulled the clinic's letter from his pocket, shielding his eyes with it.

'Tsha! That piece of paper means nothing. They may keep us all night.'

'Why should they?'

'To show they are in charge.'

'Well they are.'

'But Nomanthando is seriously ill. She may die if they delay us.'

'You should have thought of that back at the junction,' Doyle observed icily.

Alexia lifted her foot off the accelerator and glared at him. 'It was a chance, Doyle – a chance we had to take!'

As Alexia suddenly brought the pick-up to a halt, the broad beam of light spun from the windscreen on to the bonnet and into the road, where it lit up the side of a military jeep parked less than fifty metres away.

'It's too late to turn round now,' he warned.

But almost immediately Alexia, her knuckles gleaming as hard and white as dice, began to rev the engine.

'Are you mad?' Doyle yelled.

'I'm not afraid.'

'They'll shoot!'

'Let them shoot.'

'Alexia!'

'I tell you, I'm not afraid.'

'What about Promise? And Nomanthando? Jesus, you're pregnant. Doesn't the child have . . .?'

A furious banging on the rear window jolted them both.

'*Sisi*, be careful. There are soldiers hiding in the grass. Please tell them where we are going. Nomanthando is too ill. We do not want them to keep us here.'

'Better let me do the talking,' said Doyle as they drew up behind a short line of dusty vehicles.

A young soldier in fatigues ambled over. 'Wait here,' he mumbled, then sauntered off again.

Alexia's glance said, 'I told you.'

Tossing Nurse Fumba's letter on to the dashboard, Doyle leaned over and switched off the ignition.

The parking lights of the vehicle in front revealed an XG numberplate. A middle-aged couple, their marbled features illuminated in the glow of their cigarettes, sat staring out of their respective windows, like lovers with nothing left to say to each other. Ahead of them two battered pick-ups, heavily laden with sacks of maize, firewood and possibly one or two bags of *dagga*, leaned drunkenly on their axles. The soldiers were in no hurry to search them. Instead a group were quietly ordering the occupants of a Kombi-taxi travelling in the opposite direction out of their vehicle. Swathed in bright blankets, the bleary-eyed passengers grumbled openly as they spilled on to the road.

To Doyle, the soldiers' mood seemed strangely ambivalent. They did not swarm around the vehicle, harassing the driver or his passengers, as he had seen them do on previous occasions. Rather they issued their orders calmly, kept their rifles pointed discreetly at the ground and generally displayed a remarkable degree of patience in their questioning of the disgruntled villagers. Yet whenever the slender beam of a torch skidded off their faces, he detected a sign of uneasiness. Their mouths were clamped, their eyes narrow and piercing. It was as if they were reading the minds of those they'd stopped and, grinding their teeth, were constantly growling: 'Look we've no choice, we're just as helpless as you.' At the same time they made no attempt to silence the unhappy passengers, allowing them to search for their papers among the individual piles of baggage spread out on the road; those waiting at the back of the queue lighting cigarettes while they slouched against the side of the vehicle. Some wandered freely across the road to chat to fellow travellers while others went off to relieve themselves.

Doyle had no idea how far they still had to go to reach Bala, though judging by the speed at which Alexia had been driving, it couldn't have been more than ten or fifteen kilometres. The fact that he could see no lights in the distance he attributed to the cloud now hanging low over their heads and smelling of rain. A heavy downpour would mean further delay.

Meanwhile Alexia drummed her fingers on the dashboard. Insisting Doyle request to see the officer in charge, she clucked and sighed until eventually, getting no response, she swooped down and strapped on her sandals. Clambering out of the car she brushed the dust from her jumpsuit and shook her hair free. Nobody paid her any attention.

'Give me Nurse Fumba's authorisation,' she demanded, and held out her hand. Doyle passed it to her, then watched as she marched across the road to a group of soldiers who were lounging beside their jeep. At first they pretended to ignore her but he could see the subtle changes in their bearing. 'Bloody fool,' he swore, only to be distracted by a discreet knock at his window. He turned round.

'Abraham!'

'Softly, *mhlekazi*. We don't want to draw attention to ourselves.'

Doyle moved over.

'No, no. I cannot get in beside you.'

'Suit yourself,' said Doyle, with a sudden note of irritation in his voice. Had the Reverend and Alexia's suspicion of the old man left its mark? 'What are you doing here anyway? How did you get a pass?'

Stooping over his kierie, Abraham Dlamini whispered: 'I must give you something important.'

'Important to who?'

'You shall see. Here, if I can just . . .'

Ignoring the letter which Abraham pulled out of his greatcoat pocket and surreptitiously dropped into his lap, Doyle examined the worn face lit in passing by the soldiers' torches – the astute peasant brow and scarred cheeks, the cheerful mouth, flat, fanned nose and sagacious eyes. He wondered were he able to study those warm yet embattled features with the old man's own canny gaze, would he detect the same secretiveness he now saw? The same lingering mistrust? Would he see the scars as scars of a concealed anger? The shadows as shadows of resentment? humiliation? Or was this merely the result of History once again blundering on to the stage, reducing relationships to mere props?

'Please, *mhlekazi*, you must read the letter and then burn it. From what you told me about your conversations with Lieutenant Mbanjwa, I can assure you he would be extremely grateful if it was to fall into his hands.'

'How did you get hold of it?' asked Doyle, tucking the letter away in his pocket.

Abraham glanced over the roof of the vehicle at the soldiers moving about in the road. 'It was obtained this afternoon by a friend who works at the post office. You should know that Mbanjwa's men are intercepting your mail.'

Doyle shrugged. 'It's only school mail, bills, brochures . . .'

Abraham stooped low again over his kierie. 'That is the problem, my friend. From the lieutenant's point of view you are just *too* innocent.'

'You sure that's only the lieutenant's view?' Doyle remarked with barely concealed hostility. He felt the old man wasn't being entirely honest. Or was it that the arms cache buried at the bottom of the hill at Ngagabhaleko shed a different light on their friendship? The feeling that they – Alexia, the Reverend and Abraham – were toying with him, using him to conduct their own hidden battles. And yet what else did he expect? Had he expected to be told the truth? Had he, following the betrayal by his own parents all those years ago, ever again expected to know what the truth was? Perhaps he had relied too much on the old man's urbanity, on the natural and instinctive paternalism . . . He ought to have known better.

Abraham Dlamini thrust his chin forward over the turned-up collar of his greatcoat. 'I cannot speak for others, *mhlekazi*, but in any case it is only the lieutenant you need concern yourself with.'

'Mbanjwa isn't the only one who's suspicious,' said Doyle.

'It's his job to be suspicious.'

'I mean, I notice the letter's been opened.'

Before Abraham could reply there was a shout from across the road. An argument was developing in front of one of the soldier's jeeps. Doyle could see Alexia waving Nurse Fumba's letter in a young officer's face. The officer was trying to back away but Alexia, her voice rising shrilly, kept cutting him off. She was surrounded by soldiers who tried to snatch the letter out of her hand. Yet even as they prodded her with their rifle butts, she continued to hold it aloft in the officer's face. The soldiers shouted at her but contemptuously she brushed their weapons aside. Then one of them grabbed her by the hair and she screamed.

Abraham said quickly: 'That letter, it was obtained at some risk, *mhlekazi*. Fortunately the clerk who intercepted it is himself from Ngagabhaleko. He has a daughter at the school. So he knows what is going on. He understands that the Security Branch are trying to frighten you away. The parents are all aware of it. Believe me, they are on your side.'

The shouting match between Alexia and the soldiers began to escalate. As an increasing number of torches converged on the jeep, lighting up a military truck behind it, the passengers of the Kombi and the two pick-ups were herded back to their vehicles. The soldiers banged the doors, swore and brandished their rifles at those who were slow to respond. Headlights leapt out into the night like frightened animals, then froze, as if mesmerised. Alexia, her arms pinned behind her back, continued to confront the officer who now had possession of Nurse Fumba's letter and was busy tearing it up.

Abraham tapped Doyle reassuringly on the shoulder with his kierie. 'Do not worry. They will let you pass.'

'They'll have a corpse on their hands if they don't,' Doyle replied. 'There's a pupil in the back who needs to get to hospital.'

'Yes, *mhlekazi*, I realise it is urgent, but remember, that is the way it is for all of us here. Life in the village may seem slow and easy but it can be just as urgent as in the townships. That is why the pupils of Ngagabhaleko cannot afford to see you leave after so short a time among them. It will seem too cavalier. They will feel that you have not appreciated the real urgency of their situation.'

Doyle, detecting a new and disturbing note of despair in the old man's voice, dragged the letter out of his pocket. 'Sorry, Abraham. I can't take the risk. I don't know what this is about and I'm not sure that I want to know. I don't want to get involved. The country's too

143

full of urgent and unexorcised ghosts. God help you when they all break free.'

The old man's fingers closed tightly around Doyle's wrist. 'Please, *mhlekazi*, you must read the letter. It is of great importance. I am sure that once you have digested its meaning, you will not be in so much of a hurry to leave us.'

Doyle pulled his hand away. 'So you have read it.'

Abraham nodded. 'I opened it as we were approaching the roadblock. I thought that if the soldiers find a foreigner's letter on me they might become suspicious. I considered throwing it away. But then I decided to read it first. It might have contained something important. And so it did. So I took the risk of keeping it. Then by this miracle you showed up. That is fate for you, *mhlekazi*, is it not?'

'Sounds more like a conspiracy,' said Doyle.

'And you sound more like Mbanjwa. Believe me, it was meant to be like this. You will see.'

'I wouldn't count on it, Abraham. My passport's in a bag behind the seat.'

'Nevertheless, I am sure you will reconsider. The situation is surely not so desperate that you must escape.'

Doyle turned away and was relieved to see Alexia being escorted back to the pick-up, albeit with her arms pinned behind her. Quickly he leaned over to open the door. Laughing, the soldier gave her a shove. She sneared, tried unsuccessfully to stand her ground, then swore as she was bundled on to the seat. Her jumpsuit was stained with rifle oil. The beads hung awry in her hair. Doyle tried to help her but she pulled away from him. Suddenly the soldier darted round the front of the vehicle.

'*Voetsek! Voetsek kaffir!*' he yelled.

Twisting round, Doyle caught sight of Abraham hobbling across the road to the waiting Kombi. The splintering of his kierie could be heard as he fended off the blows from the soldier's rifle.

'Hey!' shouted Alexia as she slammed the car door. 'Don't tell him to *voetsek*. He's not a bladdy dog.'

Doyle pulled her forcibly by the arm. 'Don't you think you've said enough for one night?'

Alexia swung round. 'Tsha! You let them treat you whatever way they like. Look how much respect they show an old man – your

144

friend! Your only friend in the whole of Transkei. Where is your dignity? These animals think that because they carry guns they can frighten us!'

The soldier returned, pausing at the back of the vehicle to say something to Promise, who throughout had sat cradling her friend's head in her lap, motionless with terror. The girl's reply was scarcely audible as she buried herself deeper in the folds of her blanket. Nomanthando's groans had long since ceased.

'Your driver's licence!' the soldier demanded.

Alexia grabbed it from the cubbyhole and threw it through the window at him. The soldier, his face obscured by his cap, grunted as he caught it. He flicked it open, his thin lips giving nothing away. Then he stretched out his hand and carefully brushed Alexia's hair behind her ears. His fingers were long and surprisingly elegant though they smelled of rifle grease. The green, camouflage shirt, buttoned at the wrists, appeared as crisply ironed as Nurse Fumba's white tunic.

Alexia stared rigidly ahead. The soldier withdrew his hand. As Doyle watched him sling his rifle over his shoulder for a moment he thought he was going to tear up the licence coldly. But he bent down, glanced indifferently at them both and tossed it into her lap. Banging the door with his fist, he barked: '*Voetsek kaffir*, before I arrest you!'

145

17

They arrived at St Augustine's Hospital shortly after midnight where they were surprised to find two uniformed nurses waiting for them with a stretcher on the verandah. As Alexia drew up alongside the old, colonial building, with its thick stone walls and iron roof set in the middle of the mission gardens, the nurses hurried down the steps to attend to Nomanthando. They did not seem much older than Promise, but in their powder-blue uniforms with short, flounced sleeves and starched collars, they managed to speak reassuringly to the frightened girl who threw off her soiled blanket and helped them lift her friend down from the back of the pick-up.

They had barely succeeded in transferring the by now unconscious figure on to the stretcher when Alexia lurched out from behind the wheel, her face twisted with pain. Stumbling against the front of the vehicle she gave an agonised groan, her lips peeled back, her throat taut, exposing the powerful neck cords like the roots of a tree. With her fingers tearing at her midriff she slumped over the bonnet, her long hair damp and knotted against the rusted metal. Her breath came in short despairing bursts, leaving a fog on the windscreen. Doyle saw the nurses look on in horror as she pushed herself up and staggered barefoot toward the verandah, collapsing before she could reach it. Promise, clinging to the side of the stretcher, gave a stifled shriek.

Immediately the young nurses set the stretcher down. However, staring at the bloodstained figure in the pathway and then at Nomanthando lying with her arms neatly folded at their feet, it seemed they were unable to decide who they should attend to first. There was even a hint of guilt in the glances they stole at each other. Had they delivered the stretcher to the right patient? As the night-watchman came running, his boots crunching the dry gravel, Promise began to sob.

Doyle brushed past the nurses only to be met by the hospital sister.

Having punched on the verandah lights, the stocky, grey-haired figure bustled down the steps, ordered the nurses to attend to Nomanthando while she and the night-watchman hoisted up the prostrate Alexia between them and carried her indoors.

'You must excuse me, Mr Doyle,' she called out over her shoulder, 'I will be with you shortly.'

Stunned, Doyle made way for the nurses. No longer showing any sign of indecision, they lifted up the ends of the heavy stretcher and with a final reassuring word to Promise, moved swiftly past him. Promise, her face streaked with dust-dried tears, quietly climbed into the back of the pick-up. By the time Doyle had lifted up the tailboard and secured its chains, she had slipped beneath a pile of blankets and was sobbing herself to sleep on the foam mattress.

◇

The town of Bala clung like an impenetrable algae to the banks of the river Ngqika. And yet in spite of the row of shops along its unpaved main street, including a chemist, hotel and off-licence, it was little more than a dusty, overcrowded village where, like Ngagabhaleko, the boys herded cattle along the river bank, women marched out every morning into the donga-ridden countryside to search for fuel and the men were largely conspicuous by their absence.

The river Ngqika sprang up among the dull brown foothills of the Lower Drakensberg and ought to have been the town's lifeblood. But as it slunk through the dry interior it seemed to bring a dark moodiness with it; its water slow, tepid and dull; burdened by an exhausted froth around the edges where voracious swarms of mosquitoes lurked and livestock cooled themselves in its malodorous mud. Only once or twice during the rainy season did the mood change when, following a cloudburst over the mountains, the river flooded its banks, washing away the town's rapidly growing slum which would be painstakingly rebuilt from the flotsam of villages higher upstream.

For most of the time, however, it was possible to drive straight through the feeble current, by-passing the single lane bridge linking Bala with the rest of the country – as the dagga smugglers invariably did whenever army or police road-blocks sealed off the town. Everyone knew how the smugglers succeeded in avoiding the road-blocks but apart from the occasional police patrol, no serious attempt was made to seal off the various routes crossing the muddy riverbed. In that sense the river *was* the town's lifeblood. For Bala, without any other serious commercial prospect – like many a rural town it had sprung up round a mission station – had become an important centre of the nation's dagga trade.

On a hill overlooking the town, in an oasis of greenery that owed its survival to the doggedness of successive Catholic missionaries, stood the church and hospital of St Augustine. The hospital was a picturesque building rather like an English country stable, with sash windows and red sills peeking out from beneath an overhanging roof. Wooden banisters encircled its red polished verandahs; flowers grew in large earthen pots beside the glass doors, while long, looping chains protected the elegant fountain and courtyard rockery.

During the day the orange-tinged walls, which were constantly being scrubbed by hospital workers, glowed like marmalade in the sun as it slanted down through the trees – palm, pine and jacaranda, none of them indigenous yet thriving in the luxurious terraced gardens through which Doyle now strolled, putting as much distance as possible between himself and the nearby church. For even at this late hour he sensed the bubbling and unwelcome presence of Father McKeogh.

Father McKeogh, a vigorous young Irishman brought up in the back streets of Dublin, who had boxed professionally for a year before joining the priesthood, had been sent to Bala at about the same time Doyle had arrived in Ngagabhaleko. A spry figure with close-cropped hair and vivid green eyes, he had built himself a stone cottage beside the church. Here he lived with a transient community of orphans, migrants, young apprentices, doctors on temporary secondment as well as a whole menagerie of animals, among them a bad-tempered baboon, an ostrich, a clutch of guinea-fowl and an aardvark which the gardener struggled in vain to keep out of the hospital flowerbeds.

Doyle had only met Father McKeogh once. Having managed to avoid the priest on his frequent tours of the area around Ngagabhaleko, he had finally bumped into him on the steps of the church at Bala where, at Nurse Fumba's insistence, he had gone to view the enormous stained-glass windows for which St Augustine's had become famous.

No sooner had he put his head round the door than he was confronted by the effusive: 'Welcome, pilgrim, to St Augustine. I am Father McKeogh, your personal guide. Allow me to show you around.'

He had tried to slip away but found his path blocked by the garrulous priest. 'Come, come, now that you are here you may as well stay. Pardon? No, no they are not at prayer. They have just come in to escape from the heat. And who can blame them? Isn't it divinely cool in here? It's the stone floor. Naturally the high walls help the air to circulate. They also lift the roof, creating a feeling not just of space but of heavenly intervention. One can feel the Lord's hand reaching down through those splendid beams. Solid oak. God's wood. So's that lectern – hand-carved in Italy and specially shipped over. What do you think? Look around you. What do you see? Here, in a world of mud huts, we have a building that is solid stone, one people know will not be washed away by the next flood. A building they can shelter in when the storms of life become too harsh and overpowering. It's the solidity of the thing. The solidity of our faith! No, no, pilgrim please, don't go. Haven't I seen you somewhere before? Maybe you are just passing through, in which case I urge you to take one final look – examine this magnificent monument which the people here have built in the middle of a desert. Examine it and ask yourself if there is anything insubstantial about the love of God. It is the love of God that shelters and protects us . . .'

Quietly treading the gravel pathway, Doyle gave a start as he heard a garment rustling in the dark behind him. A voice called out briskly: 'Mr Doyle? Mr Doyle are you there?'

Doyle turned. 'Coming Sister,' he answered, and then promptly bumped into the thickset figure who'd arrived breathlessly behind him.

'Ah, Mr Doyle, at last I have found you. Your pupil is fast asleep in the back of the van and I didn't wish to wake her just to ask where you had got to. So I came to search for you myself.'

'I'm sorry,' he said, 'I should have waited.'

'No, not at all. I understand. Isn't the garden lovely at this hour? I sometimes walk through here myself at night when the shift is quiet. Only I dare not stay too long because there is the danger my nurses will fall asleep. I must confess that when they do that I sometimes feel like Jesus in the garden of Gethsemane.'

'How is she, Sister . . . eh?' Doyle leaned forward to read the plastic name-tag.

'Sister Mondo. I am Sister Agnes Mondo.'

The handshake was strong and vigorous. 'We were expecting you a lot earlier you know. Nurse Fumba radioed the police in Bala and they in turn radioed the hospital to inform us that you were on your way from Ngagabhaleko. Did you take the long route? I suppose you are used to driving on tarred roads.'

'We were held up by an army checkpoint. I hope it hasn't complicated things . . . How are the girls?'

'So it was the soldiers who delayed you,' said Sister Mondo, brushing aside his enquiries. 'I take it Nurse Fumba had the foresight to give you a letter. Sometimes these out-of-the-way clinics panic and they send patients to us who are then arrested on the way because they do not have the necessary documents.'

'Nurse Fumba's very thorough,' Doyle replied.

'Oh I don't mean to imply otherwise. I realise without her we would struggle. She runs that clinic single-handed. And with no waste. Her supplies are always accounted for. If she was working in one of the big hospitals in the city, she would herself be a sister by now. But you see she is a religious woman and does not like the godless life of the urban areas. . . .'

Sister Mondo paused for breath. She was a robust woman whose ample body quivered as she spoke. She reminded Doyle of Rebecca and the overwhelming energy with which she tackled even the most mundane of chores. But whereas Rebecca's joyful spirit swept one up in its warmth, Sister Mondo's was like a leaky old boat on choppy waters, vacillating between the threats inherent in her position as chief nurse and the assurances she sought to give as a woman and a mother. Her brown eyes were lively but constantly flared without warning. The lines around her mouth flickered between an obvious kindness and latent severity. There was no denying the stress locked away in her corpulent frame which seemed to leak out like an electric current – audible in the crackling of her uniform as she tugged and pulled at it in an unceasing effort to prevent it from rising above her hips. Her face sagged but the skin shone with a youthful vitality so that the strands of hair visible beneath her bonnet appeared to him to be prematurely grey. She puffed as she fanned herself with her hand although the air was cool. Doyle knew that she was sizing him up. He also realised that she was trying to work out the connection between Alexia and himself.

'My nurses tell me, sir, that the young lady was behind the wheel when you arrived. In her state that may have been unwise.'

The fragapani and magnolia trees dotted about the garden rustled in a passing, scented breeze. Doyle shivered. 'She insisted on driving.'

'Surely you did not let her have her way?'

Doyle avoided the sister's officious scrutiny. 'I'm afraid I'd had too much to drink.'

'But did she not think of her own condition?'

'She seemed reasonably fit when we left the clinic,' he replied.

'Then how do you explain – no, forgive me. I do not mean to cross-examine you like this. It's just that . . . if she was fine when you left Ngagabhaleko, than there is no obvious reason for her suddenly to be in this state. Unless of course the delay at the checkpoint . . .'

'Perhaps you could tell me, what state, Sister?'

Sister Mondo put a hand on his shoulder. But Doyle didn't know whether this was to comfort or intimidate him. Above the garden's heady fragrance he could smell a distinct whiff of formaldehyde.

'You need not be embarrassed or afraid, Mr Doyle. I want you to tell me whether this is the army's doing. I realise that if the soldiers had wanted to abuse her in any way then there would have been nothing you could do because they would have quickly beaten you up. They beat up so many innocent people who then have to come to us for treatment. As if our work is not already enough. Believe me, sir . . .' her grip tightened on his shoulder; her eyes boring into his. 'I am no friend of the soldiers. They are a law unto themselves. Why, I have even seen them march through this hospital looking for these so-called terrorists. But it is they who terrorise. They terrorise our patients. How is one to gain the faith of these unfortunate victims who are struggling to recover from ill-health? Because it is faith, and not just medicine, which heals a person. Fresh beds, clean wards, nurses, doctors, yes, they are important. But it is faith above all which heals us.'

Doyle sensed that she wanted to ask him what faith he belonged to but that something warned her against it. Quickly he said: 'Nurse Fumba would agree with you. She's one of the few Catholics in

Ngagabhaleko. As you probably know, they're mostly Lutheran round there. Nearest chapel is fifteen kilometres away. You'd have to be pretty serious about your faith to walk that sort of distance every Sunday.'

Sister Mondo nodded approvingly. 'I am extremely pleased to hear that you hold one of the nursing staff in such high regard, Mr Doyle. It is good, especially for the people of Ngagabhaleko who have been neglected all these years. But now there is a fine school and a wonderful clinic. I'm sure they must be very happy to see the two of you working in tandem. It promises much for the future.'

At the sound of approaching footsteps, Sister Mondo withdrew her hand. As she tugged at her uniform Doyle thought her eyes seemed dulled with sadness, though it might merely have been the closeness of the surrounding bushes casting their shadows over her face as she lowered her head to check her hemline.

One of the two nurses he had seen earlier came running towards them, shining a tiny, bedside torch along the path. Her plumpness meant that she too fought a constant battle to keep her uniform from rising at her hips.

'Please, Sister,' she cried, puffing, 'you must come. We have another emergency admission. A man has been shot.'

To Doyle's surprise, Sister Mondo put her arm affectionately round the young nurse's waist. 'My daughter!' she announced proudly. But then in her next breath declared: 'You will have to excuse us,' and turned, scuttling down the path.

She returned almost immediately however, alone. Her pale lips trembling. 'You see, sir, what the soldiers are doing? Now you will understand why I asked you whether anything happened to the young lady at the road-block. Here at St Augustine's we make a point of keeping a record of these things. The army must be held accountable. If you and I are expected to adhere to professional standards, then so must our soldiers. No ones dignity should be allowed to suffer. What are we if we build our nation on the same foundation as the Boers? Oh, but I'm sorry if I am allowing my emotions to run away with me. It's just that one cannot always talk so freely. Now, if you will excuse me, I really must leave you.'

'What about the girls?' Doyle called out, anxiously.

But the corpulent figure was already dashing off down the path. 'I will catch up with you later,' she cried, the sound of her footsteps across the gravel fading in the night.

◇

Doyle had no idea how long he'd been sitting on the stone bench in the garden. When he rose it felt as though the cold had inserted itself like a metal pin in his spine. Slowly he made his way back to the pick-up where he groped behind the seat for the bottle of whisky he'd packed in his travelling bag. As he put the bottle to his lips he stared at the slumbering Promise, her thin, tear-stained face surrounded by a sea of unwashed blankets. However, the girl's stoicism unsettled him and he quickly screwed the cap back on the bottle, tucking it away again in the bag which contained a change of clothes and his passport. As the whisky steadily drove out the cold, he stole across to the hospital verandah where, sprawling on the red, polished concrete, he waited for Sister Mondo to bring him news of Alexia.

Minutes later he was back at the car. The third time he threw the empty bottle away under a bush.

Sister Mondo returned soon afterwards. As Doyle struggled to his feet, she sighed and said: 'I'm sorry. We should have taken better care of you.'

Doyle waved his hands clumsily. 'How is she? The girls . . . how are they?'

Sister Mondo shook her head disapprovingly. 'They are both fine. But you my dear sir are clearly in need of somewhere to sleep. Really we should have offered you a bed. But, *hayi*!' she exclaimed, plunging her hands down the sides of her tunic . . . 'We are so full. There isn't one spare bed in the whole building. If there was a serious accident now, we would have to lay the patients out here on the verandah. And not for the first time.'

'It doesn't matter, Sister. I can sleep in the car.'

Sister Mondo continued to shake her head. 'No, Mr Doyle. That would not be necessary. Besides, there is always room in Father McKeogh's house.'

'Agnes . . I mean . . Alexia . . how is Miss Alexia . . . Xolile? Has she lost the . . .?'

'Yes, I'm afraid her pregnancy has been terminated. But the young lady is strong. She will recover. Others are not so fortunate. Now as I

153

was saying, there is always some space at Father McKeogh's. I will find someone to drive you over. I know it is not far but clearly you should not be behind the wheel. If you will just excuse me for a moment.'

'No, honestly, it's not necessary, Sister. I'll just sleep in the . . .' But the sister had already marched off and he was left with the image of her tired eyes flashing with robust sympathy beneath the bonnet pinned to her grey hair.

For a while he remained where he was, swaying unsteadily in the glare of the verandah lights. Then he stumbled down the steps and found Lieutenant Mbanjwa waiting in the pick-up.

18

Naylor unscrewed the bars on the outside of the dormitory window with his penknife and climbed out. Doyle waited until he had heard the plop of his room-mate landing in the flowerbed below before he followed, shinning down the rainwater pipe from the first floor. Quickly the two youths struck out across the school grounds.

'Bladdy hell, Doyle, you're an oddball,' Naylor panted as they approached the perimeter fence at the bottom of the playing fields. 'How could Sprinkler have got it wrong? How could he possibly have mixed you up with Seamus Coyle?'

'I thought we Paddies were all the same to you,' Doyle replied.

'Facetious swine!' Naylor swore. Then, dropping his voice so that the sawing of crickets suddenly rose, strident and sinister in the night around them, he added: 'Poor Coyle. I suppose he doesn't know his old man's kicked the bucket.'

'His old man hasn't,' said Doyle vaulting the barbed-wire fence.

Naylor hesitated.

'Jump!' Doyle urged. 'We haven't got all night. The bar closes in an hour.'

Naylor jumped. They heard a twang followed by the sound of ripping cotton. Naylor scrambling to his feet, pointed to his crotch. 'Christ! I've split my bladdy trousers.'

Doyle grabbed him by the arm. 'Come on we'll just have to keep you away from Magic Martha. She sees your ding-a-ling and you'll be in the same predicament as Coyle.'

'Been a bad year for Seamus,' grunted Naylor, struggling to keep up with Doyle as they strode down the tree-lined avenues leading into town. 'First he catches the clap. Now his old man's . . .' He broke off, trying to grab the tail of Doyle's shirt. A woman appeared in the window of a large house set back off the road and drew the curtains. In the deserted garden a hosepipe lay neatly coiled around a tap while a wrought-iron table and chairs gleamed beneath the star-studded sky. 'Hey, you . . . you mean Coyle's dad *hasn't* kicked the bucket?' Naylor spluttered.

'He's in the Bahamas,' said Doyle. 'On business. Seamus is joining him after the finals.'

'But I thought you said Sprinkler confused you with Coyle?'

'I didn't,' replied Doyle, decapitating a flower that stole out from behind a hedge with a karate chop. 'You surmised.'

'So Sprinkler got it right. It is your old man who is . . .'

'Dead. Yes.'

$$\diamond$$

It was after closing when they emerged from the hotel bar. Stopping at a take-away, Naylor growled: 'Better scoff this lot in the park. Sprinkler's got a nose for "russians".'

His speech was slurred, his eyes smoke-filled and raw. Having forgotten about the split in his trousers, it was not until they were climbing over the locked gate of the park that he remembered. But by then it was too late and as the loose material caught on a piece of sculpted ironwork it caused him to pitch headlong into the grass, crushing his hamburger beneath him.

'Jesus!' Doyle snorted, as he unscrewed a bottle of vodka. 'Next time we'll bring a bloody pram.'

Naylor rose unsteadily to his feet. As he stuffed bits of broken hamburger into his mouth he began to urinate through the split in his trousers.

Doyle raised the bottle to his lips.

'Hey!' Naylor cried. 'Save me some. I paid for it.'

Doyle held out the bottle. As Naylor reached for it, he pulled it away and ran, jeering, across the undulating lawns.

The night was clear and warm. Overhead the stars sparkled like an enormous crystal chandelier and the orange pebble pathways, the manicured flowerbeds, clipped hedges, water fountains and stone arbors all glistened in the silvery light, as though sprinkled with castor sugar.

In a dip in the middle of the park, surrounded by gently sloping banks of mowed grass, was a pond. Doyle, who had all but forgotten about Naylor, sank down on the paved edge with his legs stretched out in front of him. He took another drink from the bottle and leaned back on his elbows. After staring for some time at the smooth face of the water, he sat up and began flicking pebbles into the middle. Soon his fingers were red from the dust which he ignored, as he ignored the sound of the pebbles rattling like gunfire across the surface. Keeping his eyes fixed on the ripples he watched with a wry satisfaction as the water began lapping over his shoes. Soon the bottle was nearly empty.

'Doyle you selfish bastard!' shouted Naylor, bursting through the bushes. 'Give me some of that.'

'What happened to *paddy* bastard?'

Naylor snatched the bottle out of his room-mate's grasp. 'Smart bastard! Smart, creepy bastard.'

Doyle snatched the bottle back. 'What's bothering you, Naylor?'

Naylor swayed silently on his feet.

Doyle shrugged and picked up another handful of pebbles. As they rained down on the night-blue water Naylor made an unsuccessful lunge for the bottle. 'I'll tell you what's bothering me,' he snarled, his mouth wet and gleaming. 'Your old man's dead. And instead of going home, here you are, getting pissed; not because you're out of your mind with grief or anything like that. Bladdy hell, no! You want to piss on his grave. And your mother's!'

'My mother isn't dead,' said Doyle, staring at the ripples spreading outwards, like wrinkles on a contorted face. 'Not that I know of anyway.'

'No, but you'll be the death of her. She's on her own for Christ's sake! She needs your support. It's your responsibility. And here you are . . .'

'Getting drunk with *you*!'

'You tricked me you creep! You said Sprinkler had confused you with Coyle.'

'I told you, you surmised.'

'Christ! Doyle I bunked out with you tonight thinking it was really Coyle's dad who died, not yours. I thought we were going to celebrate.'

'We are celebrating,' said Doyle.

Naylor's eyes widened in horror. 'Your father? Your own flesh and blood?'

'He sold out.'

'So?' Naylor cried. 'He's still your old man. He helped bring you into the world. Where would you be now if it wasn't for him? And don't tell me, Ireland, because you wouldn't be bladdy born, smart-arse. Do you think . . .'

'Do you know what a hill farmer is, Naylor?'

Naylor tugged at his split trousers. 'Someone who grows hills?'

'Our farm was on a hill. Land that was fit for nothing. The valleys . . . all the fat land belonged to the Prods. Then they started to leave – IRA and all that. We heard many of them were emigrating, some of them to South Africa on assisted passages, buying up land over here. Prod land again. Fat land. My parents felt cheated. They wanted to prove that they were just as good farmers as the Prods. They wanted the Prods to see it, to acknowledge it. But the Prods were leaving, cheating them of their chance.'

'So they came out with the Protestants,' said Naylor. 'And now they're equal. What more do you want?'

'They sold out!' Doyle retorted, as the ripples, spilling over the edge of the pond, continued to soak his shoes.

'They did what they thought was best,' Naylor replied.

'For who?'

'For you. For themselves. The family. Christ! Doyle, I told you, they're your flesh and blood. Look! Look at this!' Naylor, swaying precariously near the edge of the pond, pointed to his tomato-stained shirt. 'See? See this?'

'Jesus! Naylor. You don't have to show me what blood looks like. And it doesn't look like tomato sauce.'

'How would you know, Doyle? You've turned your back on your own . . .'

'And how would you know, Naylor? You're a Boer!'

'I'm a South African. And damn proud of it!'

'A *white* South African!'

'A South African.'

'Yeah, a Prod! Living on the fat land. How much blood have you seen in your neighbourhood, hey?'

Naylor advanced recklessly. 'Don't start that crap again, Doyle. I'm not a bladdy Prod.'

'Boer!' shouted Doyle.

'Doyle!' shouted Naylor.

'Your mother was a van der Merwe, wasn't she?'

'Doyle I've had it up to here with your . . .'

'Van der Merwe's a Boer name. A Prod name.'

'Doyle!' Naylor yelled. 'I'm going to smash that fucking bottle over your head!'

Doyle put the bottle to his lips. 'Come and get it, Boer,' he sneered.

Naylor lunged wildly at the bottle. Leisurely Doyle leaned out of the way. His room-mate lost his balance, stretched out an arm for the support which was not forthcoming and tumbled flat on to his belly in the water. The loud splash was followed by a moonlit spray raining down like diamonds along the water's edge. Naylor began to flail about, coughing and spluttering: 'Doyle I'll get you for this. I'll get you, you bastard, I swear!'

Doyle got up. 'Bloody Boer,' he said, and walked away.

19

'Good evening, Mr Doyle,' said Lieutenant Mbanjwa. 'Or perhaps it should be good *morning*?'

Doyle slid in awkwardly behind the wheel, swearing as he failed to find the keys.

The lieutenant, seated on the passenger's side, smiled as he handed them over. 'Courtesy of Sister Mondo,' he said.

Doyle inserted the key in the ignition and the windscreen wipers lurched into action. 'How the hell did she get hold of them?' he scowled.

'Miss Xolile,' replied the lieutenant. 'I am told she was most reluctant to part with them. Now the sister has gone to look for a driver. You are a lucky man, sir. These ladies are clearly concerned for your safety.'

The wipers continued to lurch back and forth, leaving a trail of sludge across the windscreen. Gradually the lights of the hospital verandah began to break through and Doyle could see the frenzied mass of insects still flitting around the shaded bulbs. The tin shades were painted a glossy white and reminded him of spats as they ran in a disciplined row across the front of the building. They were the hospital's first line of defence against the hoardes of insects that swarmed up every night from the river, polished defenders who amidst the hum and ting of battle watched impassively as the corpses mounted beneath them.

'A solid building,' the lieutenant observed, echoing Father McKeogh.

Doyle flicked away a flying ant that was crushed on his shirt. 'A mortuary among the flowerbeds,' he muttered.

'In fact it reminds me of a prison,' said the lieutenant. 'The windows have bars.'

'To prevent patients from escaping I suppose.'

Lieutenant Mbanjwa frowned, then leaning forward, turned off the wipers. He patted Doyle solicitously on the arm. 'I'm sorry. Sister Mondo did not have to explain things. She remarked only that you had brought two patients from Ngagabhaleko, Miss Xolile and a pupil. I hope their condition is not too serious.'

Doyle stared at the deserted sweep of the verandah. 'No use mourning the unborn,' he said.

'The pupil was pregnant?'

'The Reverend's niece.'

The lieutenant's surprise seemed genuine. 'Oh but that is bad news, Mr Doyle. Terrible news! I would not like to be the one to inform him. He is such an upright man. He is bound to take it as a sign of God's displeasure. Oh dear! Bad news indeed. It means that we have lost a potential . . .'

'*We*, Lieutenant?'

'The nation.'

'And will the nation mourn?'

The lieutenant thrust his hand into his jacket pocket. Doyle heard the rustle of a cigarette packet. The lieutenant took his hand out. It was empty. 'I forgot,' he said, 'you do not smoke. The space in here is too confined.'

'Go ahead,' said Doyle.

The lieutenant shrugged. 'You did not mourn your father's death, Mr Doyle. Why was that?'

Doyle stared at the dapper figure dressed in a navy jacket and pin-striped shirt. He noticed the lieutenant had had a haircut. It made his crushed nose more prominent though his ears were pinned with rather more delicacy to the line above his jaw. His eyes were less bloodshot than they had been at the station. Dark, yet lucid and discerning, they induced a moment of panic as Doyle suddenly remembered the letter Abraham had passed on to him at the road-block. It was in his shirt pocket. Surely the lieutenant could see it. Perhaps that was what he had come for. If so then Alexia had been right. It had been a mistake to trust Abraham. Of course he had been aware of the old man's attempts to lure him on to the stage – it was in the nature of the villagers' desperate struggle for survival that anyone, even the most inept, be conscripted to help. So he did not feel that he had been betrayed. It was simply the clumsiness of the old man's efforts which saddened him, the waste of time and cruel dashing of hopes. For all he, Doyle, had to do was hand the letter over to the lieutenant and his innocence would be proved. He would be allowed to go free.

Innocence? Free? The words caused a bobble in his stomach. They were not words he normally used. They were Alexia's. It was she who posed the biggest threat. Not Abraham or Mbanjwa; nor even Majogo. It was Alexia . . .

'*Doyle I don't want to go back to Ngagabhaleko. I want to . . .*'

'Mr Doyle?'

He manoeuvered the letter deeper into his pocket.

'You do not answer.'

'You know the answer, Lieutenant.'

'It is not easy to understand.'

'You don't have to understand,' said Doyle.

The lieutenant gave a lukewarm smile. He seemed hurt. 'And your friend Naylor? What was his reaction when you failed to attend your father's funeral? Did he understand?'

'Naylor?'

'You were close friends after all.'

'*Were.*'

'And you never renewed your friendship when you returned to Africa?'

'After all these years? We weren't that close. In fact we weren't close at all. We merely got thrown together – the way kids do at school.'

'Nevertheless, you did meet, some months ago, I believe.'

Doyle avoided the lieutenant's watchful gaze. 'So you know about Shark Bay.'

'Did you arrange it?' the lieutenant asked.

'Naylor did.'

'I suppose it was a sort of reunion.'

'It ended in a brawl.'

'I'm sorry to hear it.'

'Spare me the crocodile tears, Lieutenant. If you know about our meeting, then you'll also know that Naylor's a member of the Nationalist Party. He's on the Board of the Port Elizabeth Chamber of Commerce and a representative of the Cape Wine Growers' Association . . .'

162

'You disapprove?' the lieutenant enquired.

Doyle continued to stare at the hospital verandah. The insects had finally ceased smashing themselves against the shades. The light was harsh. The stone walls bare. A prison? If only Alexia knew. One never did escape. Not even on the outside.

'Tell me,' he said, 'did you hire Naylor?'

The lieutenant remained silent; yet unembarrassed.

'Did you pay him to find out what I was doing here? What organisation I was supposed to belong to? Or did you think he might persuade me to work for the security forces? He tried – in his clumsy way. Cost him his boat. Very nearly cost him his life. You did send him, didn't you? What persuaded him to accept? – was it the money you offered or did he do it out of a sense of duty? Actually, on second thoughts, I'd rather not know.'

'You are disturbed?'

'Why should I be?'

'It is not a pleasant business.'

'It doesn't concern me,' said Doyle.

'But you are curious.'

'Am I?'

'He was your friend.'

'I told you, we were thrown together.'

'Then what if I were to tell you that your former room-mate . . .'

The lieutenant broke off. A strange diffidence made him lower his gaze. Contemplating the wrinkles in his tie which he smoothed down with a heavy palm, he gave the impression of searching for the right words – as if he were the one preparing to break the unhappy news about Alexia to the Reverend. After a while he looked up. His expression had changed. It had become almost blasé, indifferent. His lips pouted, like a fish turning up its nose at a piece of bait. His eyelids drooped. He left his tie lying at an angle across his shirt.

'Well I suppose if your father's death failed to move you then the fact that your former room-mate works for counter-insurgency is just as unlikely to disturb your sang . . . sangfroid, I think is the English expression.'

'French,' corrected Doyle.

The lieutenant nodded thoughtfully. Then in a slow, probing

voice, he said: 'Nevertheless, tonight I see something *has* disturbed your composure.'

Doyle turned his head away. The side window promptly threw the lieutenant's reflection back at him. 'I don't know what you mean,' he replied.

For a moment the lieutenant seemed insulted. He straightened his shoulders and adjusted his tie. 'I can see you have been drinking,' he said, 'quite a lot too. Yet it has not helped to calm you. Of course as a policeman it is easy for me to say you are tense because you are hiding something from me. But I do not think it is quite so straightforward. After all we do not just hide things from others. More importantly, we hide them from ourselves.'

'What are you trying to say, Lieutenant?'

'You see . . .' the lieutenant's reflection hovered darkly in the window. His cheeks appeared hollow, his eyes tormented. 'You see, Mr Doyle, I have been thinking about this for some time now. And it strikes me as a possibility that you have denied your father's terrorist involvement because of the shame you feel – the shame anyone in a civilised society would feel who is connected with such barbaric behaviour. Your father's activities must have especially distressed you since, as a youngster, you were powerless to prevent him from pursuing his misguided goals. It would be quite conceivable therefore, would it not, for you to have suppressed all of this in order to avoid any feelings of guilt? It is perfectly natural, Mr Doyle. People do it all the time. Really you need not feel threatened or afraid because of it – provided of course you understand what you have done and why you have done it. You have simply tried to bury your shame.'

The reflection in the window sprang to life as Doyle rounded on the lieutenant. 'Sweet Jesus! What do you want from me? Can't you get it into your head I have nothing – nothing for you, for anyone. The moment we landed here all those years ago we became nothing. You know as well as I do that my father wasn't involved in any "terrorist" activity. He was precisely the sort of immigrant this country has a history of enticing: white, semi-skilled, European and racist. You haven't offered a shred of evidence to suggest that he wasn't a member of that parasitical class. Isn't it time you produced something – other than a lot of hot air to float your paranoia on?'

The lieutenant slowly closed his eyes. It was as if the verandah lights had become too bright. Doyle, for the first time noticing a tiny scar cutting across the corner of his brow, almost hoped that the lieutenant would produce the evidence . . . a list of names maybe, of acknowledged ANC members at the time, or of a cell which, unknown either to him or his mother, had operated from the farm . . . some mention in captured underground documentation . . . evidence that one, Seamus Doyle, had been a bone fide *comrade*, had given his life for *the cause*. If nothing else, at least the lieutenant's fears would have been well founded. For without the evidence he was like a drowning man. And a drowning man will do anything to save himself.

For the moment however, the lieutenant's eyes remained shut.

Doyle said: 'All parents let their children down in the end. It's how they live with their fallibility afterwards that counts. Mine didn't try to hide it. They flaunted it. It became their crutch. Their excuse. Catholics are always more likely than Protestants to point the finger at themselves. By the same token they are more likely to look to be excused. Would you have excused them, Lieutenant?'

The lieutenant looked up. The scar seemed to swell. He felt it gently with the tip of his finger. 'You are a difficult man to understand, Mr Doyle. One who has become, if you don't mind my saying so, by your own definition more Protestant than Catholic. For it seems you are determined to point the finger elsewhere. Indeed you appear to have built your whole life upon a principle of . . . condemnation.'

'Of loyalty, Lieutenant.'

'But you are loyal to no one. You belong to no organisation. You are not even married. A man of your age and you have no children. We Xhosas could not exist in such isolation.'

Doyle let out an audible sigh of relief. 'So, at last you recognise I am on my own?'

The lieutenant nodded, sadly. 'Now I accept it's true. Quite clearly I overestimated you.'

'History, Lieutenant. You may put it down to your country's History.'

'Yes, but we are not just History's puppets, Mr Doyle. We are also its creators. That is why I believe my estimation of you has gone down. If you had expressed your solidarity with at least some small part of society – it would not have mattered which part: establishment or anti-establishment – by joining some organisation, some group which was prepared to defend its vision, then I can say, my admiration would have remained as it was in the beginning. But here you are entirely alone. Always alone. Even when you leave our country and fly off somewhere else, there too I'm sure you will be by yourself. Yet I cannot believe anyone would choose to live like this. Without the company, without the love and respect of our fellow-beings we are nothing.'

Doyle, inwardly triumphant now that his unsuitability for the part in their play had at last been recognised, put a hand on his former co-star's sleeve. 'Let's just leave it there shall we, Lieutenant? You won't goad me.'

The lieutenant sighed and pushed open the car door. 'No, sir,' he said, looking up as a posse of armed and uniformed policemen materialised on the far side of the verandah. 'I probably shall not be able to goad you. But just in case you should have second thoughts, allow me to warn you that over the next few weeks there will be an extensive security drag-net in operation. Many people will be caught up in it, maybe even some you know at Ngagabhaleko. It would be as well for you to be on your guard – against friend and informant. You can never be sure these days. Sometimes the two are one.'

Doyle saw that the policemen were posting guards on the corners of the verandah. Losing no time the rest of them hurried toward the entrance, their boots leaving prints on the polished concrete. In their silent frenzy they reminded him of the insects descending upon the lights, their shadows long and tapering, their eyes glazed, red. Where had they come from? He hadn't heard their vehicles.

The lieutenant said: 'If you will excuse me.'

Doyle pointed to the verandah. 'This why you showed up tonight . . . to drag-net a hospital?'

The lieutenant smiled enigmatically as he stepped out of the pick-up. 'I hope you haven't become paranoid, Mr Doyle. We have many fish to catch. Now if you will allow me, I shall bid you goodnight.'

Doyle watched as the lieutenant climbed the verandah steps, pausing half way to check his inside jacket pocket, before disappearing noiselessly through the screen door.

The door was still flapping like a fish's gill when, in the uneasy silence (no screams, no protests; where was Sister Mondo now, he wondered, to record this brutal invasion?) Promise stuck her head round the back of the cabin.

'Please, sir, the police, they frighten me.'

He gestured to the seat vacated by the lieutenant. 'You'd better come in here.'

Immediately she leapt over the side of the vehicle and scrambled in beside him. 'Why they come with so many guns to the hospital?'

He helped her with the blanket which trailed behind her. Her sleep-wracked body gave off a warmth that was fragrant and comforting.

'I don't know,' he said. 'Why do they come with any?'

Rubbing her cheeks vigorously with both hands, she shivered: 'My eldest brother is a soldier. He is in the Transkei army. Last year he was promoted to the position of corporal.'

'What are you afraid of then?' he asked ruefully. Promise didn't seem to know. Or perhaps she didn't have the time to explain. Pulling the blanket up over her shoulders she ducked into its dark, deep folds as a man with his arm in a sling burst out on to the verandah in front of them. He was tall and thin, dressed only in a pair of shorts. His eyes had a look of wild desperation about them as he sized up his options and took off to the right.

Within seconds the verandah was seething with policemen, tawny uniforms fanning out in front of the scrubbed stone like a spray of mud from a passing vehicle's tyres. They all seemed to point, to shout and brandish their weapons as though they were the ones under attack. A lightshade was noisily smashed, its white orb sent spinning into the night. The freshly shaven scalp of Lieutenant Mbanjwa gleamed beneath the naked bulb.

A guard raised his rifle horizontally across his chest to bar the fugitive's way. The fugitive swung round almost falling over as his bare feet stuck to the cold concrete. He stared helplessly into the unlit garden. Would the night shield him from the policemen's bullets? Perhaps there were policemen out there already. Waiting for the excuse to fire.

Doyle heard Mbanjwa's voice above the undisciplined babble of the rest of the men. He ordered the fugitive to stop. But he already had stopped. Frozen by his own indecision. The policemen closed in.

Suddenly there was an even louder voice barking at the men. Pursued by her two young nurses Sister Mondo charged across the verandah. Her bonnet had been knocked askew and one grey stocking lay bunched at her ankle, like a bruised swelling. 'No! No!' she yelled as she swept to the front elbowing aside those who towered over her in their dusty boots and heavy fatigues.

'You can't take him away. He is too ill. Who do you think you are? We are a hospital. He is one of our patients.'

'Please Sister,' he heard Mbanjwa appeal, 'you must not interfere.'

'Interfere!' she exclaimed, brushing the lieutenant aside. 'This is a hospital and I am in charge here.'

'I'm sorry, Sister, but . . .'

Seeing his chance the barefoot fugitive bolted toward the edge of the verandah. Without breaking his stride he leapt over the flourishing Christmas bushes and into the night, jettisoning his sling which dangled like a broken flower from the dark leaves. A policeman raised his rifle.

Immediately Sister Mondo threw herself between him and the wounded fugitive. 'No! What do you think you are doing?' Her voice was shrill and set the nerves tingling down Doyle's spine.

The policeman's finger curled around the trigger.

Against the black rifle-stock Sister Mondo's hair seemed almost white.

'No! No! You can't do this. We are a hosp . . .'

The barrel leapt like an electric current in the policeman's hands. Doyle felt Promise shudder beside him. Sister Mondo took a step back, hovered on the edge of the verandah and then, clutching her neck, crashed through the wooden banister into the bushes below.

PART TWO

Prologue

The clatter of helicopter blades drowns the noise of the car's engine as it climbs a narrow coastal road over steep cliffs. Beyond a turquoise sea a knuckle of land breaks through the horizon. The driver of the car gestures excitedly to the woman beside him who nurses a leaky flask, and to the boy in the back. As the fat-bellied helicopter sidles down in front of them, spilling its eggs over the gorse bushes, the driver spins the wheel around causing the car to leave the road. The shiny sea opens out beneath them. They glide effortlessly toward the knuckle of land, their path intercepted by a formation of geese whose wings, the boy notices, are torn and clotted with blood. He also notices blood leaking from the flask which the man and the woman pass back and forth between them. Horrified, he attempts to leap out of the car but it is his parents who are sucked out as the doors burst open. He watches as they plunge toward a silent void that opens in the sea, the force of their fall blowing the doors shut again behind them, imprisoning him in the back of the vehicle as it too plummets down in their wake. The boy screams, banging his fists against the window.

Suddenly a bird appears at the wheel, its feathers soft and radiant though it is clearly exhausted and makes no sound. In its hunger it pecks at the leather steering cover but its beak is chipped and blunt. It is soon thrown off balance by the constant veering as they hurtle toward the void.

The boy clambers into the front to catch the panic-stricken bird, thrusting his arm through the wheel. Immediately the bonnet of the car lifts and they begin to sail over the sea – a black, violent sea whose towering waves reach up, crashing against the windows. The boy hangs on blindly to the wheel. Blind and yet exhilarated. For the loud buffeting by the wind and the waves fills him with a frenzied excitement which leads him to emulate his father's gesture, a triumphant fist raised in the air.

But no sooner has he removed his hand from the wheel than the vehicle is swamped by a tumultuous wave that sends them spinning out of control. Hurriedly he searches for the bird, finds it and tucks it under his shirt. Soothed by the warmth of its feathers against his skin, he settles down again behind the wheel. The waves rise furiously to meet him . . .

171

20

Their placards appeared slightly more dog-eared than before, but their message, which he glimpsed through the collapsed frame of one of the classroom windows, remained just as clear, in spite of the swirling mist that deadened the sound of their chanting.

'TEACHER – SPY! TEACHER – SPY! TEACHER – SPY!'

If only they knew, he sighed. But then how could they? And even if he told them – *showed them the letter* – would they believe him? Would their reaction be any different from his own? Majogo would surely laugh, just as he, Doyle, had laughed at the lieutenant's assertion that his father, far from being an innocent victim, had in fact been *planting* the landmine when it had gone off, killing him.

Well, Mbanjwa had been right! The dapper figure's suspicion, born of historical mistrust, had been justified. There was no such thing as an innocent white man. All one had to find out was whose side he was on. The lieutenant had come up with the obvious answer. Majogo swore the – equally obvious – opposite. He wondered what the rest of his pupils would say if they were to learn the truth. Would they retain the same confidence in him as before?

For the moment they had other things on their mind. Wrapped in their greatcoats and blankets they poured over their exam scripts while he roamed between the desks, tripping over the outstretched legs of the doughty Promise who, though still clearly affected by the previous night's shooting had insisted on returning to Ngagabhaleko with him in order to write. Hunched, bleary-eyed, her hair in knots, she looked up at him and smiled. Her answer-sheet remained largely blank. He had tried to dissuade her from coming to school, but even though it was only a trial exam his suggestion had appalled her. As indeed it would have appalled her classmates, all of whom remained determinedly deaf to the chanting of 'TEACHER-SPY! TEACHER-SPY!' filtering through the broken windows.

He knew that sooner or later they would expect him to do

172

something about Majogo. 'We mustn't judge, *mhlekazi*,' Abraham had advised. But hadn't the committee done just that? Without even talking to the boys. It was strange but he was beginning to feel a certain amount of sympathy for Majogo, beginning even to feel afraid . . . The boys were isolated and vulnerable.

He was equally afraid for Abraham. The weapons buried in the veld were no longer a secret. He was at the mercy of the Reverend and his stewards – a potential victim of his own side's anger, like his, Doyle's father, all those years ago, according to his aunt's letter. He wondered whether the old man had returned safely in the Kombi? Doyle now understood why he had risked being beaten up by the soldiers at the road-block. For the letter, which he yet again dragged from his pocket, had altered everything. It had stripped away his 'innocence' and armed him with a truth which the old man would undoubtedly admire. Yet it was a truth that had come too late. It was out of date. Its age made it dangerous and unreliable, made him afraid, not only for the boys or the old man, but for . . .

'. . . *would've broken your Uncle Dermot's heart*,' he read, hoping the pupils would not see his hands shaking; already his pulse was racing, his stomach churning. '. . . *Dermot always used to say: "put everything up front. Honesty's the best bullet-proof vest". Only the Brits got him in the back. A long time ago it was. You only just started school. You must have cried every time I seen you. 'Cause you were close, you and your uncle – and your dad. The Holy Trinity your mum and me used to call you. There goes the Holy Trinity we'd say as we watched you go down the street to the pub or the dogs or the match, depending like. Seeing you stuck in the middle of the two, I used to think you were a novice taking the Holy Orders. Only they weren't so holy, not with all that gambling and drinking going on and you gawking like the wee'n you were. I don't suppose you'll be having greyhounds where you are now. Plenty of women though to take their place, running around like we're always seeing them on Survival Special, without a stitch to cover their bones. Them Survival programmes is now all – ag well you never were one for the TV except when it came to the news and you wanted to know everything about what was going on in the world. Got that from your granda – him always boasting about the time he was in America and then Australia. And where did he end up? On his brother's farm near Cloonacool in Co. Sligo, good as it was for nothing but the wind blowing through the bracken. All those years away and for what? But least he had the satisfaction of ending his days among family. Strange word that must be to you now, Seamus.*

But at the end of the day, it's family that counts. Turn your back on your family and you turn it on God. Sending money every year doesn't absolve you from that sin. You hear me? One would think you had no shame. Or is it shame that keeps you from these shores? Well let me tell you, we tar and feather nobody nowadays.

And here's something else that ought to shame you. Long ago your mother swore me to secrecy over this but what's the use of secrecy when it only adds to the suffering which all these years the poor woman has had to bear. She always was a proud woman your mother though it didn't pay her well. She was the bravest and strongest of us sisters. Even the Brits couldn't get her down. So, Seamus, you'll understand it's not easy for me to see her reduced to a shadow of her former self, saying things like, "he'll be back, Mary, isn't he my son? My own flesh and blood. All I have left in the world. Didn't I bring him up not to hate or to hold bitterness against anyone in his heart? God's my witness, he'll be back, innocent as the day he was born."

But you know while innocence and ignorance sometimes seem to us like twins, they really live on opposite sides of the street. So let me fill you in on a few of the details which your proud mother has kept from you all these years in the hope (what fools we women are) that you would somehow keep your innocence – though in my opinion you lost it before your father died, even before your Uncle Dermot died. You lost it the day the first Brit soldier stuck his clodhoppers through the door. That's the way we Irish have been losing our virginity for years.

'Course it was only natural for you to be against leaving home but the fact was your father was forced to leave and it was useless him running off to America or some such place because it would be easy for him to be tracked down. He thought in South Africa he'd be safe from the more bloodthirsty of his own countrymen.

But an Irishman is born a political animal – something your mother to this day stubbornly refuses to accept. That is why she tried to protect you from the truth. And still tries. But now I am telling you the truth, Seamus, which is that your father became involved in the underground movement out there. I forget the name but you'll know it. He provided a safe house the way he used to on the farm at home – until those five Provos got ambushed and the organisation accused him – God forgive them – of selling out to the Brits. Ijits! Bloody ijits! Anyway, your father gave the black fighters a safe place to hide from the army and the police. And he helped them to transport guns and explosives. It was while he was helping to transport a landmine that he was killed when it went off unexpected. The police there knew what happened but they turned it into a propaganda stunt, reporting that an innocent white farmer had been blown up by terrorists. Sounds like they learned a trick or two from the Brits.

Now when your mother told me all this, I tell you Seamus we sat and cried buckets. How lonely and bitter those tears we shed. And now, so many years afterwards and I'm thinking of you, of the life you have built not out of the mortar of innocence but ignorant steel. It reminds me of a fella I read about who sold his worthless Connemara farm and took himself off to America and now the new owners have just discovered coal on the place!

However, thanks to God's grace, you still have the chance to make up for everything you have lost; the chance to reclaim your past, which it is every true Irishman's duty to do. So what I'm asking is, how much longer are you going to make your good mother suffer? She is getting on in years and can no longer manage on her own. I agree she brought much of it on herself but if you had any shred of decency left in you, you would at least pay her a visit so that she can explain everything to you. You owe it to her. And to yourself. You can't spend the rest of your life hiding in the jungle. God finds us all out in the end. And may he forgive me for any harsh word I have spoken to you. May you, Seamus, forgive me. Like your mother I wish only to see you return home. You will surely brighten the lives of two lonely old women . . . Your loving aunt, Mary.'

◇

It was mid-afternoon when Doyle returned to his hut. Having learnt from Rebecca that her brother had remained overnight at a neighbouring village and would probably not be back until the evening, he decided to try to get some sleep. He had had precious little in the past forty-eight hours, what with his overnight visit to the hospital and the night before that being forced to watch the Reverend and his stewards dig up Abraham's secret cache of arms . . .

And yet within minutes of lying down he was on his feet again, reaching for his aunt's letter, reaching for a glass and the whisky beside his bed.

It was a while before his hands stopped shaking. By then he had downed a succession of stiff drinks. Allowing the letter to slip from his fingers he lurched over to the window, pulled the curtain aside and through the glass, shattered by the previous evening's stoning, drank in a deep draught of air. The air seemed to make his head spin. It was hot and dry, the mist having lifted, exposing the school's whitewashed buildings like freshly laid eggs in an unprotected nest. Unprotected? He remembered Majogo. But everything was quiet. There was no sign of the boys.

175

He shivered with pleasure in the silence. He wanted to wrap it around him, wanted to pull in the walls of his tiny hut so that the stillness would last forever, cutting him off from the noise of the village, from the sound of his own heart beating. For something in him was coming alive. Like a mysterious ether it was stealing through his veins, breathing into the sluggish blood a new vitality. The whisky seemed helpless against it, merely slowing its progress, dulling the pain, the sense of intrusion. Feeling a sudden wave of nausea, he pulled the curtain back over the window and in the gloom poured himself another drink.

He was staring at the bottom of the empty glass when he heard the sound – one he still instinctively recognised – of police vehicles racing past the mission. He lunged for the door, swung it open and through the dust caught a glimpse of a Land Rover and Black Maria heading toward the school.

Half pulling on his sandles, he shuffled outside. At the mission gate he bumped into Alexia, who refused to let him pass.

'They are lancing the boil!' she announced triumphantly. 'Soon the infection of these *tsotsis* will be gone!'

But she didn't look in any way triumphant. She had a swelling above her right eye, sustained in her fall outside the hospital. Shadows spread like bruises down the hollows of her cheeks. Physically the tension – the wild and brittle petulance – was gone. Her jaw sagged. Her mouth hung open.

Doyle stretched out an unsteady hand toward her. 'You . . . you should be in bed. The only reason the hospital sent you home was because they didn't have any free. Come, Alexia, let me help you.'

Whether it was because she clung so tightly to the gate-posts, or because he was drunk, his grip on her arm proved ineffectual; his fingers like sand which the breeze brushed away.

'I will go when the police have left,' she declared. And with her eyes sunk deep in their purple sockets, she defied him to push his way past her.

Doyle stumbled over to the house, put his head round the door and shouted for help. But the mission appeared deserted. He swore as he returned to the gate. 'Jesus, woman, you can hardly stand!'

Alexia tightened the cord of her hospital gown, which was obviously a child's as the hem failed to reach her knees. The sleeves ended above her wrists and even with the cord fastened the front barely closed. Her hair which was uncombed hung in greasy locks over the frayed collar. She made no effort to brush the fringe from her face.

Again Doyle held out his hand. 'You're only making things worse.'

'Ha! It's not me who is making it worse, but you. Why are you running to school? We all know what the police are going to do. They are going to make your life easier by removing those *tsotsis*.'

'But I'm the . . . It's . . . It's my job to protect . . .'

'Protect? You mean you want to throw yourself between the police and the children, like Sister Mondo? You – a hero? Tsha! They will slaughter you. And what for? Because it was you who allowed those *tsotsis* to demonstrate in the first place. You did not want to take the responsibility for expelling them. You did not want to become involved. Now you want to protect them? What sort of madness is this?'

Doyle threw up his hands in despair. She was right. It was a kind of madness. But how could he explain it? His own thoughts were confused; his body somehow in conflict with itself; his mind already leaping ahead, wondering whether he could climb over the fence without falling and making a fool of himself. There was no other way out of the mission, except by the back gate. And she clearly had her eye on that. Weak as she was, she would easily outsprint him.

Feeling the sun which was burning down out of the hard, blue sky, intensifying the effects of the alcohol, he leaned over the barbed wire. 'I'm not another Sister Mondo,' he panted. 'I'm not going to throw myself in front of their guns. It's just . . .'

The top strand of wire was loose. As he pushed it down it was like dipping spaghetti into a pot of boiling water. It sagged and fell away. He realised he could have climbed *through* the fence. But by then it was too late. He crashed to the ground, leaving his sandal behind on the jagged barbs.

Alexia refused to let go of the gate-post. 'You fool!' she cried. 'You will kill yourself even before you reach the police.'

Doyle struggled back on to his feet. 'I sh . . . shouldn't have to do this,' he gasped. 'Alexia get out of the bloody way! If you don't want to help, I . . . I . . . Those children are my respons . . . Jesus they are my . . .'

He broke off, trying to get his breath back. There was a strange tidal hissing in his ears. His vision seemed blurred. Or was that the heat, the silver haze dancing along the top of the fence? Yet he could see she remained unmoved; could tell that it required an enormous effort for her simply to stay on her feet. Physically broken. Spiritually unbowed. Africa, it seemed, in transition. What would come next? Rehabilitation? Or total destruction?

Screams coming from the school yard told him the children were running away. He could hear the vicious crack of a sjambok followed by the muffled crashing of desks. Majogo and his band must have been trying to find sanctuary in the classroom.

'It's nothing to do with you,' said Alexia as he started at yet another loud report from a police whip. 'Let those who put Majogo up to it take responsibility. This is their doing. It's what they want.'

Doyle looked questioningly at her. 'You know who put them up to it?'

'Ask your friend,' she said.

'You mean Abraham?'

'To him we are all just cannon-fodder.'

Doyle waved a finger clumsily at her. 'That's not true. You . . . you know it's not true.'

'Then what about the guns he hides?'

'You only have your uncle's word.'

'Tsha! Did he not take you to see them?'

'Yes . . but . . .'

'And weren't his stewards also present? They know. Everyone knows!'

'They only know what the stewards have told them. And since the stewards work for your uncle . . .' He paused, swaying in the hot, still air. His shoulder ached where he had landed on it. His eyes stung. His sandal still hung mockingly on the barbed wire. 'You sure your uncle didn't put you up to this, Alexia? Maybe you and he came to some sort of an agreement? I mean how come he isn't suspicious about us? How come he was so ready to believe you'd slept with the *induna*?'

'Put me up to what?' she replied, scornfully.

'Trying to get me to leave Nga . . Nga . . gabhaleko,' he stammered.

'Tsha! I do not need his help in that.'

'Maybe he needs yours.'

Alexia spat feebly on to the red earth.

Doyle said: 'How do you know your uncle hasn't seen you creep into my hut at night? Maybe he's put Majogo up to this to frighten me away.'

'You are a fool, Doyle. The Reverend is doing everything he can to protect you. You saw how those policemen behaved at the hospital last night. If they should link those weapons to Abraham and, since you are friends, the old man to you, then you are finished. You think the village is a place to hide, a place to throw away all your responsibilities?'

'Throw them away?' he laughed, bitterly. 'On the contrary. It's you who's preventing me from carrying out my duty. And if either you or your uncle are trying to discredit Abraham on my account, or have put Majogo up to this in order to scare me away, then you should know . . .'

'What if Dlamini is the one who is behind those *tsotsis*?'

'You should know I won't be scared.'

'Then,' said Alexia, without any sign of emotion, 'your friend may be the death of you.'

Doyle wrenched his sandal off the fence. 'The old man's innocent I tell you!'

Alexia tucked the collar of her pink gown under her chin. 'He is guilty. In this world all men are guilty. And they carry a guilty conscience which they hide from each other. The old man hopes that by playing on your guilt he can persuade you to stay and become involved in the struggle.'

'What guilt?' said Doyle.

'Tsha, you are white. So you are guilty. He knows. He has known all along. You are a fool if you think you can trust him. You cannot trust people just because they are poor and downtrodden. You say you do not expect people in this country to trust you, but now you are prepared to trust them. What kind of thinking is this? It's the thinking of a guilty man. We, the poor, the blacks, we too are guilty. We too must bear our shame. I am ashamed when I think of my uncle satisfying himself on my sister. I want to be sick with shame.'

'Alexia. Alexia, please,' he pleaded, as she turned and slumped

179

over the gate-post. She began to cough and he could hear the bile rising in her throat. As she spat it out it unravelled like an elastic thread down the front of her gown. He tried to steady her on to her feet, but she pulled away, digging her fingers into the dry wood.

'Last night you saw an innocent woman shot in front of you. Now you feel guilty. And you want to help. By doing what? By fighting with the police? Here? In this God-forsaken place? Go home, Doyle. If you must fight, go home! We do not want any more bloodshed . . .'

As she spoke he became aware of an ominous silence in the school yard. The children had fled. He could just make out the weathered faces of their parents in the distance, their aunts, uncles and grandparents, all of whom had hurried up from the village, only to find their roles reduced yet again to those of extras. Against the towering backdrop of land and sky, uniformed figures were marching back briskly to their vehicles.

'Alexia,' he groaned, 'let me through.'

She laughed. 'You are a fool, Doyle, a drunken fool.'

'Drunk, I admit. Fool? We shall have to see.'

'To be driven by guilt is a mistake.'

Doyle put his hand on her shoulder as he squeezed past her. He could feel her strength ebbing away. His mouth dry, his heart pounding, he staggered up the road toward the school.

He was too late. Majogo and his friends had been rounded up and were being bundled into the back of the police van. Majogo, who was the last to enter, saw him coming and immediately began to chant: 'Teacher! Spy! Teacher! Spy!' The refrain was quickly taken up by the others. Even as the metal door was securely bolted, and the Black Maria's engine sprang to life, their voices could be heard, chanting: 'Teacher! Spy! Teacher! Spy! Teacher! Spy!'

Doyle glanced back over his shoulder at Alexia, stumbled and fell.

21

'Really *mhlekazi*, you must not worry. My brother he come back. All his life he come, he go, he come, he go. We used to this thing. We know the Lord Jesus bring him back safe.'

Yes, but when, Doyle wanted to know. When would the old man be returning to Ngagabhaleko? Why hadn't he let anyone in the village know where he had gone; how long he would be away? Why hadn't he got in touch, sent a message via the bush telegraph? Didn't he realise there were people who were concerned for his safety?

The questions were repeated endlessly over supper at Rebecca's – to which Doyle now found himself regularly invited. It was Rebecca's way of reassuring him that her brother was indeed safe. 'Any day he come, *mhlekazi*. He find you here, he happy. And the Lord he happy also. He watch over my brother, truly. He watch over all of us.'

She was also concerned for Doyle's health and tried to dissuade him from drinking so heavily. But the truth was her maternal ardour and religious certainty only unsettled him even further and drove him back to his hut, back to the solace of his whisky.

And so the days passed in a haze of heat and alcohol; the admonishing truth of his aunt's letter eventually succeeding in driving him out into the veld where he plunged down the steep and arid slopes of the burning hills and then had to crawl back up on his hands and knees, with the shrill ha-ha-ha of the *Hadeda* in his ears. He got caught in the summer storms; blundered into herds of grazing cattle; stumbled over ploughed fields where wide-horned oxen and their drivers stood panting in the middle of the quivering landscape – running and rippling in light-tripping waves, splashed with colour where the women spread their washing out on the banks of the river to dry. He could hear their laughter whenever he passed, could see their questioning glances. Once he came upon a small group of herdboys playing football and joined in. He didn't care whether or not he made a fool of himself. He had to see the joy on their faces, hear the insect-like whirr of their tiny legs as they leaped over the tufts of spiny grass. He had to share in their brief happiness because it was all there was until Abraham returned, to confirm the truth he already knew. The truth that was like a thunderclap echoing among the hills, a flash of lightning, around which gathered the dark clouds of unease . . .

Every day he hung about the old man's kraal. But the waiting was tearing him apart. Half of him wanted to read and re-read the letter, the other half to flee into the fields. Only the whisky was holding him together. But not even it could fully absorb the shock when, one afternoon, he arrived at the old man's kraal and found the buildings had been ransacked. Doors had been kicked off their hinges, windows smashed. Bits of furniture lay scattered and broken. In what seemed a futile gesture, a large water butt had been emptied over the remains of a disembowelled mattress.

His reaction as he entered the front hut and saw the old man's meagre possessions strewn upon the floor was a mixture of self-loathing and anger. He felt angry with himself, over all the time that he had wasted. It was as though in some way he was responsible for the destruction; could have prevented it. 'Hey! He's not a bladdy dog,' he could still hear Alexia shouting at the soldier who had harried the old man across the road back to the Kombi-taxi. He could have done something to help; at least got out of the car to protest.

He stooped and picked up a round commemorative plate from the floor. It was cracked and broke in his hands as he was examining it. For a brief moment he stared at the two halves – at the British royal family rudely separated - before hurling them across the room where they smashed like confetti against the wall.

Numbly he began to pick his way through the wreckage. Through his anger there filtered a deep sense of sadness. He put his hand in his pocket where he kept his aunt's letter. He knew nothing would be the same again. There would be no tranquil shrine to return to; no innocent games of dominoes on the bench in the doorway while ragged clouds sailed overhead and chickens nosed about the yard. The letter had seen to that – almost as much as the Security Branch whose work he assumed this act of vandalism to be – Mbanjwa's drag-net in operation. It was as though, indirectly, his aunt had helped them to kick in the door. 'God finds us all out in the end,' she had written. And if not God . . .? He had to admit Mbanjwa had come pretty close. Had he got his hands on the letter . . .? Here he paused, looking up anxiously. What if the kraal was being watched? If Mbanjwa's men were waiting outside? The letter posed a threat. Aside from an obvious interest in its contents, Mbanjwa would also want to know how he had come to receive it.

A brief search among the wrecked drawers revealed a box of matches. Doyle took the letter out of his pocket and set it alight, his hand trembling, though he was by now quite sober. He watched as the blue airmail paper slowly browned and curled round the edges, the yellow flame licking his fingers. He wondered how he would feel in the morning when he woke and found the letter missing. Maybe it would seem like a dream, like a storm that had passed overhead without breaking. How would he know, without visible proof, that it had reached him at all; had ever existed; was real? He looked round for somewhere to dispose of the ashes. The destruction of the old man's hut – wasn't that real? The shooting of Sister Mondo? What more did he want? How much longer could he keep the truth at bay?

He scattered the ashes over the torn lino and with their charred smell clinging to his hands continued to pick his way through the debris, righting a broken chair, gathering the old man's clothes in a crushed suitcase, rescuing an old photograph from its shattered frame. The photograph, of a young, robust woman in Victorian dress, lifted his spirits. She was staring directly at the camera, not entirely comfortable but unafraid and without any trace of shyness in her patient and conscientious gaze. Her hair was swept back from her forehead, exposing a broad, strong face. She did not smile. Even so there was a warmth in her cheeks and an unfussy air in the way she posed with her feet squashed into a pair of flat shoes. These were planted on either side of a bulging briefcase, her arms forming a modest V down her front. It was obvious she was waiting for the ordeal to be over; wanting to get on with things.

Hurriedly he pocketed the photograph, cast a final glance over the ransacked interior, then stepped out into the glare. He was about to make his way across the village to Rebecca when he heard his name being called: 'Mr Doyle! A moment please! Mr Doyle! Hello sir.'

He squinted up into the sun. An open umbrella loomed like a buzzard circling against the sky as the Reverend Xolile picked his way down the hill, scattering the small herd of village goats grazing on the fresh shoots brought about by the rain.

'I fear the days of Dlamini's residence are numbered,' said the tall figure in black, swooping down upon him. 'See how already the rain has dug a trench to his door?'

Doyle hung back in the shadow of the kraal.

'And all we have had so far I am told is a few drops.'

He ignored the Reverend's outstretched hand, eyeing him warily. He was surprised how much the Reverend seemed to have aged in the weeks he'd been away – attending a business management course in the Transvaal. His face appeared fatter, his eyes dull and yellowed. Sweat trickling down his greying temples left his skin stained like old blotting paper. There were lines around his mouth, a thin stubble creeping across his cheeks. Doyle could see something of Alexia – the bed-ridden Alexia – in this strangely demoralised figure whose suit was crumpled, cuffs unbuttoned and collar smudged.

'I was on my way to see Dlamini's sister,' the Reverend announced. 'As you know she is one of our longest serving parishioners and I am anxious to hear what she has to say about her brother's absence.'

Unable to avoid being gathered in like a chick under the umbrella's wing, Doyle thought he detected the smell of brandy on the Reverend's breath.

'Such fortitude,' the Reverend sighed, pulling a large, white handkerchief from his jacket pocket and dragging it across his brow. 'Our women put us all to shame, wouldn't you agree, Mr Doyle?'

Haggard, wistful eyes followed Doyle as he backed into the light, stumbling up against the wall of the hut. 'You sure it's Rebecca you wanted to see?' he asked, his voice catching in the dryness.

The Reverend Xolile began to mop his cheeks. 'I'm told Dlamini's sister has been looking after you. Is this true? You are a lucky man.'

'News travels,' said Doyle.

'In this case it did not have far to go. I have just come from the mission where my stewards have been filling me in on the things that have happened during my absence. That is how I heard Dlamini has disappeared. My niece tells me she saw him being beaten at an army road-block. Now I'm wondering whether he has been . . .'

'Detained? I didn't think you cared.'

The Reverend glanced at his dirt-stained handkerchief. 'You do me an injustice, Mr Doyle. Mr Dlamini and I have very different views on the way the struggle should be conducted. But I can assure you neither of us would like to see the other come to any harm. We are of the same flock and our destinies are linked.'

'Sure!' Doyle retorted with a unexpected vehemence. 'What about the guns you and your stewards dug up the other night? Did you think of the danger you might . . .?'

'I was afraid they would get you into trouble, Mr Doyle, through your association with Mr Dlamini.'

'And the old man? Didn't you think you might be endangering *him*?'

The Reverend tucked the handkerchief back into his pocket. 'Of course, but if you will forgive me for saying so, you are rather a novice in these matters whereas the old man knows better than anyone in the village how to survive. Believe me, he is a wily old fox.'

Doyle swung round, pointing to the front of the hut. 'Care to take a look inside the fox's lair, Reverend?'

The Reverend Xolile's puzzled gaze followed him to the door – hanging at a peculiar angle like a drunk trying to cross the threshold. Doyle waited while the umbrella was folded, then watched as the Reverend plunged into the wrecked interior. He did not follow.

Lurking near the doorway where he and Abraham had passed the cold winter afternoons drinking coffee and playing dominoes on the wooden bench that now lay smashed beyond repair, he listened to the Reverend's disconsolate sighs while his glance wandered to the top of the hill. A group of young children whom he had seen earlier outside the kraal were playing with an old bicycle wheel. He could hear the steel rim rattling over the sharp stones and the clack of their sticks as they steered it round and round in a monotonous circle. Their laughter sounded surprisingly faint. Perhaps it was because they were bored or the sound got swallowed up in the dongas. Maybe it was the dust. It reminded him of the crater of a smoking volcano . . .

'Is this how you found it?' the Reverend asked, raising his umbrella.

Doyle nodded.

'But not a single item has been left undamaged. Really such destruction is unnecessary. Our people are poor enough as it is. How could anyone hope to replace all . . .'

Doyle turned aside angrily. 'What the hell does it matter? The rains would have washed it to the bottom of the hill anyway, right?'

'No,' cried the Reverend, pinching his fingers as he tried to shut the broken door. 'Not like this. Mr Dlamini would have been able to rescue his belongings. Now he is left with nothing. Of course he is not a man who is very much concerned with worldly goods. He would hardly have lived in such a simple manner. But there are one or two items he has always treasured. I tried to look for them. Perhaps you saw them, Mr Doyle? The photograph of his deceased wife, her teaching diploma which she gained after being fired from her cleaning job in Durban; his own BA certificate. And, of course, the typewriter. Mr Dlamini did such a lot of work on that old machine. As you know he typed the school committee's minutes. He also frequently helped the church . . .'

'They've taken it,' said Doyle.

'They?'

'I think we know who *they* are, Reverend.'

The Reverend abandoned his fruitless attempt to close the sagging door. 'I'm sorry, but this is something of a shock to me. I can see you are angry. Then you will understand my own confusion. Really, I did not expect to find . . . But why did my stewards not inform me about this?'

'Shouldn't be too difficult to figure out.'

'Perhaps they are still unaware. Perhaps they have not yet seen the kraal. Could it be you are the first here?'

Doyle pointed to the band of children playing at the top of the hill. 'They were here when I arrived.'

'In that case the village already knows about it. But what reason could my stewards possibly have had for not letting me know? I wonder . . . It is possible they assembled very early in the morning at the mission in anticipation of my arrival and so the news has not yet reached them. Otherwise they would surely have informed me.'

'Unless they were trying to protect you.'

'I do not understand.'

'They don't want you feeling guilty.'

'Guilty?' exclaimed the Reverend, running his fingers round the inside of his collar. 'Forgive me, but what is it I have done?'

Doyle bent and picked up a stone. He flung it vigorously at a pair of long-haired goats that were advancing into the yard. 'The site where the guns are buried will tell you,' he said, the goats fixing their pained eyes on him. 'I think we ought to take another look.'

'Now?'

'Why not?'

'What do you hope to find?'

'The reason Abraham's kraal has been raided,' said Doyle as the goats continued to stare at him with sulky eyes.

'You believe the police have uncovered those weapons?'

'I believe someone's tipped them off.'

'But I only showed them to you, Mr Doyle.'

'And half a dozen stewards.'

'They are quite trustworthy.'

'All of them?'

'Each and every one.'

'Let's put them to the test then,' said Doyle, watching the animals turn quietly away, their heads bowed, the long strands of hair dragging through the dirt.

'I do not think that is necessary, Mr Doyle.'

'There's only one way to find out, Reverend.'

◇

They rested at the top of the hill; Doyle clearing the stale taste of dust and whisky from his throat; the Reverend dabbing the inside of his collar with his handkerchief. The children seemed to have mysteriously melted into the earth, leaving behind their spokeless wheel, spinning lazily on a flat stone. The air remained hot and sticky and the light, bouncing mercilessly off the stones, caused both men to screw up their eyes – the Reverend's dominated by a brace of crows' feet, imparting a weary, moribund air; Doyle's translucent northern features hardened by sunburn and lack of sleep.

The gaze of the two men followed the same arc: from the iron-roofed mission planted in the centre of the plain to the freshly greened slopes of the village below, where rows of mud bricks lay baking in the sun. The village was expanding, huts with their golden thatched roofs springing up overnight. For every kraal like Abraham's threatened by a storm, half a dozen new ones appeared. Soon the river would boast the population of a medium-sized town along its muddy banks.

In the distance the hills floated on waves conjured up by the heat. But while heaven and earth fused in this girdle of water, the Reverend – ignoring the small band of children whose bald heads popped up out of a nearby donga – gestured with his umbrella toward the slopes of an adjoining hill. 'That is the one, but I must warn you, Mr Doyle, it is farther away than it looks.'

The children's heads swivelled round, then swivelled back again. Doyle casually picked up their wheel. After a false start which elicited a few bewildered giggles, he set it rolling down the stony incline. With their wide eyes fastened on him he thought for a moment they were going to let it roll all the way down to the bottom on its own. But then a tiny figure dressed only in a pair of yellow briefs pulled her grubby fingers from her mouth and began to run after it. Soon the rest of the children were scrambling like ants out of the donga.

The Reverend said: 'It is very hot for walking.'

Doyle pointed to the shade afforded by the large umbrella.

'Actually it is not just the sun, Mr Doyle. The doctor says my heart is no longer as good as it used to be. I am not yet as old as your friend, Dlamini, but then he is a very unusual man. To live so long. And be so strong!'

'I don't mind going alone,' said Doyle.

The Reverend eyed him mournfully. 'It would not be good for you to be seen on your own near that place. If you promise to go slowly I shall accompany you, though on one condition. You see that mud building on the far side, the square one, where the zinc roof shines? It is one of our churches, just a small, local branch. The people that side are very poor. I would like to call in there on our way back. There is something I think may be of interest to you.'

22

Two hours later the Reverend, his hand waxen with sweat and trembling, pointed his umbrella through the trees. 'I believe that is what you expected to see, Mr Doyle.'

At first Doyle's gaze wandered aimlessly among the acacia thorntrees strung out like skeletons along the parched slopes below. But, as yet another herd of goats trawled the hoary branches for shoots, leaving behind tell-tale signs of snagged hair, he gradually began to pick out the camouflage uniforms hiding in the shadows. He counted three, four, then six and seven, before he spotted the shallow hole in a clearing surrounded by armed policemen.

Inside the hole two men, one dressed in a pair of football shorts, the other in rolled-up jeans, were wielding shovels. Both were lean and strong and the dark red soil reflected the rich texture of their skin suffused with sunlight. Back to back the two men slid the long-handled shovels into the earth while the policemen looked on; tense, pulsating figures in the watery haze.

Doyle scanned the trees surrounding the clearing and was startled to find in among the thorns swarms of children whom the police appeared to ignore. They made little noise in spite of their numbers, squatting bareheaded in the baking sun, a few with infants strapped to their backs so that from a distance their bulging eyes and humped postures reminded him of toads. The eyes and ears of the village, he wondered how much sense they made of it all – the two men digging among the thorntrees, the police, armed, watchful, ignoring the sweat streaming down their stony faces; the silent resignation of the two men, the smell of goats, of fresh soil and fear.

'If it's any consolation,' Doyle said, standing close enough to the Reverend to catch again the lingering smell of brandy, 'Christ couldn't rely on his stewards either.'

But the Reverend, whose stubborn expression betrayed an increasing vulnerability, remained adamant. 'No, Mr Doyle, this is not the work of my stewards. That even one could have done such a thing is unthinkable.'

'How can you be so sure?'

'I am sure. They would not contemplate such a terrible deed.'

'Not even for thirty pieces of silver?'

'They are all good men,' said the Reverend.

'Chosen by you?'

'They were elected by the Church membership.'

'Nominated by you?'

'Nominated by individual members, Mr Doyle.'

Doyle swatted a swarm of midges away with his hand. 'Democracy's no insurance against betrayal. Your stewards are all poor and poverty as everyone knows eats at a man's soul.'

'I assure you,' replied the exhausted figure, warding off the same swarm of midges with his umbrella, 'these men are all of the highest integrity.'

'Integrity!' Doyle exclaimed. 'Jesus. *Someone* tipped off the police. How else do you think . . .'

But as he fixed his hostile gaze on the Reverend, it suddenly dawned on him that that someone may have been none other than Alexia, acting, as it now seemed likely, without her uncle's knowledge. He realised it had been a mistake to show her his aunt's letter though by doing so he had hoped she would understand why any attempt to drive a wedge between himself and Abraham was bound to fail. Had he thought about it more carefully however, he would have recognised the danger, seen himself drifting further and further away from her, drawing closer instead to the old man . . . to the heart of the struggle.

Of course he could always deny having received the letter. But what would Alexia's reaction be? Or had she already told the Reverend the truth about their relationship? Perhaps that was why he had showed up at Abraham's kraal. Why else the urgency, the pretence that he had been on his way to Rebecca's? Why, in spite of his niéce's harrowing experience, no mention of her at all?

Doyle felt his arm being tugged. 'Come,' said the Reverend. 'It is futile to stand here guessing. Whoever is responsible will bear it on their conscience. Let me take you to our humble church.'

190

The small, wooden sign nailed to the front of the building read: Welcome to Sidi Lutheran Church Ngagabhaleko. Pastor: Rev. B. Xolile. As they ducked through the doorway bits of dried mud trickled to the floor.

It took a while for their eyes to adjust to the gloom. Doyle heard the Reverend set his umbrella down, pat his pockets in search of a match then, realising he hadn't brought any, utter a lugubrious sigh, before offering his sincerest apologies. But Doyle sensed the Reverend was rather relieved by the darkness for it helped to hide the deep lines of uncertainty in his face which the sun had so ruthlessly exposed.

Though the floor of the church had been recently smeared – Doyle had noticed a plastic bucket outside filled with copper-coloured water over which a blue dragonfly skimmed like a piece of porcelain – the smell of dung was offset by the fragrance of freshly cut reeds, used in the village to weave large circular mats. These now covered the floor, filling the interior with a pleasant lushness which helped to keep out the heat and at the same time preserve an air of vigour and fecundity.

The mats were springy underfoot and creaked as Doyle squeezed past the Reverend. He had only gone a few paces when he banged his shins against a bench and heard something roll on to the floor with a gentle thud. He bent to pick it up. It was a marrow, one of many he was astonished to discover, along with pumpkins, beetroots, squashes, maize and spinach, all carefully arranged in earthy pyramids half-a-dozen rows deep at the front of the church. There were straw baskets and tablecloths, a sprinkling of fresh leaves to decorate the walls and a flower-festooned pulpit in front of a plain wooden cross. In the corner stood a blackboard. Someone had written in large letters: 'The Lord welcome back Reverend Benedict Xolile after his long absence.'

Seeing a piece of chalk lying on the floor, Doyle picked it up, hastily rubbed out the Reverend's name and substituted 'Abraham Dlamini' followed by a large question mark. Tossing the chalk into an empty collection plate beside the board, he headed for the door.

'Mr Doyle,' cried the Reverend, moving rapidly to intercept him.

'Wait, you misunderstand me. I did not bring you all the way to show you . . . I was not even aware . . .'

But Doyle brushed aside the Reverend's outstretched arm. 'What does it prove? The church is subject to the same laws as the rest of us. Who's to say your stewards haven't betrayed you? They . . .'

'Please!' cried the Reverend, his hand hovering nervously like a bird above Doyle's shoulder, 'I did not bring you here to defend my church.'

'Of course not!' said Doyle sharply.

'No,' replied the Reverend, withdrawing his hand into the safety of his midriff, 'but if you will give me a minute to explain.'

Doyle flung the door back forcefully on its hinges. Once again mud spattered on to the floor.

The Reverend's voice seemed on the verge of breaking. 'Please, hear me out, Mr Doyle. I can understand your frustration. Mr Dlamini is a close friend and his absence is of great concern to you. But if you will allow me to . . .'

'Continue covering up for your stewards?'

'No, sir.'

'Then?'

The Reverend paused, took a deep breath. 'This has nothing to do with my stewards. I merely hoped that by bringing you here and showing you what the villagers are capable of producing under the most difficult circumstances, you might be encouraged to have a little more patience. Patience, Mr Doyle, that is the lesson the people of our church are offering you. It takes time to grow crops such as these. As you know the soil is very poor. It must be fed, nurtured like a baby. But with what? For there is no money to buy expensive fertilizers.'

'Expensive!' Doyle hovered in the pool of light by the door. 'You think patience is cheap? How many people in the village have died waiting for things to improve? Waiting for the church to come to their rescue? What has the church done for the poor in this country other than preach patience? How do you think things are going to improve? Who is going to improve them – the Boers? How many generations have gone to feed *that* Christian monster? Don't you think it's time people stopped waiting? Time they began to defend themselves? Tell me, Reverend, why is it the poor, the broken-in-spirit, who are always asked to be patient?'

The Reverend's face hardened in the light. 'Broken-in-spirit? I do not think so. What you see here in front of you represents the efforts of a determined people. The villagers would not have produced such crops had they given up hope. Few outsiders understand this. It is not what they expect of village life. To you the spirit of the village people may appear weak and fragile. Yet it survives. Now how is that . . .?'

Feeling the sun on his back as he held the door open, Doyle waited for the Reverend to continue. Patience? There had to be more – more to their gruelling walk up the long and sinuous path to the church, to the imploring voice. And that telling smell of brandy.

'The spirit of the village people survives, Mr Doyle, because here we do only what we know we can do. No one ploughs more than they can sow. Instead they study the land which has been allocated to them, whether by the Boers, their chief . . .'

'God?'

'Even God – and they say to themselves, now what can we do with this scorched piece of earth? Can we plant beans here to provide nitrogen and then follow with potatoes? Can we try pumpkins or spinach or shall we leave it fallow? How much water shall we need, how much manure? No one says: "If only I had that plot over there".'

'Maybe it's time they did,' said Doyle.

The Reverend frowned. 'No. That would break their resolve.'

'It would end their poverty.'

'There is no guarantee of that, Mr Doyle.'

'Least they would get their land back; break the stranglehold history has on them.'

'They will break it anyway.'

'But when?' cried Doyle waving his arms, allowing the door to swing shut behind him. 'How much longer do the people of Ngagabhaleko have to wait?'

'They themselves will decide. Believe me it is better you do not become involved. At least not in the manner you may be contemplating. That would be a terrible . . .'

The Reverend's voice trailed away in the dark and pungent interior.

193

Doyle said: 'So Alexia's told you?'

'She is concerned for your safety. We all are.'

'What exactly did she say?'

'She said that you received a letter from home.'

'Did she say how I got it?'

'She told me the police are intercepting your mail. And that Mr Dlamini ensured you received it. It is a worrying development.'

'Did she tell you what was in the letter?'

The Reverend hesitated. 'She . . . she explained how your father . . .'

'Go on,' said Doyle.

'. . . how he died here in Transkei fighting on the side of our people. She said that she was afraid you might try to emulate his noble gesture.'

'Noble?' Doyle's eyes narrowed. 'I don't think that's the word your niece could have used, Reverend.'

The tall figure bowed his head, resigned. 'It was indeed a noble gesture, Mr Doyle.'

Doyle hung back quietly in the dark.

But then as the door creaked behind them, the darkness split open like a gourd. A child with a large gap in her teeth put her head round the edge and whispered something to the Reverend in the vernacular before disappearing again.

The Reverend straightened his jacket. 'If you don't mind, Mr Doyle, I think we should take a minor precaution. I stress, it is only minor. But it is better to be safe rather than sorry in these matters. If you don't mind getting your trousers a little dirty, please, I ask you to crawl in under the pulpit. Fortunately it is dark in here and all this produce will help to conceal you.'

'From who?' said Doyle, alarmed, yet allowing the Reverend to steer him gently by the arm. 'Who is it I'm supposed to be hiding from?'

'The police,' said the Reverend, 'they have recovered the guns and are coming back this way.'

'To the church?'

'I understand their vans are parked nearby.'

'But why should they connect – Jesus, Reverend! What have your stewards been up to?'

The Reverend's grip on his arm tightened. 'This has nothing to do with the guns, Mr Doyle. Alexia told me you saw the police shoot a ward sister at the hospital. Your presence here, where there are no witnesses, may make them feel it is a perfect opportunity to prevent you from testifying should the matter ever come to court.'

'But surely you're a witness.'

'In Africa no black man is ever a witness. We are invisible.'

'But the police could come back tomorrow, next week or month . . .'

'You will be at school where you'll be safe.'

'Among children?'

'From now on,' said the Reverend, 'you should go nowhere alone.'

'You aren't just trying to scare me?' said Doyle, hesitating, before going down on his knees beside the pulpit – a makeshift affair knocked together with rough planks smelling of rats' urine, which was covered in a white linen tablecloth. 'You aren't still trying to frighten me into leaving?'

'It is not my intention to frighten you, Mr Doyle.'

'Though you'd prefer I left Ngagabhaleko. Alexia . . . our affair . . . it hasn't been easy on you . . .'

'Please.' The Reverend lifted the edge of the tablecloth.

Doyle looked up from his crouched position. 'I don't understand why you should go to all this trouble of protecting me. After all the embarrassment we must have . . .'

'Ssh!' whispered the Reverend, dropping the tablecloth over Doyle's head. 'They are here.'

◇

But the police whom the Reverend had prudently met outside, did not enter the church. It was clear from the brusque tone of the officer in charge that they were in a hurry to get back to their vehicles, though when they had gone the Reverend revealed that some of the children had boasted to them of the church's harvest and, not expecting to find anyone present, they had made this small detour in the hope of carrying off some of it for themselves.

Doyle crawled out from his hiding place. From behind a crack in the door he watched the policemen make their way along the contour of the hill, driving the two shirtless figures in front of them with the white gunny-sack slung from a pole which they supported on their shoulders. They marched swiftly, confidently, scattering the goats from their path. The children trickled by quietly in their wake, like the abandoned eggs of some serpentine monster. Soon they had rounded the bend and all that was left was the silence impaled upon the thorns.

'So!' a relieved Reverend Xolile exclaimed, adjusting the table-cloth over the pulpit. 'You think I wish you to leave Ngagabhaleko because of my niece?'

Doyle shrugged as he brushed the dirt from his knees.

'It would not be very professional of me, especially since our school finds it difficult to attract qualified teachers. Our children need you.'

'At any cost?'

'Surely, Mr Doyle, you have seen that for our people education is everything. It is the one way of escaping poverty, of preparing themselves for a better future. It is also a way of holding on to their self-respect.'

'Tell me Reverend,' said Doyle, aware that his clothes smelled of rat's urine, 'did Alexia tell you she lied when she said she'd slept with one of the *indunas*?'

The Reverend spread his broad hands out over the pulpit. 'She did not have to. It was obvious she was trying to protect you.'

'Not herself?'

'No,' the Reverend said firmly. 'That is not in her nature.'

'How long have you known . . . about us?'

'Oh . . .?' The Reverend's hands fluttered skywards. 'For quite some time now. In fact I even knew when she went behind my back to begin studying with you. But please . . .'

His voice once more sounded on the verge of breaking, causing Doyle to retreat uneasily in the dark. It was as if he were pulling on the strings of a kite and the further back he crept the higher it soared; it wasn't he that was in control, it controlled him, causing him to stagger up against the wall at the back of the church.

'. . . you must not think, Mr Doyle, that I have been playing some sort of game with you. The fact is my niece has been a very difficult person to live with and you have taken some of the burden off my shoulders. You will appreciate how angry she is at the world. Indeed she has felt that way ever since her parents . . . as she puts it,

196

"abandoned her for the struggle". Such a person is not easy to console. Nor does she wish to be regarded as just another casualty. What she wants is her own individual life to bear fruit.'

There was an uneasy silence as Doyle slunk between the empty rows of benches at the back where the floor lay uncovered and his shoes trod noiselessly on the smooth dung surface. The air was cool and damp; the darkness elastic. In front of him loomed the pyramids of soil-encrusted vegetables. Where was Alexia now to back him up? But then . . . would she? The silence was as harsh as the heat; even the crickets seemed stunned.

Then the reed mats creaked as the Reverend, abandoning the pulpit, shuffled slowly to a vacant bench near the door where a sliver of light was enough to drain his face and bleach his temples.

Doyle said: 'Has she told you she'll be unable to have any children?'

The Reverend's knuckles cracked alarmingly. 'On my return to the mission this morning my niece told me many things. It was the first time in all the years that she has been living with us that I was able to feel like a parent to her. Undoubtedly the experience she has recently suffered has brought her closer to the rest of the family. It helped her to confide in me not just as an uncle, but a father. It was in that spirit that I offered her the advice I did.'

'Advice?' said Doyle, the word creeping surreptitiously from his lips, like a caterpillar from a cabbage leaf. 'What advice did you give her?'

The Reverend turned his head away from the light. 'I don't know whether she has told you of an elder sister of hers . . .'

'Revival?'

'Alexia and Revival were very close. But after Revival ran away they did not see each other again. Well, just last week I managed to track her down in Atteridgeville, near Pretoria. I told her about Alexia and asked whether it might not be beneficial to all concerned if her younger sister came to live with her for a while.'

'Atteridgeville? It's not quite London or Paris is it? It's what she used to dream of . . . I don't know whether she still does. She hasn't been round for a while.'

'*Hayi*, no; but Revival has been very successful, Mr Doyle. She is married to a doctor. She has two children, both at school. She is

197

herself a trained physiotherapist. They have a house with plenty of rooms and a fine garden.'

'And she agreed to Alexia staying with them?'

For a moment the Reverend's eyes had to search the dark for him. 'Yes, she agreed.'

'It's a risk,' said Doyle, venturing slowly up the aisle. 'What if it doesn't work out?'

'I am confident,' said the Reverend, 'that Revival and her husband are fully qualified to deal with the situation. And I don't mean just clinically qualified. Those two have so much love. Everyone they meet is made to feel welcome and important. *Everyone.* Yet they are not religious. They are just full of the spirit of life. There are people like that in the townships you know. History has failed to crush them.'

'Have you spoken to Alexia about this? What about her exams? I know she's still studying because she sends her work over to me to mark.'

The Reverend, rising suddenly to his feet, seemed to sway, like a dead branch in the wind. Perhaps, Doyle thought to himself, a part of him had just died; the part he and Alexia had always regarded as hard and unbending – the clean-cut figure in expensive suits, the tall, elegant chairman of the school committee, regional representative of the Lutheran church, veteran of countless conferences, the Right Reverend Benedict Xolile. Yet behind the collar was a figure of bewildering modesty, a shepherd who didn't always know what was best for his flock; who, as it turned out, had no more answers than the rest of them.

'Perhaps,' the Reverend remarked, leaning unsteadily on his umbrella, 'it was wrong of me to think of my niece as a patient, because the love and the cheerful spirit of Revival is also in Alexia herself. It's true she has been reckless in the past. But this morning when I spoke to her I saw little of that recklessness. What I saw was a young woman – still a bit impatient and with a bold tongue – who has learnt from her suffering; who knows what it is like to make a sacrifice for others. She has loved and found herself rejected. Yet she is not angry or bitter. Nor has she given up all hope, though she has few illusions.'

'London? Paris? Weren't they illusions?'

The Reverend bowed his head in quiet surrender. It was, Doyle thought, as if the police had succeeded in plundering the church's harvest and left him alone in the desecrated interior; an old and broken man.

'Yes. And so, it seems, are Pretoria and Atteridgeville. You see I'm afraid Alexia is no longer in favour of the idea of leaving Ngagabhaleko. Yes, I know it is a complete turn around by her. But as for the reasons . . . well, it's true she is determined to write the examinations, though that is not her real reason for staying. The real reason I am not at liberty to say. I am under oath. However . . .'

The stooped figure looked up and then chortled unexpectedly. It was a sound that seemed to unlock others outside: the bleating of goats, and crickets, the bellow of a hungry ox followed by a woman's laughter and the far off cry of a herdboy, his whip shattering the dry air like glass.

'. . . I can reveal to you, Mr Doyle, that it is her birthday next weekend. And that we shall be giving her a party, to which you are of course invited. She will be twenty-one.'

Motioning for Doyle to follow, he turned to open the church door, adding: 'Maybe we shall also have a party for you one of these days. And a cake with just a few more candles.'

'A cake?' said Doyle, struggling to clear his throat.

'But of course, you are still young,' beamed the Reverend, as they stepped out – not into the glare but into the purple glow of an evening that had stolen unexpectedly upon them; 'which means that you will be able to give me a hand so that I may make it back to the mission in time for the special service we are holding for my niece, and others who are recovering from illness, though I fear it shall be dark by the time we reach there.'

23

He is the seed.
He is the sun.
He is the rain.
The man from Northern Ireland.

He tolerate any abusive speeches without punishment.
He never beats the students.
He just sighs at the foolish ones.
The man from Northern Ireland.

We thank God who bring him here.
God has reasons.
God he also care for
The man from Northern Ireland.

It was late at night. A heavy fog rolled over the village while it slept. The faint sound of thunder rumbling in the distance marked the tail-end of the storm which had struck earlier that afternoon, bringing welcome relief from the heat – at a price. For struck by lightning, a kraal had gone up in flames, leaving two children and their grandmother dead. For hours the family's anguished screams could be heard above the crashing of the rain, ending only once the rain had abated and they had fled in a state of shock to relatives in a nearby village.

Alone in his hut, which was lit by a single candle on the table beside him, Doyle ploughed remorselessly through a pile of exam scripts, the dull routine filling in the hours left empty by Alexia's withdrawal and the continued absence of Abraham Dlamini . . .

Even as the candle shrank and the temperature outside began to drop, silencing the chorus of frogs, he persevered . . . 'the life of an ox', Alexia had called it . . . 'always ploughing the same furrow'. If only it were true. If only he could go back . . . back to . . .

Mazeppa's just a name now,
A memory beached upon the yellow sand
Of a young man's heart.

Mazeppa's just a song now,
A scratched record in an old fifties juke-box
playing . . .

Doyle's red pen hovered over the page. There were no marks for faultless handwriting. Overriding the examiner's instructions – an all too common complaint – would incur stringent penalties in the final.

. . . in a deserted shebeen.

Mazeppa's just an artefact,
A broken, joyless piece . . .

He had not spoken to Alexia since Majogo's arrest. Only that morning she had left with the Reverend for the christening of one of his grandchildren in Johannesburg and something told him that she would not return. Despite reassurances that arrangements for his niece's birthday party were going ahead and that he would not allow anything to delay their getting back to the village in time for it, Doyle had seen in the Reverend's chastened expression the hope that, having been reunited with her sister, Alexia would decide to remain behind in the city, forging a new life for herself under Revival's filial eye. *Revival!* The chance seemed too good to be missed. And yet . . .

A broken, joyless piece in the hands
of a common thief.

Doyle's pen slid viciously across the page. He was running out of scripts, running out of candle. Already he was down to his last.

He turned suddenly as the pale orange flame flickered in a draught and saw a young child, wrapped in a blanket, standing in the doorway. The child's eyes were dull and heavy with sleep. It made no attempt to speak, merely holding out its fist from which Doyle rescued a warm and sticky bit of paper wrapped around a tiny object. The object turned out to be a domino – the double six! It brought a modest smile to his lips, though as soon as the child had slipped away he hurriedly pulled on his sandals and raced outside.

The note asked him to wait in a donga beside an abandoned kraal. As he crouched, alone and shivering in the fog, listening to the muted sounds from the village, he found himself fingering the innocuous piece of wood as though it were a secret talisman or . . . rosary. He even caught himself mumbling a *Hail Mary, Mother of God*, which was brought to an abrupt end by a rush of wet earth as someone leapt into the donga behind him. He shot to his feet.

'No! Don't turn round, *mhlekazi*. It is better you don't know who we are.'

The voice, a boy's rather than a man's, carried a hint of desperation which surprised him. Maybe it was someone he'd recognise. Someone he knew. It might be one of his own pupils. At least they hadn't given themselves away by addressing him as '*titsha*'.

'If you will just follow this donga to the foot of the hill and wait there. We will meet you again. We will go stage by stage so that nobody may see us together.'

'Where are we going?' Doyle asked.

'*Hayi, mhlekazi*, it is better you know nothing.'

'But . . .'

'Please, you must trust us.' The voice sounded hurt.

Doyle paused, thoughtfully rolling the domino over in his hand. His heart beating furiously against his chest, he set off finally along the bottom of the donga. There was no time for second thoughts, for thinking about pulling out. The fuse was lit.

The stages of his journey varied in length. Some lasted a few minutes, others ten or fifteen. At the end of each – marked either by a termite mound, a solitary thornbush or ravine – he was met and told where to head for next. After numerous detours and seemingly endless descents into ever deeper and deeper valleys, all in the grip of the irrepressible fog, he inevitably lost his sense of direction. In fact he was no longer even sure that those who led him to the door of an isolated hut were the same youths who had met him in the donga, or that his escort wasn't alone, for he had heard no sound between them, and once, when he had got lost, it had taken a while for him to be located.

He was left outside the hut, a semi-derelict building whose gouged walls suggested the presence of cattle resting in its shade during the day. He knocked softly. There was no reply. Bending down he squeezed the double-six under a crack and knocked again. This time it was opened by Abraham Dlamini who laughed. 'So, you are learning. It's good to do these things with a sense of humour. Otherwise . . .' He swept his kierie round to indicate the hut's bleak interior, 'one may end up in a cell much worse than this.'

The hut was bare. Old thatch dangled from the rafters which had been torn loose in the wind leaving mud blocks teetering overhead. Some had already crashed to the ground and lay split open like dried cheeses. Abraham had used these to encircle a fire which burned feebly at the back. He tipped a block over with his boot and motioned Doyle to sit down.

'At least we have the luxury of some coffee,' he said, pointing eagerly to the water heating in a smoke-blackened billycan.

Doyle, whose clothes were damp, started to chivvy up the fire.

Abraham produced a tiny envelope of instant coffee. 'Your aunt's letter must have come as a great shock to you, my friend,' he said, grinning broadly. 'Just imagine, when I saw that road-block, I was seriously thinking of getting rid of it!'

As the warmth from the fire gradually stole through his clothes, Doyle looked up into the old man's sanguine face. 'You took a risk. If it had been a *police* road-block . . .?'

'It was worth it, don't you think?' said Abraham, tapping him lightly on the knee with his kierie. 'Besides, I am sure you would have done the same for me.'

'Would I?' said Doyle.

'Of course!'

Doyle gripped the end of the kierie. 'I saw what the Security Police did to your kraal. And to the pupils at school. They were whipping the kids in the playground. I wanted to stop them, but I was too drunk. Yet the only way I would have been able to stop them was by being drunk.'

'There is nothing unusual in that. You have seen for yourself how even in a place like Ngagabhaleko the number of shebeens is growing. For some people it is the only way of shouldering the burden. We cannot all be fighters, the . . . how do you call them . . . death or glory boys?'

'I'm afraid I made a fool of myself.'

'But you wanted to stop the police, didn't you? The last time we spoke you talked only of leaving Ngagabhaleko. So you see, it was worth it.'

Doyle shamefully let go of the stick. 'You're too old for all of this, Abraham. You should let the younger ones take the risks.'

'*Hayi*. It is the old who have the least to lose, *mhlekazi*. For younger people such as yourself the price is much higher if you are caught.'

'The old don't fight,' said Doyle, rubbing the smoke from his eyes. 'They retire to the village, where they make up for the time they missed with their children by spending it with their grandchildren.'

Abraham pointed to the water, which was beginning to boil. 'The old may fight, my friend, provided they have sons of their own in the front line in order to make them more cautious.'

'How many do you have?' asked Doyle, pouring the water into two empty baked bean tins. 'How many sons do you have in the front line?'

Abraham set his kierie down on the floor beside him. Stretching out his bent hands, he warmed them over the steam rising from his coffee. He wore his greatcoat over a pair of khaki overalls with a woollen balaclava pulled down over his ears. The greatcoat was unbuttoned and his boots were without laces. Although his face shone boldly, like a brass rubbing in the glow of the fire, he could not hide the sudden air of dejection that came over him, the lonely and disconsolate air, Doyle thought, of an army deserter who, too late, regretted having abandoned his unit. Yet there was no trace of self pity in the old man's voice as he whispered through scalding mouthfuls of coffee.

'I had three sons, *mhlekazi*; two of them big and strong, who worked on the mines; one thin, like you, who was very brave. I lost all three. Some will say it was not my fault. The young are sometimes careless. But I was their father. And to lose three of ones own children in . . . in . . .' He broke off, swearing as he burnt his fingers on the tin mug.

'You lost all three in the struggle?'

Abraham rubbed the tips of his fingers ruefully. 'The struggle? Yes I suppose we call it that, just as they call it "the troubles" in your country, am I right?'

He looked up and Doyle saw that in spite of the heat of the fire, his eyes were cold and hard.

'. . . You see it is a way of compartmentalising ones pain, shunting it to the side so that one may carry on with what is normal, with what the authorities want the people to think is normal.'

'I . . . I'm . . . sorry,' Doyle stammered, 'I didn't mean it to sound like that. I suppose I must have said a lot of things over the year which hurt you. I didn't realise. You never mentioned your sons. You always seemed so . . . so relaxed, playing dominoes and drinking coffee, sometimes teasing Rebecca. I've never understood how the people in this country could hide so much pain. You never really see it. They show no obvious signs, everyone behaves with such restraint, such incredible dignity. Where's the anger? Why doesn't it come out? Surely you can't go on hiding it?'

Carefully tilting the tin in his hand Abraham poured some of the coffee on to the fire, dousing the flames which Doyle had allowed to flare up over the protective barrier of mud bricks.

'No *mhlekazi*,' he sighed through the steam, 'we cannot afford it. There would be too many deaths to wallow in. People would become cold and indifferent.'

'Dignity has its price too,' said Doyle, huddling closer to the warmed bricks. 'Dignity and patience. They are the two pillars which so much suffering in this country rests on. Every morning at school I take the register and find myself calling out names like Faith, Beauty, Sweetness, and Promise. You keep turning the other cheek, Abraham, and more of your people will die.'

Abraham pulled the greatcoat round his bulky frame. 'Yes that is also true. And I will admit that recently I lost another son. Well, strictly speaking not my own. But of course in traditional society a boy may have many fathers and I was one of the fathers to this young man. He was about your age.'

Doyle poured some of his own coffee out on to the fire.

'You saw him,' said Abraham.

'Here, in the village?'

'At St Augustine's. He was the man the police shot.'

'But I thought he escaped. They shot the nurse, Sister Mondo . . . fell from the verandah right in front of the pick-up. I can remember I wanted to get the hell out, but there was Promise screaming, terrified, and Mbanjwa, who earlier had offered to drive me to my father's grave, losing control of his men; there was no telling who they'd shoot at next. And then Alexia . . . she'd just had a . . . Jesus! I wasn't sure what had happened. Everything that night was so . . .'

'*Mhlekazi*?'

Doyle looked up from the fire where the image of Sister Mondo flickered sinisterly in the flames, her blue tunic bulging at the hips, her kepi awry, revealing the grey, almost white hair as she flung herself in front of the raised rifle shouting: 'No, you can't do this! We are a hospital.'

'*Mhlekazi*,' Abraham whispered urgently, 'just answer me this question: if you had had a choice, would you have preferred not to have received the letter from your aunt?'

'I don't understand.'

'Well, correct me if I am wrong, but I think it has gone some way to restoring your faith in life, has it not?'

'What's that got to do with the man who died, or Sister Mondo?'

'Their deaths are not the reason you have decided to throw your lot in with us?'

'Let's just say I've recovered my original script, Abraham.'

'Ones script can never be wholly original, *mhlekazi*.'

'Well, at least I no longer need to feel ashamed over the parts I've inherited.'

'Ah, that is what I hoped to hear!' exclaimed Abraham, raising his tin like a champagne glass in the air. 'It means Mbutu's death was not in vain.'

'Mbutu?'

'He was the clerk at the GPO who intercepted your letter when it was headed for the Security Branch. Unfortunately someone saw him do it and tried to blackmail him. The blackmailer even went to Mbutu's house to tell his wife. You can understand, a woman with a fine house in the town, five children and a husband with a steady job. She did not want Mbutu to jeopardise all that. Not for . . .'

'A white man?'

'For any man.'

'Why didn't Mbutu try to get the money from me?'

Abraham ran his tongue along his teeth as though trying to get rid of the taste of the bitter, black coffee. 'Mbutu knew the man wasn't really after the money. He wanted his wife. His wife had once been the blackmailer's girlfriend, but then she left him to marry Mbutu. So it was an old score that was being settled.'

Doyle shifted uncomfortably on the hard block. 'You're saying that to make me feel better.'

'Indeed not. Mbutu understood the situation he was in. Unlike yourself he was not a reluctant playwright. He took the responsibility for his own script. And now that you have made the same decision there is no need for you to feel guilty.'

'It might have ended differently.'

'If you had paid the money, you mean? No, *mhlekazi*. The blackmailer was the part written into Mbutu's script which he did not have any control over. He accepted it with humility.'

'We could have got rid of him,' said Doyle.

'You mean killed him?'

'If that was the only way.'

Abraham growled as he shifted the phlegm in his throat. Emptying the remains of his coffee over the fire, which hissed and crackled as the drops skidded like mercury over the glowing coals, he tucked his chin into the depths of his greatcoat and appeared to fall into a deep reverie. It was only broken when a live coal exploded and sent sparks pinging against the tin mug dangling from his hand. When he spoke again his voice was dry and cracked, like charcoal. 'The solutions to life's problems, *mhlekazi*, do not lie in death. When the blackmailer realised Mbutu would not give in he tipped off the police. But did he gain the woman he desired? The following morning she herself shot him. Now he is badly wounded and she is in hiding.'

Doyle turned his head away from the fire to stare at the shadows flickering on the wall around them. He now saw that the fire was his own life and now that it had been rekindled it was impossible to ignore the shadows it threw up; the shadows of those like Mbutu and his wife whom he had never known, or his father whom he had seriously misjudged . . . Alexia, misused . . . the Reverend distrusted. He had to fight down the urge to throw the rest of his coffee over the flames, to try and bring the shadows under some sort of control. But control was impossible. One could not enjoy the fire without the ghostly presence of the shadows . . . his mother suffering the instinctive urge to cocoon her only child from the world . . . Sister

Mondo attempting to shield her patient from the policeman's bullets . . . Promise cradling her friend's head in her lap . . . All unselfish actors who gave themselves up into the hands of the playwright, yet without losing any of their dignity. It was this 'submission', this self-sacrifice, that lay at the heart of their nobility. In Africa it was true the elements – the land, the sea, the mountains – were the stars of the show. But that Africa was a show for Europeans, imagined by Europeans. The *real* stars, Doyle knew, were the shadows in the background . . . like the youth, or youths, who had earlier led him through the fog to Abraham; the tiny child clutching the piece of paper with the domino in its hand, who might once have been himself, sent under the Brits' noses with a message from his father to sheltering Provos.

◇

'*Mhlekazi?*'

Doyle gave a start as Abraham nudged him gently with his kierie.

'I have some other news, concerning a certain young man.'

Doyle saw the heavy creases in the old man's skin lighten, like sand that had just been washed by the tide. Rejuvenated, crab-like eyes popped out of their shell.

Doyle said: 'It wouldn't be Majogo would it?'

And the eyes swivelled round with delight. 'You need no longer worry about the organ-grinder, my friend.'

'There wasn't one?'

'Oh but there was, though it wasn't the person you suspected, namely the Reverend Benedict Xolile.'

'I've changed my mind about the Reverend,' Doyle confessed.

'I'm glad to hear it. You were always a little hard on him. Perhaps it was your anti-clerical nature. Or else you were afraid that he would find out about you and . . .'

'He already knows.'

'Ah! That is good.'

Doyle leaned back in surprise. 'What do you mean, *good?*'

Abraham's coal-scuttle laugh seemed to make the bricks around the fire vibrate.

'Now, now, *mhlekazi*, there's no need to be alarmed. I only meant . . .' He paused, glancing at his watch. 'I'm sorry, I shouldn't

208

have made any comment. It's none of my business. Besides it's getting late and there is still something I must discuss with you.'

'The organ-grinder,' Doyle reminded him. And found he wasn't surprised when Abraham revealed that it was the Security Branch who had set up the boycott, though when the old man had finished he was forced to brandish his kierie in front of him like a schoolmaster trying to restrain an unruly pupil.

'But what the hell were they after? Surely they weren't trying to close the school down, were they? They must have known they'd have a real riot on their hands. Maybe that's what they wanted. Jesus I should have guessed it. I mean . . . a boycott! It was almost a give-away. It was totally out of keeping with . . . But why would they want . . .?'

'They were after you, *mhlekazi*. They used Majogo as the bait.'

'Why me?'

'Because they couldn't believe that anyone would voluntarily come to such a remote place as this. There had to be an ulterior motive. Then when they dug into your past and discovered your father's involvement, well, they were certain of two things: either you would lead them on to something much bigger via Majogo – you would of course be appalled at the boy's amateur display and so would try to organise something more professional – or they would be able to limit any damage you might cause by leading you up this . . . cul de sac, so to speak.'

'What happens now that they've taken Majogo away?'

'It means they have changed their mind about you. You are not the man they at first suspected. It is excellent, *mhlekazi*, you have given us the perfect cover.'

'You knew about this all along?'

'Nothing concrete, but we had our suspicions. Like you, we knew the boycott was out of keeping with the character of our children.'

'Then why didn't you tell me? Or the school committee? All that agonising, over whether or not to expel the boys, for nothing.'

Abraham averted his eyes as a feather of smoke drifted towards him out of the dwindling fire. 'To be honest, it served our own purposes. It allowed us to see how you would react to Majogo. After all we too are wary of liberal heroes. But more importantly, with the police distracted by you it gave us the opportunity to get on with our own business.'

'Smuggling arms?'

'If you are referring to those the police recently took away, well we had to give them something to keep them happy. And besides, such distractions are useful. I believe you too, *mhlekazi*, were dragged out one night to see them.'

Doyle huddled over the shrinking fire. 'I thought the Reverend was trying to frighten me away from his niece. Turned out he was warning me about you.'

Once more the old man's craggy face seemed to light up. 'Ah well, the Reverend is an honest man. He might seem a little ambitious to you at times, but in these rural parts a minister is expected to be well dressed, exemplary in his behaviour, a sort of ambassador for the area. If he walks anywhere his parishioners buy him a bicycle. If he cycles they buy him a vehicle. He is a man they want to look up to.'

It was Doyle this time who looked at his watch. The fire was almost dead and the cold was beginning to creep up through the dung floor. He said: 'So distracting the police gave you the opportunity to get on with something else.'

'Explosives, *mhlekazi*. For a long time we have been ferrying explosives across the country.'

'Mines?'

'You mean like the one that killed your father? Yes, we have carried many landmines also.'

Doyle smoothed over the ashes of the fire with the bottom of the tin and said painfully, 'If only I'd known. If only all those years ago I had known . . . It isn't only the people of Ngagabhaleko who need someone like the Reverend to look up to. We all do. To a child, a boy, a father is the closest hero. But if he's lost before the boy has had a chance to grow up then he loses the will to fight for what is right. The child ends up, like Alexia, like myself, fighting for no one, trusting no one . . . Alone, we fight for survival . . . the barest minimum. I suppose it's no surprise we drifted together. We're two of a kind. But then it was just as inevitable we'd end up on our own again . . .'

'*Mhlekazi*,' said Abraham, resting a warm hand on his shoulder, 'you are no longer alone. Together there is a lot we can still do – must do. Time is short. Now there are some few mines we need to shift. We need to do it before the children return to school.'

Doyle gave a shudder as the cold continued to seep up from the floor. 'What has school got to do with it?'

'Well, you see these things arrived rather unexpectedly and with all the police running around we thought the safest place, which was also the emptiest, would be the old church. Obviously we must get them away before the pupils return after their short break.'

'To where?' asked Doyle, feeling the urgency in the old man's fingers tightening round his shoulder, drawing him in.

'To Bala.'

'When?'

'This coming Saturday.'

'It's Alexia's birthday.'

'Yes, it is another useful distraction. If you agree to help us, you will receive a message from the hospital to come and collect the body of Nomanthando. The girl died yesterday. I'm sorry, *mhlekazi*, I should have told you.'

'Jesus.'

'Nurse Fumba will give you a letter of authorisation. There will be a coffin to carry. Fortunately the girl's family have not objected . . .'

A quiet almost imperceptible knock at the door saw Abraham struggle to his feet. There was no light in the hut now that the fire was out, but Doyle, holding his breath, heard him shuffle across the floor, grunt as he stooped, then return to the fireplace where he dropped a second domino in Doyle's hand. With another of his eccentric chuckles he opened the door.

Following a brief conversation outside, of which Doyle could only just make out the words Bala and *isibedlele*, Abraham returned to the back of the hut, plodding doggedly on his kierie. He shoved out a hand and pulled Doyle up cheerfully by the front of his shirt. 'Well, now your chance has come, my friend. Our people in Bala have acknowledged they are ready to receive the mines. All we need to do is give you the rest of the details. But remember . . .' he paused, gripping Doyle tightly by his shirt, 'you are taking a risk.'

Doyle held up the domino which Abraham had handed to him in the dark. It was another double-six.

'It is the same risk which claimed your father's life,' said Abraham.

Doyle slipped the piece into his pocket. 'And the lives of many others,' he said.

'Yes, and many others,' Abraham sighed, scattering the ashes of the cold fire with his kierie.

24

It seemed only moments before he had been watching the sun drop below the distant hills and yet already a blue-black sky reflected the lines etched deep in his face as he stared out of the mission house window. The hollows of his eyes were illuminated by the flickering light of decorative candles which earlier in the day had adorned Alexia's birthday cake but now were gathered on the window sill shedding petals of green and blue and yellow wax into a china bowl.

He was alone in the room. Most of the guests had left or were in the process of leaving; the rustle of cotton and crimplene fading into the back yard where children ran among the barking dogs and fires subsided beneath large three-legged pots that stood empty. From the kitchen looking out on to the yard came the sounds of crockery clanging against the sides of an enamel washbasin, of plates being packed away in bags and cardboard boxes – much of it having being borrowed – of glass tumblers rattling on a metal tray, an explosion of cutlery scattered over the lino floor followed by shrieks of laughter. In the passage outside a child was singing quietly to herself, her wistful melody drifting in and out among the noisy farewells; the countless conversations being conducted through windows and across the veld where the rattle of the Reverend's car marked the bumpy progress of a group of elders who were being ferried home.

In the bruised and tender silence separating the front of the house from the back, Doyle found himself listening out for Alexia, anticipating yet dreading the approach of her languid footsteps. He knew he owed her an apology – more – he owed her much more! She had the right to demand anything of him and he had no right to refuse. And yet he knew he would refuse because he owed even more to those shadowy figures thrown up on to the wall by the fire, those same unselfish actors who had perished, unnoticed, on the stage . . . Mbutu, Nomanthando, Sister Mondo . . .

This was not an excuse, an attempt to wash his hands of her. On the contrary, he now felt increasingly drawn to her. How proud and stunning she had looked in her long African robe, its red, green and gold flashes sweeping down over her right shoulder; on the left her hair gathered in an ornate cone, sparkling with ribbons and beads, offsetting the natural beauty of her face, its scarless purity.

Entering the crowded room where the curtains had been drawn so that the decorated cake glistened like freshly fallen snow in the candlelight, she had briefly closed her eyes as though offering a short prayer of thanks – a prodigal child not only forgiven but applauded for her courage, her breathtaking elegance, above all for bringing a touch of glamour to their lives.

Moments later, with the candles extinguished and the curtains drawn back, forcing the elders to screw up their faces, it seemed to Doyle that she sank the long-bladed knife into the cake with a strange diffidence, the heavy fruit clogging the silver blade which became unwieldy, and that she shamefully lowered her head as though the broken icing were an omen, a sign of impending misfortune . . . If only, he had felt, watching her clumsily slide her finger along the blade to clean it, she could return to that evocative world of 'Mazeppa'. If only they could both return and start again, rubbing out their lines, their onerous script, like the tide rubbing out their footprints in the sand. If only they could wake again and find they had the beach all to themselves . . . drive back together to Ngagabhaleko, arguing over the merits of Desdemona's slavish love for Othello; over the Moor's weakness which had cost her her life.

Perhaps they could still return. Perhaps she would write her finals and they would celebrate her passing by going back to the same ramshackle hotel. Or was that too much to ask? Mazeppa . . . *'just an artefact, a broken, joyless piece in the hands of a common thief'* . . .?

The answer lay in the deep lines in his face reflected in the window. For the lines evoked an even more pressing anxiety. In fact he had been staring at two faces, the one hidden and obscure, like a painting concealed beneath a later work on the same canvas; the other more immediate and easily recognisable – revealing his concern over Abraham's failure to contact him. He had received no message from the clinic, had had no call to collect Nomanthando's body from the hospital, no confirmation that the mines had been transferred to the coffin in the back of the pick-up parked outside the school building

. . . Staring through the candle-lit window Doyle waited, as he had waited anxiously all day for Abraham's signal.

Outside, the yard lay deserted. The laughter in the kitchen had subsided, a weary silence beginning to steal through the house. The child in the passage scrambled to her feet gathering together the paper wrappings she had been carefully folding. Her melody grew pensive. As it faded into the belly of the house the buzz of crickets advanced on to the porch.

In the china bowl on the windowsill the tiny candles threw out their last fitful light. One by one the shrunken wicks sank into the molten pool of wax. Emitting a faint smell of paraffin the wax moulded itself round the inside of the bowl which glowed snugly, spreading its warmth across the base of the window. Doyle traced his finger lightly over the glass. Suddenly it seemed to twist and melt in front of his eyes, becoming a buckling, crackling inferno with long flames scorching the night sky. He flung the window open and realised he was watching the school burning.

'Titsha! Titsha!' A posse of children came running through the front gate.

Dashing out on to the porch Doyle immediately hid behind a pillar as a squad of police vehicles raced past the mission. They did not stop at the school however but sped on down the hill to the village like sparks thrown out by the fire. Sprinting through the dust thrown up by their tyres, Doyle arrived at the school yard to find Alexia waiting in the shadows.

He brushed past her, jerking open the door of the pick-up. He cursed as he failed to find the keys, then releasing the handbrake began pushing the vehicle across the yard away from the flames, startling those villagers who had come running to help by ordering them to remain outside the perimeter fence.

Finally he pulled violently on the handbrake and jumped into the back of the pick-up. Holding up the coffin lid with one hand he probed the false bottom with the other. It was empty! He banged the lid down angrily, leapt over the tailboard and ran back across the yard. Ducking through the entrance he heard a voice call out after him. 'Doyle wait! It's too dangerous!' It was Alexia and they were the first words she had spoken to him since the day of Majogo's arrest.

Without replying he darted up the main aisle and found to his horror that the derelict pulpit was surrounded by burning debris. A fallen rafter with a length of corrugated-iron roofing still attached to it lay across the top of the front row of desks along which the fire was rapidly spreading, throwing up balls of smoke that bounced off the inside of the mud walls – they at least would not burn and gave him time to think, time, he realised, already wasted pushing the pick-up harmlessly out of the way. It was a move he now regretted because he had nowhere to hide the mines and would have to transport them across the yard in full view of the villagers. But first he had to salvage them, clear the area around the pulpit.

'Doyle are you mad, do you want to be killed?'

He peered through the billowing smoke and saw Alexia crouching in the doorway.

'Go away!' he shouted, kicking the burning rafter from the desks so that it crashed to the floor, the corrugated-iron slicing through the layers of dried dung.

'What are you doing?' Alexia yelled at him. 'You are spreading the fire.'

'Jesus, will you go away!' he shouted again and began manoeuvring the blazing desks out of his way, the scalding metal blistering his hands.

Alexia kicked the door impulsively. 'Don't be a fool, Doyle. Get out now. There isn't time.'

'For what?' he grunted as he put his shoulder to the pulpit and strained to shift it clear of the large hole it covered.

'You will be blown to pieces!'

Doyle paused . . . choking on the thickening smoke. Then, incensed, he rammed his shoulder against the side of the pulpit and sent it toppling.

'How much do you know, Alexia?' he bellowed. 'How much do you bloody well know?'

Alexia screamed as a desk near her burst into flames. 'Doyle, please, you must come away. It is useless. You can't do anything now. The fire is too big.'

Doyle fell to his knees and sweeping aside the burning debris – a class geography project on rural pollution stinking of rubber and disintegrating plastic, piles of charred exercise books, fragments from the roof – he began scooping out the soil from the uncovered hole.

Soon the sweat shimmered down his neck, slithered and shone in the rancid soil. It was a race to get to the mines before the fire did, before the roof collapsed and blew up the building; a race he dare not lose. And yet he found himself driven less by the fear of the impending explosion than by the police presence in the village. For there had to be a link between the two, even if they had ignored the fire, gone racing down the hill. They would be back. He knew they would be back. For someone had . . .

'Alexia!' he barked. 'Was it you? Did you tell the police?'

Just then he caught sight of a piece of sacking and began feverishly to scrape away the soil. By now his fingers were black with dirt and ash. He breathed in the hot smoke, the stench of rubber, tasted it, wiped it across his face, into his eyes; his throat was rough and dry. Whenever he swallowed he heard his ears pop.

'Quick! Shift up. I will help you. Hurry or you will get us killed.'

Doyle found himself being elbowed aside by a grim-faced Alexia who, slipping an envelope out from under her robe, dropped it on the ground in front of him and began clearing away the loose soil while he stared at her.

'Read it,' she hissed.

Doyle's blackened fingers left clear prints on the white envelope as he tore it open. 'It's a birthday card.'

'Read it!'

'It's in Xhosa.'

'The signature you fool. See who it's from.'

'It's . . .' he coughed as the smoke gripped his throat. 'It's from the colonel.'

Alexia's eyes flared as a bundle of papers nearby caught fire. 'The colonel warned *me*, Doyle, not the other way round. He says in his message the police received information from sources elsewhere in the country about explosives in Ngagabhaleko. He warns there will be a raid.'

Doyle stared at his blackened prints on the pink card where the silver key embossed on the front sparkled with a fresh innocence in the glow of the fire.

'I did not blackmail him,' Alexia volunteered.

'Then why . . .'

'Because he says he suspects you are involved.'

217

'You mean he was trying to warn *me*?'

Alexia winced at the crack of a rafter snapping in two, the red candescent arms pivoting round like the hands of an illuminated clock. A sheet of corrugated-iron tore loose and plunged toward them, snagging at the last minute inches above their heads. Her robe now dull with ash, she continued to dig out the soil with her bare hands.

'No, Doyle, it was not the colonel's intention to warn you. He did it because he wishes to trap me. He knew I would inform you of the raid. That way he could say that I was involved in these guerrilla activities with you and so instead of me blackmailing him, he could blackmail me. He could threaten to have me arrested as an accomplice if I told anyone what he had done to Revival when she was young.'

Doyle stared as if hypnotised at the sugar-brown sacking appearing beneath her fingers.

'We are lucky, Doyle, that the colonel is no friend of the Security Branch. Otherwise he might not have chosen this moment to act as he did. But it will all come to nothing if we are still here when the police return. Then we shall be caught red-handed.'

Alexia quickly brushed away the last of the soil, found the mouth of the sack and lightly unfolded it. 'I saw the police when they came rushing past. I suggested to Mbanjwa that he search a certain kraal in the village which has been abandoned for some time. I wasn't sure whether he would believe me. But when I told him things were no longer the same between us and therefore I had no reason to protect you, he seemed satisfied.'

Doyle's mouth was dry. His tongue seemed to swell and flounder against his lips. 'Jesus,' he gasped. 'You might have warned us earlier.'

As Alexia's hand probed the mouth of the sack, tiny pellets of rat droppings spilled over her wrist. She did not flinch.

'I did warn you.'

'How?'

'By starting the fire.'

'You!'

Alexia leaned forward and cautiously peered into the foul-smelling sack.

218

'*You* started the fire!' Doyle exclaimed.

'I knew you wouldn't believe me if I told you the police were coming to Ngagabhaleko. You would have dismissed it the way you dismissed the Reverend's warning about the guns. You thought he was trying to scare you. Why should you have trusted me? You did not trust me even when I helped to get you released from jail . . .'

A rush of charred timber collapsing to the floor like crumbling birthday cake caused Alexia to withdraw her hand swiftly from the mouth of the sack.

'Doyle the fire was a warning for you to stay away from the school. I did not think you would be so foolish as to risk your life like this. After the way your father died? But maybe it is the way you also wish to die. To be blown up as if you were just a piece of wood. Maybe it is the only way you can forgive yourself for all the years you have wasted, for being wrong about him.'

'And you?' said Doyle, sliding his arms round the sack in an attempt to lift it out of the hole. 'Why are you risking your life?'

Before Alexia could reply they heard a vehicle skid to a halt in the yard outside. Hurriedly she pulled him to his feet and with the rows of fiercely burning desks illuminating their way they raced to the door where, hurdling over a fallen rafter, they found their path blocked by the blonde-haired Naylor.

'Shit, still messing about with black meat, Doyle!'

Doyle felt his legs give way beneath him. Leaning on Alexia who tried, unsuccessfully, to squeeze past the broad-shouldered figure, he gasped: 'I wouldn't go in there, it's a bloody furnace.'

'Oh yeah?' said Naylor, squinting over their shoulders. 'You call a few burning sticks a furnace. It's a mud hut. You can't burn . . .'

Another rafter tumbled from the roof bringing down a cascade of hot metal sheeting which skewed on to the floor at Naylor's feet, sending a shower of sparks into his face. Like Alexia earlier he did not flinch. In his former room-mate's eyes it seemed to Doyle there burned another, much fiercer fire.

'This your work, Doyle? What you trying to do? Get rid of the evidence? Stupid bastard. Stupid paddy bastard! We had you tagged all along man. Thought you could hide behind the black bitch hey? No chance. We come to collect.'

'Collect?' said Doyle catching a glimpse of the holster under Naylor's jacket.

Naylor, whose neck seemed to burst out of his collar, swung round to address a figure hanging back in the night, a figure averse to the heat of the fire but whose creamy smooth jaw Doyle instantly recognised as the flames licked hungrily at its shadow.

'See, Lieutenant. I told you this is where we should have looked first. All that crap you spouted about hell hath no fury like a woman scorned. Black meat man. She's just black meat. I know this guy. I know him better than his own mother. He's got a sick mind. Shit, stashing explosives away in a school! Endangering the lives of a bunch of innocent children!'

'The pupils are on holi . . .' Doyle bit his tongue.

Alexia scowled. 'We are wasting time. The furniture is burning for nothing. We should be trying to save it.'

Naylor's lip curled like a burning ember. 'You're right, we are wasting time. So which of you is going to show me where you've hidden the stuff?'

Doyle put his hand up to shield his face from the increasing heat. 'I don't know what you're talking about. We were just trying to get some of the desks out.'

Naylor stabbed the bright, white flame of his finger at Doyle's chest. 'Don't fuck around with me, hey!'

As Doyle retreated Naylor grabbed him by the throat. 'Listen, I don't care if this fucking roof caves in on top of us. But you and I are going to take a walk. We are going to go through fire for each other. We are going to risk our lives. We are going to be the men we should have been the night your father died . . .'

Naylor rocked furiously on the balls of his feet, his face flushed, his eyes wild, almost glazed in their ferocity. Doyle was reminded of Nomanthando. In this same room she too had grabbed him by the throat, her sour breath spilling into his face. It was as if the demon she had left behind had claimed another victim. Naylor's formidable frame wracked by the same primeval terror. .

'It was a long time ago,' he said.

Naylor's grip on his throat tightened. 'It's not that long ago you bastard. I can remember every minute of it. You shat on me that night because I was a South African, a *white* South African! You called me a fucking Prod! A Prod you reckoned who lived on the fat land. Well let me tell you this is still the fat land and that's the way it's going to stay. Neither you nor your terrorist friends are going to change that. What we change is what we want to change. No shit like you is going to hold a gun to our heads. Jeez, I've waited a long time for this. I don't know how many fucking liberals I've nailed since I've been in this business, but in my mind every single one of them was you – the arrogant bastard who walked away and left me floundering in the water. I was drunk. I could have drowned, Doyle! But did you give a shit? No. "Bladdy Boer", you said, and walked away.'

Half-choked by Naylor's frenzied grip on his throat, Doyle felt his body sag. There appeared to be no hope of stopping the fire from spreading; his former room-mate's resentment flaring into a self-destructive conflagration that would incinerate them all. His heart and lungs bursting, he saw Alexia steal up through the smoke beside him. But just as the certain touch of her fingers sent a shiver of momentary relief down his spine he felt her own body give a sudden and involuntary jerk. With the shrill sound of tearing metal, followed by a despairing thud, a section of wall collapsed.

Ghostly figurines of dust rising in the glow of the fire left behind a mysterious silence. His throat freed, Doyle drank in the draughts of fresh air which momentarily flattened the flames and sent them crawling under the furniture on their bellies.

Through the gap on the far side of the room, behind the pulpit, he saw the villagers lining the perimeter fence. Some had brought with them buckets of water, others grass brooms with which to beat out the fire. But this play again was offering them only bit parts. Even with the school – *their* school – burning centre stage, they were forced to remain in the wings while the protagonists continued to fight over the past.

The first to recover, Alexia shoved Doyle toward the door and a brief, fleeting glimpse of safety – a sky studded with stars sloping down over the yellow coned roofs – before Naylor dragged him back by his collar.

'Oh no, my china. You're not walking out on me again. I want to know where you've hidden those mines. You, me, we're going to stand in the middle of this fucking fire until you tell me where they are.'

Surrendering to the hold on his collar Doyle gave a despondent sigh. It all seemed so petty. This wasn't a struggle for freedom, a fight for justice or truth. Even now the truth was being burnt to the ground around them — books, papers, a class map of Africa shrivelling to a brown, gossamer skin at their feet. Naylor had turned it into a fight between two schoolboys: two former room-mates venting their long-standing hatred for each other. There was no higher principle to appeal to here. It was simply revenge.

Yet was it fair to blame it all on Naylor? For Doyle himself was a prisoner of History. Far from setting him free, it could be argued his aunt's letter had sent him reeling back into the cell, back into the past . . . a violent past, painted over with the blood of misguided martyrs . . . like his father. Perhaps Alexia and his mother had been right all along. Perhaps they had foreseen where the struggle would lead. And yet to give in without a fight . . .? To the likes of the Boers? the Brits? To give in to the likes of Naylor whose face was twisted with rancour, a figure trapped in his own self-consuming hatred as he dragged Doyle closer to the fire.

'Come on Paddy, time for your moment of truth. If you haven't hidden those mines in here then you got nothing to be scared of except a few minor burns. Better than being blown up hey? Least you get a chance, not like those walking past a bin in the city when it explodes. Did you ever stop to think about them, the innocent wives and children? You ever thought about that hey, *hero*?'

Kicking the sheets of corrugated roofing out of their path, Naylor forced Doyle toward the middle of the room. Boldly Alexia leapt in front of them.

'Jeez, kaffir, what do you think you're doing?' Naylor growled.

Over Alexia's right shoulder Doyle could see the pulpit blazing in the background. Charred rafters lay smouldering near the uncovered hole, like the burnt out skeleton of animals caught in a veld fire.

'Listen bitch, if you don't get out of our bladdy way . . .' Naylor reached under his jacket.

Quickly Doyle stepped between them. 'Forgotten the innocent wives, Naylor?' Naylor's hand came out empty, a marbled fist which he crashed through a burning desk-top. 'Let's go!' he barked.

'No Doyle, he can't force you.'

'Alexia, the man has a gun!'

'Tsha! You are afraid of his gun but not of being blown to pieces. Doyle you are mad. He is a Boer. He wants to kill himself. He wants to die.'

'Then let him die. Why are you stopping him?' said Doyle.

Swooping down over the desk which Naylor had smashed, Alexia lifted a chunk of blazing wood which she brandished in Doyle's face. 'It's you I'm stopping. You do not have to take part in this madness. That is what these Boers want. They want all of us to commit suicide with them. They cannot win the struggle, no matter how long they try to hold out. All they can do is take as many of us as possible with them to their death.'

Doyle felt the close heat of the burning club. He could see the flames licking her hand, her eyes bright with tears.

'Alexia,' he said reaching out, trying to prize her fingers loose, 'there are thousands of Naylors. We can't ignore them, just wait for them to go away. They have to be . . .'

'No Doyle,' she cried, the club singeing her robe as she broke free of his grasp, 'they do not all have to be defeated. Just as the Boers cannot destroy all of us, so we cannot defeat all of them. Only they can do that. Only they can destroy themselves. Besides, there will always be Naylors, just as there are Mandelas. These people do not belong just to the struggle, but to life itself. Maybe that is what you are afraid of – not this madman's gun, but the fact that the struggle will go on forever. You are not a hero. You are really running away . . .'

Doyle lunged forward, knocking the club to the ground.

'See!' she cried, defiantly shaking her blistered fist at him. 'You are afraid! You would rather die than face a life of struggle, as our people must do. You and he are the same, madmen disguised as heroes, cowards hiding behind a false bravery. Instead of the real challenge outside, you challenge each other in here, knowing that you will both die – happy to die because that is your escape.'

'Alexia that's not true.'

'Prove it, Doyle.'

'But you know it's not . . .'

'Then let your friend go, let him find the mines by himself. If you truly value your life fight to save it. Fight to continue the struggle. To live. It is not selfishness Doyle. It is the most important fight of all.'

223

Before Doyle could reply he felt Naylor's fist thud into his chest. 'Let's go, Doyle!'

Winded, Doyle found himself spun around, facing the fire.

'No, Doyle!' Alexia cried. 'He cannot force you.'

Doyle screwed up his eyes as he stared into the flames. It could only be a matter of minutes before the remaining rafters came crashing down, before the area around the pulpit . . .

'Chicken?' Naylor snarled.

Doyle paused, his mouth dry, his pulse racing.

'Come on, I've waited long enough!'

'No Doyle, it's madness!'

The flames licked lazily at his cheeks like a sjambok from whose slender tip sparks flew. He felt no pain. Stumbling over a burnt out desk, he grasped the hot metal in his hands and flung it aside. Once more sparks leapt out at him.

'Doyle!'

. . . sparks that suddenly froze and in a dark and fragile silence led him to recall the candles reflected in the guests' eyes as they swarmed round the cake, their cheeks, like Alexia's, puffed in anticipation of her blowing the candles out, their silence a silence in which hope and terror seemed momentarily fused.

'Doyle . . .?'

He turned. Alexia held out her hand.

'Screw the kaffir, Doyle!'

Without warning Doyle whirled round, grabbing Naylor by the front of his shirt. Blindly he began dragging the startled figure through the flames.

They had only gone a few feet when a sheet of iron roofing burst free, plunging toward the pulpit. Doyle heard Alexia scream as a searing flash followed by a tumultuous blast split the mud walls wide open, sending blazing rafters soaring high into the night sky where stars and embers fused in a colourful pageant and the resounding crash of iron seemed long, drawn out, before the blue-gold fragments rained down upon the open veld.

Hurled to the ground, Doyle saw over and over again the brief, incandescent glimpse he had caught of Naylor, tall, blonde and virile, being flung like an old book into the yard.

25

'*What do you call it . . . a cone . . . cairn? A cairn. No marble, just a pile of stones . . .*'

Doyle stared tearfully at the site of his father's grave. It lay in ruins, the stones scattered in thick mud. In the aftermath of the previous night's storm the mud glowed like melted-down gold. It was heavy underfoot and yet light to look at, light and alluring. For this really was gold – in the form of vast tea estates dominating the surrounding hills, where no spare inch of land lay empty, the steepest gradient shimmering in its new found wealth.

No spare inch of land – except around his father's grave. And even that was in the process of being cleared for cultivation, a trailer nearby revealing that some of the stones had already been gathered up ready for transporting when the workers returned after the weekend. Clearly this was not a land for looking back, for preserving memorials to the past. It was a land that promised fresh hope for the future, a redeeming wealth unimaginable in places like Ngagabha-leko. This was a land that had already set its sights on the next century.

But *could* it escape its past?

Ignoring the trailer, Doyle wiped away his tears and began gathering the stones up out of the mud, setting them down on his father's grave. He did not feel bitter about its ruined state. If anyone had neglected it, he had. If anyone had failed to fight for its preservation he had. If anyone had wished it would wither away . . . There was no one else to blame. He had said no prayers and sent no flowers. He had shed no tears except those as a boy and they had been for his own unhappiness. Now each stone that he prized out of the mud was like a brushed away tear as it fell on the grave.

To those watching in the background – Alexia, her uncle and the Security Branch men led by Lieutenant Mbanjwa who were waiting to escort him to the airport – it must have seemed these were tears of penance. He thought of them more as tears of relief; and the pain, as each sharp stone cut his hands, as the pain of recognition. For every tear was an affirmation of the past. He was no longer covering it up, but bringing it out into the open. He was setting each stone where it could be seen. Setting one on top of the other.

Wiping away the mud from the stones, he allowed the sun to sweep into their open fissures. And in those same sun-lit fissures he could once more see his father – dark, broad-shouldered with long curly hair, olive-green eyes – and his mother, pale, slight, thin-lipped, standing together in their bare feet on the stone floor of the farmhouse kitchen while soldiers with pickaxes first dug up the yard, then the barn, then the living room and finally, toward dawn, the kitchen, using those same pickaxes to smash the hundred-year-old flags that had once been the floor of his great-grandfather's cottage, and beneath which, a government spokesman in the following evening's paper claimed, a large number of weapons had been discovered, though none had.

He could see them standing in the corner by the cold fireplace, half-naked and defenceless. His father ruffled his hair, trying to calm him. His mother tucked him against her thigh. He was ten years old and his fingers left bruises in their skin. Bruises that ran like a chain to their locked hands. And when the sparks flew as the iron pickaxes struck the stones those same locked hands shielded his eyes so that he would not see their tears. But he saw them now.

That was why each stone he set upon the grave could never be simply a mark of penance. It was more. It was a gradual re-telling of the story. A relaying of the stone floor which the Brits had ripped up. An effort to reconstruct the foundations that had later given way when the 'people's army', having taken to fighting amongst themselves, had begun to suspect its own followers and forced those like his father to flee for their lives. If only his father had told him they had been hounded out . . . But then how could he have? The locked stones were the locked hands shielding his eyes. And yet . . . Doyle paused, squatting down on his haunches, his fingers torn, his breath coming in short, hot gasps . . . if that were the case, then there was an argument for dismantling the grave rather than restoring it, for going back, stone by stone, through the wasted years . . . Waiteh . . . Bitter Creek . . . Colombo . . . slowly dismantling the illusion that he could ever have been free of the past; or that anyone could be protected from the truth.

Indeed as a monument to his 'innocence', it made him feel decidedly nauseous. And suddenly he was having to lower his head over his knees as a thin trickle of bile shot up out of the back of his throat. Spitting out the sour liquid he waited for the empty swell in his stomach to subside and with it the painful recollection of his cruelty to Alexia, his distrust of the Reverend. Both of them even now – after all the waiting and uncertainty they had had to endure since the blast at school, from which it had at first seemed Alexia might never recover – continued to wait for him. Alexia still in a wheelchair, the Reverend patiently shielding her from the sun with his umbrella. Africa once again waiting, always waiting, waiting, waiting . . .

Far from being a monument to his innocence, his father's grave had become a symbol of self-indulgence. For it was his own and no one else's suffering he saw, had always seen, as the boorish Naylor had pointed out all those years ago. Only now, he felt, rising hurriedly to his feet, lifting the topmost stone from the 'cairn' with its dried mud flaking off in his hands, he had the power to put an end to it. All he had to do was scatter these few stones and the grave would be no more . . . yet another white man's footprint erased, another stumbling block to Africa's freedom cleared out of the way. The waiting over . . .

But as he lifted the large, cracked stone to his chest, his feet apart, his body braced, preparing to heave it on to the back of the trailer, he heard Alexia call out, her voice strained yet gentle. 'No, Doyle. There is no need to punish yourself. You must restore it. It is your duty. The Company cannot plant over it if it is maintained.'

Trying to gauge the distance between himself and the trailer, Doyle felt the weight of the stone sink rapidly through his arms, across his shoulders and down into his chest. His foot slipped in the mud and he only just managed to keep his balance. With the sun burning down on the back of his neck, he fell to his knees and shamefully set the stone back in position. Only then did he look round at the injured figure in the wheelchair, who vigorously waved him on.

◇

227

Poor Doyle, thought Alexia. He did not know which way to turn. Trying to make sense of the past had only made him more confused, more idealistic, more bogged down in the mud. When would he learn – when would the white man ever learn – not everything in life made sense? Not everything could be brought under ones control? For a start the past would always be a battleground. It would always be fought over, reclaimed and re-written. That was what his aunt's letter had done. It had re-written Doyle's past, softening the hard ground of his despair; preparing it for Abraham Dlamini, Nomanthando and Sister Mondo to leave their modest impressions, changing the barren into fertile soil. Only for the soil to be turned into mud by his mother's denial . . .

'. . . I told Mary no such thing, Seamus. She knows it and God too is my witness. It's true your father had to escape from the back-stabbing Provos, but he did not become involved with the underground movement in South Africa. God forgive the woman for lying, even if she was only trying to help. But I will not have you return under a cloud of untruth. Mary herself has promised to confess everything to Father McFaul, although she is trying to hold out until you return. She is a stubborn woman as you well know, so perhaps you may spare a thought for her soul, even if you have damned mine for all eternity. I do not ask you to come back against your will . . . only that you forgive her, her lies . . .'

Which way was the man to turn? With each suck and sigh he appeared to sink deeper in the mud. First he wished to restore the grave; then to demolish it. If only he could look at each stone as though it were a mirror, each reflecting a little piece of the truth, a little piece of himself. For then he would see the despair which had brought him to Ngagabhaleko, and held him prisoner there; recognise the relief given by his aunt's letter, the fear . . . So many mixed feelings, all boiling to the surface. It was as if he had wanted to die in the fire – not as a martyr in the liberation struggle, but in order to destroy the fervour of his emotions . . . the shame of so many lost and wasted years; as if only death could put an end to the horror and self-pity . . .

Naylor had got it totally wrong. Doyle wasn't the subversive he had spent all his time hunting down. But then Naylor was just as lost, just as driven by the unseen past. And so another life had been wasted. For Naylor she could feel no sorrow. For Doyle on the other hand . . . struggling, layer by muddy layer, to come to terms with the truth?

'Yes, Doyle,' she swore softly to herself, 'stand and stare at that damned stone, at that piece of the truth. What do you see? Do you see the pain you have caused? Not mine – for my pain I alone am responsible. Do you see – do you *feel* the pain you have inflicted upon yourself? For so many years your cynicism acted as a painkiller. But your conversion to the struggle . . . that pain was even worse! For now your friend, Dlamini, is in jail while you are free. See how thoughtful the Security Police are? Even now they are waiting to put you on the plane, bound for home. For Ireland.

'And yet what do you leave behind? The grave of your father? Look again into the mirror. Do you see the burnt out school? The kids playing aimlessly in the veld? Did you not think that by carrying on teaching you could still take part in the struggle? That education can also be for liberation? Maybe the children are just helpless victims to you, a price that must be paid. Then what of the old man? Your friend with whom you spent all those hours talking and playing dominoes. All his life he has managed to avoid being captured. Now he sits in the stinking cells at Umtata. Why is it he must suffer while you escape?

'White man, don't think I don't love you. For truly you are a child. And what woman cannot love a child, even when the child shows no love in return? Yet you did show some love. Remember when we returned from Mazeppa how you persuaded the Reverend to let me accompany you? You felt sorry for me when I told you how the Boer government had executed my father. It's true, pity is not the same as love. But from your hard heart! That was something. After that I knew you were not the person you thought yourself to be. There was love somewhere inside you, shielded by the past, by the memory of how your father had betrayed you. Every now and then it would put its head round the door, again like a child, peeping into an empty room. Remember how you sat up all night with Promise Mhlongo and her friends, watching over Nomanthando? Or how you waited for me at the hospital? How you sheltered Promise in the car when the police fired at Sister Mondo? Remember how you always stopped to give a lift to the villagers along the road? Or how you rescued

Abraham Dlamini's photograph of his wife from the kraal? You see, Doyle, even you are capable of love!

'So why is it everything you touch turns to stone? Even I sitting here in this wheelchair, I too am turned to stone. Is it because the struggle is more important to you than any person? Then look carefully at that stone in your hand. Look again at the mound of stones growing taller before your eyes. Who are you honouring? Not a hero – your mother's letter makes it clear – just an anonymous individual. And how many of them have we not buried in our country over these past few years? How many of them have not been buried in your own country? And has the struggle succeeded? Here? Or over there?

'So why, even now, can't you see what you are doing? Is it a tear in your eye? Or just some . . . tsha! You are like a bird flapping in the mud. Someone throws a stone at you and you jump. From another direction – another stone. You jump again. You are beating your wings in vain. Your new idealism will not help you to escape. All it will do is make you a prisoner of the struggle, another martyr to the cause. Only, without intimacy, without love – for *someone* not just something – the cause becomes . . . a quicksand into which individuals, even whole communities, are sucked and disappear. Yes, you can fight for the cause, but you cannot love it or be loved by it. We can only love others by caring for them, by touching, feeling, wanting them, sharing their pain. Without pain nothing is ever complete. The pain is the sharp edge of the stone cutting your hands and drawing blood. But how much of it do you feel, I wonder? Oh I know you are sorry and have said so many times for the pain you have caused me and my uncle. But what is the use of that when you are ready to jump at the first stone thrown at your feet?

'If you truly feel the pain, then why do you not show it? Why do you not look at me, look into my eyes? Maybe I was just a body to you, something to satisfy your animal hunger. Yet you did look once – in the fire. I remember what I saw – a jewel of light crushed by the fear and confusion. You and your friend Naylor were the same – madmen disguised as heroes. You were both happy to die that night, because death would have set you free. You showed what many African men have shown – a willingness to die because living is such suffering.

230

'Well I could have saved you if you had let me. If you had turned your back on the fire. But your anger was too strong. And your idealism was at least a thousand degrees hotter than the flames. Others also could have saved you. Rebecca Dlamini for instance, who pulled you out of the ruins after the mines exploded. But by then it was too late. Your "struggle" for liberation had been "won". Promise Mhlongo too could have saved you. In that at least she would have been able to boast of some success. Instead she sits moping in the village, having failed her exams.

'Why did you not give us a chance? You think we Africans can only receive help and never give it? Believe me, we are full to capacity with love. But what's the use? The white man cannot see it. Even now, rather than put your arm around me, you hug a pile of stones. What are you looking for there? The final absolution? Look, even when you have collected every stone, all you will have gained is a breathing space. There will always be another stone, another piece of missing truth. For the final stone is mysterious and elusive, the self always incomplete. It cannot be any other way. We are not God. We are only a part of God. So stop searching for more stones.

'Come . . . the Security Police are getting impatient. This chapter in your life may be over, but for them, Lieutenant Mbanjwa and the rest of us, it goes on. Tonight my uncle preaches at a brand new church in Nurse Fumba's village. Even though she is a Catholic she will be present in the Protestant congregation. Yes, Doyle, there is a lot you could have learned in Ngagabhaleko. All we can do for you now is pray . . .'

$$\diamondsuit$$

Hitching up his sweat-soaked shirt Doyle stood back. Already the ground away from the grave was dry and cracked. By the following day the surrounding plantations would have lost their emerald sheen, the workers wrapped in faded shawls resembling desert bedouin as they crept across the dusty slopes. The grave would have resumed its slide into dereliction, the tears of pain and penance absorbed by the earth, the changing earth, one moment quagmire, the next blowing away like ash in the wind; yet changing only on the surface, where the last stone now lay at his feet, the grave almost complete.

Brushing the mud from his face Doyle turned toward the Rever-

231

end. The Reverend Xolile nodded and set aside his umbrella. Aided by Lieutenant Mbanjwa he carefully steered Alexia's wheelchair over the uneven ground so that she could plant the wooden cross they had brought at the head of the grave. Spurning their offers of help she leaned forward banging the sharpened end into the ground with her fist. When she had finished she looked up and in her eyes Doyle could see the reflection of large white clouds crossing the sky. In the distance the wild 'skreee' of an African goshawk echoed across the hills.

GLOSSARY

abelungu white people
amaqaba Xhosa traditionalists
bundu rural area; bush
buti brother
Hadeda Ibis (bird)
Hayi No! (Also used as a general exclamation)
induna chief's appointees; assistants
inkosikazi literally 'female chief', but used normally as a polite form
  of address
intshiyani birds
isibedlele hospital
jondolo small hut
liqgira witchdoctor
lobola bride price
mawethu friend
mhlekazi Sir/form of address
molweni hello
nkozi chief
Sala khakuhle! Farewell (literally 'stay well')
sisi sister
tsotsi thug; villain
umlungu white man
Unjani How are you?
voetsek Afrikaans for 'bugger-off' – used towards dogs/animals